A Natural History of the
HEDGEROW

A Natural History of the
HEDGEROW

and ditches, dykes and dry stone walls

JOHN WRIGHT

PROFILE BOOKS

First published in Great Britain in 2016 by
PROFILE BOOKS LTD
3 Holford Yard
Bevin Way
London
wc1x 9hd
www.profilebooks.com

1 3 5 7 9 10 8 6 4 2

Printed and bound in Italy by Printer Trento s.r.l.

Design by Jade Design

Typeset in Joanna by MacGuru Ltd

A CIP catalogue record for this book is available from the British Library.

ISBN 978 1 84668 552 1
eISBN 978 1 84765 935 4

CONTENTS

PART III   NATURAL HISTORY

PART IV   HOW BOUNDARIES ARE MADE
         AND MAINTAINED

To my friend Richard Pearson, who is more
at home in a hedge than most.

Summer hedgerows in West Dorset.

Introduction

A PREOCCUPATION WITH HEDGEROWS

I spend a large proportion of my time wandering along hedgerows, examining walls and banks and clambering in and out of ditches. Even a drive along a country road or – more dangerously still – a motorway, will have me glancing out of the window to see what is growing by the wayside. A favourite game in my family is to count how many cherry plum trees we can spot on a trip from our home in Dorset to, say, Oxford (147), though it could just as well be wild parsley stands or apple trees we are counting. Lethal as these distractions may be, at least they do not slow me down, but a walk from one end of 100 metre hedge to the other can take me half an hour and any companions soon get bored and walk on ahead. 'But aren't you interested?' I might ask rather pompously. 'Look at this elder tree that's had its bark rubbed away by a deer,' or 'Here's an oak apple, let's see if the wasp has flown,' or 'This plant will have you dead in half an hour if you eat it,' and so on.

What interests me most are the mysteries – plants I do not recognise at all, fungi that I can put a genus to but not a species, things that could be animal, vegetable or mineral. I would like to think that such an attitude is not unusual; after all, many of my friends are enthusiastic naturalists of one sort or another, but, sadly, I do not think that this is the case.

I often take people on mushroom and hedgerow forays and while a few can tell an elder from an alder they are in the minority. The people who join me do so to learn about wild foods; what can be found in hedgerow, wood, pasture and meadow that tastes pleasant, won't have them in A&E and are free. I duly oblige, but I try to show them more – much more. I think that, on the whole, I am successful, though it is not always easy to tell. On a few occasions my success has been immediate and obvious. I am proud of what I do, though I take no great credit for it; it is just the everyday delight of an enthusiast, sharing the objects of his passion with others. I just slow people down and invite them to look.

For those who are willing to go slow, there is much to see; much more than might be imagined. Part III of the book, the largest part, covers the natural history of Britain's hedges in some detail. It tells the stories of hawthorn and blackthorn, of oak and elm and a dozen more hedgerow trees, but also of those organisms that depend on them or cohabit with them. Some are obvious, like the endless stands of cow parsley that appear every spring, others are very much more subtle. The hawthorn, for example, supports dozens of microfungi, many micromoths and macromoths, several galls and scores of other organisms.

This is what makes a walk along a hedgerow so much more than just a bit of exercise or a breath of fresh air. My particular interest is largely in hedgerow trees and plants and what may be called their 'diseases' and symbionts – organisms living in symbiosis. This may disappoint those with an interest in vertebrates, be they bird, bat or badger. I do, however, write of the relationships these animals have with their hedgerow habitat. Reptiles and amphibians barely get a mention except to acknowledge that they too can find a home in a hedge or wall.

Quite how unique hedges are to Britain is not sufficiently appreciated. For example, the 'tunnels' sometimes formed by roadside hedges, notably in the south, are almost unknown in other parts of the world. I am fortunate in that where I live I can see half a dozen hedges just by glancing out of my office window at the hill above my village. Most people in Britain live in towns and may not see a rural hedge at close quarters from one year to the next (I was a townie once, so I mean no criticism). Those fabled visitors arriving from outer space would have, literally, a very different view. From the air the landscape is dominated not by towns and cities, not by roads and factories, not even by forest or bare heath, but by a coast-to-coast network of hedges and fields. They might assume that the entire population spent its time creating and tending this truly vast construction. Not so long ago, they would have been right.

Once a year or more, many of us become like those aliens for a few minutes. Returning from a holiday in Greece or Turkey or anywhere else, we see what they would see and it takes our breath away. Beautiful as our holiday destinations may be, they cannot compare to the lush, green patchwork visible beneath us as we take the descent to Gatwick, Heathrow or – my personal favourite – Exeter in Devon.

What, these extra-terrestrial visitors might wonder, are all those lengths of hedges for?

Religious observance? Installation art? Some among those who live on this island often wonder too. The answer is that there is no single use for a hedge, but many. It may simply be a way of controlling and sheltering stock; a means of protecting crops and stock from unwelcome animals or from theft; as a defence against soil erosion, or as a resource for timber, food and medicine. These are practical matters, but there are also more psychological and social issues, such as the demarcation of private property and privacy. Which of these are important at any one time – and it may be several of them – determine the fate and nature of the hedge. If a hedge ceases to be valued, then the land it is on is usually reclaimed and put to better use. For a thousand years hedgerows were almost entirely dispensed with in about half of England and Wales, after which they were widely replanted only, more recently, to be dispensed with all over again in many parts of the country.

To the list of hedge use we must also add one further consideration. Before the advent of intensive agriculture, hedgerow natural history was not specially valued. The large tracts of land that had been more or less left to nature made it an also-ran in the natural history stakes. Now that our wildlife habitats have been so drastically reduced, hedgerows lead the field. While few of the agricultural reasons for planting or retaining hedgerows remain that relevant today, their importance as a natural history habitat cannot be overstated.

As well as hedges, the book discusses other types of field boundary, including hurdles, dry stone walls and fences, while their various methods of construction are described in Part IV. Part I sets the stage with an historical account of when and why these boundaries were first made, how the various forms waxed and waned over the millennia, and how this has affected those organisms that make up and live in a hedge. While farming can sometimes be ecologically benign, it is often destructive of the natural world and as agricultural practices have changed over the centuries, so have the number and variety of wild plants and animals that live on the land. The open-field system of the Middle Ages, for example, had little use for hedges and swept away the enclosed fields that had existed before its creation. With its demise and the increasing enclosure of common land from the seventeenth century onward, thousands of miles of new hedge were planted, while the common waste (uncultivated land) was destroyed and its rich flora, fauna and mycota lost.

In Part II the full extent of these gains and losses are explored. The losses have been caused by man: sometimes as a result of eking out a living from the land, sometimes through simple greed. Much of our hedgerow heritage has been depleted over the last seventy years. Fears for its survival, expressed during the 1970s, went largely unheeded in the agricultural subsidy rush of the 1980s and 90s. While the excesses and mistakes of the past are beyond our control, we have the knowledge, the ability and the responsibility not to

Less a few substantial anachronisms such as the rhododendron in the centre, this is a nice extant example of the 'waste' which came and went during agricultural expansions and contractions over the millennia.

repeat them. Today hedgerow loss is understood by most people to be a bad thing and hedges are protected as never before. Unfortunately, many of those remaining are in a poor state of repair. Having outlived their usefulness – large arable farms need no hedges – they have been left to wither. Pastoral farming, for which hedges are certainly useful, often make do with barbed wire. Even when a hedge exists, barbed wire is often used as the primary physical barrier and the hedge left to do its best, or its worst.

Some effort is being made to address these problems, but we must face the fact that many hedges are doomed in the long term. Those that survive, however, must be cared for with informed and sensitive cutting and repairing regimes. If a hedge flourishes, then the organisms that depend on it will do well. It is neither particularly onerous nor expensive to look after hedges and it often it involves not doing something (such as verge cutting) – or at least doing it at the right time and with a little more thought.

This is a personal account of the hedgerow because, for me, hedgerows are a personal matter. They are our common heritage and we should delight in them and protect them as though they were our personal property. In one way they truly are our property, as we enjoy historical and statutory rights to their bounty. Hedgerows were once a source of timber, of medicinal herbs and, crucially, of food for ourselves and for animals. Picking blackberries, stinging nettles, hazel nuts or sloes is less of a tradition and more a part of our biological heritage. It is something we are meant to do. In the past, and to some extent the present, the hedgerow was a resource that was essential to life. While the close behind every house grew vegetables and the fields might supply a subsistence quantity of corn and occasional meat, the hedgerow and the waste ground were essential for providing some nutritional variety for the rural population. A piece in *Jackson's Oxford Journal* of 1778 gives a hint of the value of this free source of food: 'The present is the greatest Nut Year that has been known for a long Time past; the Hazels are every where bending beneath the Weight of their Produce, and as it were by their friendly Curves, inviting the Hand of the Rustic to pluck their Clusters.'

Much of the information in this book on the structure of hedges is from personal observation while that on the natural history of hedgerow plants and fungi is from long personal experience. Much else comes from talking to many people for whom the hedge is as much a personal matter as it is to me. For the historical section, I have spoken to experts and used the published works of a secondary and, wherever possible, primary nature; my debt to the giants of the field – C. J. Barr, Richard Muir, Oliver Rackham, W. G. Hoskins, Max Hooper and many more – is deep. It is presumptuous in the extreme to claim that I have stood on their shoulders, but I trust that at least I have not stepped on their toes.

A few housekeeping notes: I have attempted to be explicit when writing of hedges and hedgerows, but on occasion 'hedge', 'hedgerow' and 'fence' are used to refer to any agricultural boundary.

Latin names are provided for every species for which there may be doubt when providing a common name alone. Dimensions of distance and area are a mixture of metric and imperial, and their use depends on context. When discussing the post-war period, I mostly use metric. Land measurements, such as rods, poles and perches, are only mentioned infrequently.

1 mile = 1.609 kilometres
1 yard = 0.914 metres
1 foot = 30.48 centimetres
1 acre = 4046.85 square metres
1 hectare = 10,000 square metres (2.47 acres)

PART I

THE PAST

Chapter 1

IN THE BEGINNING

Every year I visit the New Forest in Hampshire to explore its huge number of species of fungi. The best places to find rare and interesting specimens are the old enclosures of pine and birch, beech and oak. These are interspersed with grassy clearings and separated by open areas of grass and heath. The ensemble created appears primal in a way matched by few other places in Britain. The New Forest has by no means been left unaffected by man, but the management it has received has been both practical and, for the most part, considerate; here, the natural world is allowed the upper hand.

Was this the type of countryside encountered by Britain's post-Ice Age immigrants – the Mesolithic settlers – once the tundra had lifted its icy hand? The trees might have been a little different: elm and lime were much more common in lowland England than they are now, though neither would have thrived in the acid soils of the New Forest. And the grazing animals essential for maintaining grassy clearings and more extensive grassland would probably have been aurochs instead of ponies. But did the grassy glades and open grassland that give the New Forest so much of its varied and cheerful character exist in prehistoric Britain? In fact, it has long

Ancient beech in the New Forest.

been suggested, and is part of common perception, that before agriculture took possession of this land, it was carpeted from coast to coast by closed-canopy, primeval forest – a considerably more forbidding prospect than that of the park-like New Forest.

As someone who spends a great deal of time in forests, I can say with some authority that they are not good places to find food. Berries and nuts form on the trees of the wood edge, seldom on canopy trees (the naturalised sweet chestnut being a notable if unreliable exception) and the few edible roots that exist belong to grassland and edge habitats. Edible leaves too are found much more out of the forest than in it. Fungi can be collected in some abundance, but they appear irregularly and make a treacherous dinner for those without a good folk knowledge of what is edible. The main source of food in woodlands is game, but hunting in dense woods is fraught with difficulty.

It is attractive therefore to fancy that park-like conditions prevailed and that post-Ice Age settlers found a welcoming home. This idea has been supported by the Dutch forest ecologist Frans Vera who, in his *Grazing Ecology and Forest History* (2000), makes a strong case for a semi-open landscape.' One of his main arguments is the disinclination of oak, a common tree then as now, to seed success-fully in closed-canopy conditions. He argues that oak saplings would require a nursery of bushes in open grassland to establish them-selves and form the basis of a new, or at least moving, forest. Vera also persuasively explains away the lack of grass pollen found in the archaeological record. If grassy glades existed to any great extent, then one would be entitled to expect grass pollen. However, he points out that grass extensively grazed by aurochs and wild horses is usually kept short and seldom produces its flowers, so that such grassland is more likely to contain windblown tree pollen than grass pollen. Conservationists wishing to find a model of a primal landscape and ecology have seized upon Vera's conjecture.

Appealing as the idea of a large park may be, plenty of academics have argued against Vera's view, and a dense blanket canopy is still considered the most likely arrangement of the landscape. The tell-tale signs of extensive grassland such as grass pollens, dung beetle remains (indicating grazing animals), sub-fossilised, low-branched trees (as opposed to high-branched, forest canopy trees) are largely absent, whereas evidence for extensive forest exists in abundance. That would not have been the entire picture, of course, and some open upland areas of grass or heath, reedy flood plains, saltmarsh and grassy coastal fringes would have existed. There would also have been some breaks in the wildwood caused by soil conditions, disease, fallen trees and fire.

Thus it seems likely – but no more than that – that the canvas upon which British civilisation was drawn was initially an almost continuous forest. Did the early settlers find it an attractive aspect? It would seem not. The evidence that the wilderness was not entirely to Mesolithic man's liking is suggested by signs – such as charcoal and pollen – that he set fire to large parts of it. While many fires are likely to have been caused by lightning, some archaeologists believe that humans had a considerable and repeated impact on the forest cover.

Countering this idea is the fact that even when trees are felled and left to dry, setting fire to closed-canopy woodland is simply not possible. There are repeated and extensive fires in dry weather in the New Forest, but these are of bracken, gorse and heather, never of oak and beech. Wartime experiences confirm this, as broad-leaved woodlands steadfastly refused to burn even when inadvertently bombed with incendiary devices. Even cutting a tree down in the first place is all but impossible with stone axes, and primal woodland trees would have been enormous. On the other hand, it could be argued, there was a relative abundance of the much more flammable Scots pine during the Mesolithic period, and Mesolithic settlers tended to favour the less densely wooded upland areas, notably chalk, where the trees are shallow-rooted.

An alternative hypothesis is that natural clearings in the forest, caused by trees blown down during storms, were used.[2] The fallen trees could then have been cleared by lopping off and burning the branches, with unturned roots burnt in situ and the trunks hauled away. Any new growth could easily have been controlled with stone tools, fire and grazing animals. However they were created, these clearances were piecemeal affairs; the wholesale removal of the wildwood would have to wait for the Neolithic introduction of agriculture and the efforts of their better equipped Bronze Age heirs.

Mesolithic man was a hunter-gatherer and, as suggested above, unbroken woodland is not particularly bountiful for either hunter or gatherer, so they sought to change it into broken woodland. Charcoal is the chief, and obvious, indicator of ancient forest fires, as it forms dateable layers in the soil. But there are other signs such as pollen and fungal spores which show the organisms that existed before and after a fire. One study found a succession of plants replacing the lost trees, which included stinging nettles, meadowsweet, members of the carrot family and hazel, as well as the grasses which may have been the primary goal of those lighting the fires.[3] An area cleared in this way would form an oasis of plants edible to humans, complete with an edge habitat in which fruit and nut-bearing trees would become productive. Hazelnut shells are the most commonly found plant remains in middens from the period and this would provide a satisfying explanation for why hazelnuts – which are disinclined to form reliably in canopy conditions – managed to contribute such a large part of the Mesolithic diet. Hazel trees are also more resistant to fire than the oak, lime and elm trees that might be shading them, and would survive as productive, isolated trees in a newly opened environment.

More important than any newly gained access to hazelnut butter and nettle soup is the attractiveness to grazing deer, pigs and aurochs of a grassy, herb-rich clearing, replete with succulent growth from tree stumps and surrounded by low-growing trees. More important still is that a clearing concentrates the animals in one place, allowing them to be hunted much more easily than in close woodland. A sensible place for such clearings is near water, providing an irresistible magnet to prey. Support for the existence of such animals in newly created clearings is provided by the contemporary increase in the spores of dung-loving fungi, the bones of red deer and Mesolithic microliths (small shards of flint used for preparing carcasses).[4]

These clearings often regenerated quite quickly as grazing animals soon learned that the attractive new diner was also a very dangerous one. Clearings were soon abandoned by prey and predator alike and a new one established elsewhere. Some, however, have lasted a very long time indeed. The heathland of Iping Common in West Sussex is believed to be a Mesolithic clearing that, once heather had become established, was unable to revert to woodland.[5]

It is a moot point whether the Mesolithic 'enhancement' of the natural environment counts as farming or not and so, for the purposes of this book, whether the clearances created, designed in part as a trap, can possibly be counted as enclosures. If you have an enclosure then, by definition, there must be a physical boundary. The boundary in this case will be trees and could, with a pronounced raising of an eyebrow, be called a 'hedge' albeit a hedge with only one side. It would not be stock-proof in the recognised sense of impenetrable to animals, but it would not need to be; the grass is definitely greener on the inside (for a while at least).

Clearing an area of woodland for agricultural purposes is so common a procedure, right up to the present day, that it has acquired a name: assarting, from the French *essarter* meaning 'to clear and grub up trees and bushes'. A clearing made in this way is called an

The hedges here embody the tell-tale curving front edge of an assarted landscape.

assart and we will see more of them later. Just how extensive Mesolithic assarts were is not known for certain but they are unlikely to be related to any nearby settlements as Mesolithic people were nomadic, settling for only brief periods in any one place. So if an area were cleared, it would be revisited once grasses and other plants had established themselves and then eventually abandoned as its utility declined.

Chapter 2

THE NEOLITHIC CLEARANCES

It has long been accepted that Neolithic peoples inherited a virgin landscape from their Mesolithic predecessors but, as we have seen, this was not entirely the case. Somewhere between 4300 and 4000 BCE a new way of life, long experienced by inhabitants of the Near East, found its way to Britain. Whether its arrival was sudden or gradual, and whether the existing people and their culture was entirely replaced by another has long been debated. Recent DNA analysis suggests that only 20 per cent of the population at this time were new arrivals, but they brought with them a revolution.[1] This revolution was, of course, agriculture. The new way of life did not just arrive in the form of boatloads of people bringing new ideas; it also came as crops and domesticated animals and as a technology.

Arable farming required that the work of the earlier nomadic peoples be continued and expanded and large areas of forest cleared. Again, the evidence that this took place can be found in the extensive layers of charcoal and occasional dumps of charred logs discovered in archaeological digs, along with the pollen extracted from dateable samples of deposited peat or soil. It seems that Neolithic man preferred the fertile and well-drained chalky areas of southern

Britain to those of clay and sand. As well as being well drained, there was less dense forest cover to clear and soils that were easier to dig or plough.[2]

The extent to which these peoples expanded and when and where this took place is not known for certain (and there is no academic consensus on the subject), but the new arrivals did not remodel vast areas of the British landscape into field systems, as their successors in the Bronze Age did, rather they cleared small areas for farming. This was done irregularly over the two and a half thousand years of the Neolithic period – a process of clearing, cultivating and allowing arable land to become pasture, and often, eventually, abandoning it to nature. The Neolithic farming enterprise waxed and waned, with a considerable hiatus in arable farming around 3400 BCE when the pollen record consistently demonstrates extensive grassland in some places and a return to woodland elsewhere.[3] But even if farming seems to have failed for a while, cereals were grown in Britain for a long period, and would have been enjoyed by animals (wild and domesticated) as well as humans, a fact that early farmers would have quickly discovered. This, then, is the first time that the inhabitants of Britain faced the problem of keeping vegetation and animals apart. Enter the British hedge.

If one were to look for evidence of Neolithic field systems as vague rectangles in aerial photographs or as distinct ridges visible from ground level or, more energetically, from metre-deep excavations into peat bogs, one would look largely in vain and assume that Neolithic man was a hunter-gatherer after all. The evidence that they planted crops and kept domesticated animals comes from digs which have exposed such things as grain (spelt, barley, emmer, einkorn and wheat) impressed into pottery shards, grain storage pits (often put to later use as rubbish pits), quern stones for grinding grain and the bones of cattle and sheep.[4] As an aside, it is worth noting that barley appears to have been the grain most planted by the late Neolithic period and that barley is used to make ale. Beer may be the very basis of civilisation.

So field systems, or even the odd single field, are almost absent in the Neolithic record, but that doesn't mean that they didn't exist.

A circular stone enclosure of uncertain vintage on Dartmoor.

Below the 5,500-year-old South Street Long Barrow in Wiltshire is an area of cross-hatched chalk. The primitive plough used at that time, the ard, was little more than a pointy stick attached to a beam. This was dragged across the land, scratching a groove into the thin soil and the chalk beneath. Lines of scratched grooves do not make a ploughed field, so the ard was drawn again across the field at right angles to the grooves. Such cross-hatching is found in several sites in Britain, although the marks seem too deep for such a flimsy tool and it has been suggested that a rip ard was used instead. This considerably more robust plough, consisting of a hook designed to rip up the soil, was used in the original preparation of established grassland. It may be that the ground was either being prepared for arable or – less encouragingly for those searching for evidence of agriculture – simply for the building of a barrow.

There are a few hints of very early field systems and even stone boundaries in Britain: circular plots surrounded by the remnants of stone walls exist in Cornwall, Nottinghamshire and Yorkshire, and on Dartmoor and the Shetland Islands, but these are of doubtful provenance. For an unquestionably Neolithic field system one must look to the Céide Fields and nearby sites in County Mayo, Ireland. These were discovered in the 1930s by schoolteacher Patrick Caulfield, who noticed the regularity of the stones that he uncovered while collecting peat. His son, Seamus, who had studied archaeology, examined this remarkable site further in 1970. Five and a half thousand years old, it had been protected by the ravages of time and the attentions of humans by deep blanket bog. What was revealed was an extensive rectilinear field system enclosing 1,000 hectares with more nearby. The fields are up to 700 metres long and 150–200 metres wide running vaguely north, further divided (but not always) by east-west walls into smaller fields of about 250 metres. Such an arrangement is termed a coaxial system and simply means that the fields are roughly rectangular with the longer walls of each field forming a continuous line, in appearance like a brick wall laid on its side.

The walls which define the Céide Fields are unsophisticated constructions. Slightly triangular in section, they are no more than 80 cm in height and look as though they were just chucked there as long heaps of stones. Pollen evidence suggests that they were used for pasture, but what such a low wall would be for is unclear.[5] It could well have been just a tidy place to put the stones as the land was cleared (a 'consumption wall'), or perhaps they were a form of stock-proofing, though this would only have worked if the animals kept inside were hobbled. Alternatively, the wall simply defined areas of ownership or, at least, responsibility. Walls they most certainly are, however, and our first encounter with a hedge, albeit one of stone and in the wrong country.

One might imagine that the Céide Fields form a model for Neolithic farming and that a similar system would be found across the water. But, as already stated, despite raised hopes and the possibility that some Bronze Age field systems might be found to be earlier, no definite British Neolithic field system has been discovered.[6] It seems likely that Ireland embraced what is sometimes called the 'Neolithic package' with more enthusiasm than their British contemporaries. This may have been because Ireland was considerably less abundant in wild game, making cultivation a tempting prospect, or perhaps it was because its north-west coastal location was on a Neolithic trade route.

The British Neolithic peoples seem to have been a little more itinerant than their Irish cousins, clearing areas for rough pasture, ploughing or hand digging small areas here and there for cereals until the soil became depleted, and then simply moving on, whereupon the land reverted to woodland. It has been suggested that some practised a version of the infield-outfield system of agriculture that was to become widespread in later times.[7] Cattle and sheep would be ranched in large, unbounded outfields, herded by man and perhaps dog, then returned to an infield enclosure at night. The infields would have rotated between arable and enclosure, the soil in the enclosure benefitting enormously from the dung and the plough-like effect of hooves, making subsequent ploughing for arable much easier. The reversion to pasture is frequently attested by the pollen of pasture-loving plants like sorrel and plantain.

Sometimes, however, Neolithic farmers lingered for a long time. At Hockham Mere in Norfolk the cleared area continued for 300 years before reverting to woodland. Agriculture was not the sole means of sustenance for Neolithic peoples and they continued to hunt, fish and forage like their Mesolithic forebears. The great Avebury Stone Circle in Wiltshire is surrounded by Neolithic sites containing the remains of wild boar, aurochs and deer, as well as plant foods such as hazelnuts, sloes and crab apples.

Infield-outfield aside, if the British Neolithic people employed hedges to separate livestock from crops (and wild animals from both), it is likely that they were dead hedges, ones made of dead wood – what we might now call a fence, though no doubt one of a decidedly rustic nature. Such fences barely last more than a few years, but their presence can exist for thousands in the form of post holes. In establishing an assart it is possible to improve the surrounding, gappy forest perimeter by piling up brash or even weaving hazel into the existing trees, though whether this was done is debatable.[8] There is, however, some evidence of live hedges having been made in the sudden increase in the pollen traces of blackthorn and dog rose. This suggests that small fields, probably for managing cattle, were enclosed by thorny hedges, which could also provide food in the form of berries.[9]

It is also worth considering the possibility – the likelihood even – that boundaries weren't always needed. If you wish to keep deer from your corn, you simply leave some poor soul out in the field to shoo them away with a great deal of shouting and stick waving, a time-consuming method that is still used today in simple agrarian communities.

Chapter 3

THE BRONZE AND IRON AGES

Only a single topic book such as this would conflate so long and varied a period as that from the commencement of the Bronze Age to the close of the Iron Age, a period of two and a half thousand years. Although there was little advance on the rather part-time approach of the Neolithic peoples during the Early Bronze Age, beyond the establishment of fields in predominantly upland and coastal regions, the period as a whole saw the population embrace agriculture as a more permanent and organised way of life. Such was the continuity of the field systems used, it is possible to extend this time frame, in some places at least, through to Saxon England and even beyond. A second reason for treating this long period as one is that establishing the dates of a field system is extremely difficult, despite the best efforts of hundreds of archaeologists. Like film stars who have had 'work' done, some field systems are considerably older than they appear, and seem to have slowly made their way back through time from a first assessment as medieval, through Saxon, Roman and Iron Age to that of the Bronze Age. Fields, or rather, fields systems, can be long-lived creations, gaining permanence by usage; the plough and subsequent soil erosion building up material at their boundaries. In

Barely visible, the remnants of a Bronze Age field system at Burrington Ham, Somerset.

this way they can prevail while historical periods pass. And today the landscape still shows signs of these ancient field systems.

For example, a little to the north of the famous Cheddar Gorge in Somerset lies Burrington Ham, an overgrown outcrop of the Mendip Hills. Many years ago, a friend who lived nearby took me there, explaining that there was something ancient he wanted me to see. It is an unprepossessing site, criss-crossed with grassy paths made slightly treacherous by trip-hazard rocks every twenty-five yards or so. A little disappointed at the conspicuous lack of stone circle or medieval castle, I asked him what we were looking for. 'You have just walked over them,' was his puzzling reply. The rocks that had proved a mild nuisance along the path were not natural, he explained, they were the remains of the stone walls of a Bronze Age field system. Although we could see only portions of them, they extended under the dense bracken for up to forty-five yards: six of them, all parallel to one another. These were the oldest field boundaries I had seen at the time and they made me think of the hands and lives of those who had built them, maybe two thousand years before Christ. I was, at last, impressed.

A well-preserved length of ancient stone wall which is probably part of a reave.

A similar, but much more extensive, Bronze Age field system on Dartmoor went unsuspected until fairly recently, despite having considerably more obvious signs of its existence on the ground. It had been forgotten rather than discovered, as the presence of these lines of stones was known to early nineteenth-century archaeologists, though not understood by them – the stones were thought to be trackways, despite being conspicuously unsuitable for such a purpose. Rediscovered in the 1970s by landscape archaeologist Andrew Fleming, these stones are the Dartmoor reaves, a name that is thought by some to have come from *rǣw* the Old English for a 'row' *(not according to the* OED *which claims 'origin unknown').*[1] They extend for miles over the slopes of Dartmoor covering 10,000 hectares. Twenty major field systems make up the reaves as a whole and they are resolutely rectilinear.

The effort of establishing fields and building these stone walls seems out of all proportion to what could be gained from this cold, wet and forbidding land. I once camped for a few days on Dartmoor in order to investigate its fungi and had to be rescued by some friends. They could not understand my plight (I have never been wetter in my life), as the weather in Exeter, where they lived, had

Ancient field system traces in West Dorset.

been pleasant and mild. However, back in the Bronze Age the soil of the newly cleared Dartmoor would have been better because the climate then was 2C° warmer.[2]

Stone walls, both ancient and modern, are found all over Britain, and can survive for thousands of years. But what of lowland Britain, where hedges dominate and one might imagine field boundaries to be more ephemeral? Thirty-five years ago, when I first moved to my part of Dorset, I lived in an isolated, modern farmhouse of poor construction and hideous aspect. It was cold and damp. However, what the house lacked in comfort was made up a thousandfold by the view of the surrounding countryside. I could see thirty miles over the hills without a single dwelling to disturb my gaze, and the house overlooked the narrow coombe valley in which much of the farm lay. In the evening the setting sun would cast shadows over the herb-rich grassland of the opposite coombe side and bring into relief strange rectangular markings, about sixty-four metres from side to side. It was clear, even to my then inexperienced eye, that they marked out a field system. Commander 'Snowy' Eyre, my colourful landlord (secretary of the hunt and well known for chasing foxes, matrons and maids with indiscriminate enthusiasm), had told me that when he took on the farm after the war, the man from the Ministry of Agriculture had said, 'Take your plough around the farm, Commander', so I assumed it had been he who had removed the hedges surrounding those ghostly fields.

As I came to learn about indicator species and understand grassland a little more, I realised that Commander Eyre was not to blame; the hedges had been gone for centuries. What I could not work out was how old the fields actually were, but would no doubt, if pressed, have suggested medieval. In fact, they are much older 'Celtic' field remnants, laid out in the Iron Age or, just possibly, earlier still. They were coaxial – arranged in a rectilinear fashion – which is typical of many 'Celtic' fields, although this name can apply to irregular ancient fields too.

In academic writing on field systems, the 'Celtic' field appellation is always in quotation marks, denoting that the fields are not necessarily Celtic (Iron Age) at all and may be earlier or even later. It was an archaeology officer of the Ordnance Survey, O. G. S. Crawford, who made the rather hurried assignment of these fields to the Iron Age in 1923. A champion of the use of aerial photographs in the study of landscape history, Crawford is probably better known for lumbering everyone with 'Celtic' fields that are not, necessarily, Celtic.

While the stone boundary remains of the Bronze Age fields at Burrington Ham or the much more extensive field system of Dartmoor are fairly uncommon, the type of ancient field found on Snowy Eyre's farm is not. In fact, I can see some through the tiny window of my attic office on the other side of the same hill. In West Dorset they appear everywhere on the chalk downland, remnants of a once much larger system. The most beautiful Dorset example is found in the Bronze Age Valley of Stones near Little Bredy. Here, approximately seventy individual fields can be seen, laid out in a coaxial pattern, and all with an orientation of north-west to south-east. The most remarkable aspect of this layout is that it seems to take almost no account of the local topography; a plan of the site would work just as well were the land flat, instead of being what it is, extremely hilly.

A similar, and much larger, field system can be seen (just) in the

Ancient field system at Valley of Stones, Dorset.

Piddle Valley, a few miles east of my own Frome Valley. In his *Fields in the English Landscape*, Christopher Taylor notes the same neat, coaxial patchwork fields, several hundred of them extending for over 800 hectares.[3] The field system again shows little regard for the geography by appearing to cross flood plains and even the River Piddle itself. Scores of similar systems have been discovered and described in Dorset, most of them on the chalk downs, though the Piddle Valley system is the most extensive. Dating is, as always, very difficult, but a Bronze Age origin for many or most of them seems likely.[4]

So common are such glories here that they were once thought to be a Dorset, or at least Wessex, specialty, but they are common almost everywhere on the chalk downlands of the south including more easterly locations such as Black Patch on the Sussex Downs. Traces of them have now been found all over Britain, indicating that these regular field systems may have extended through much of England and Wales, if not in Scotland where coaxial systems certainly existed but were less extensive and more fragmented.

Quite how extensive they were is not easy to say. Even within the areas in which they are clearly evident, they survive only on marginal land such as steep hillsides, where the plough has seldom passed since the fields were abandoned centuries or millennia ago. It is not possible to infer with any certainty that the surviving field forms are representative of those which existed in river valleys or fertile plains. Indeed, marginal land by its very nature is often farmed differently. However, there is sufficient evidence to suggest that the landscape over this period quickly filled with small fields laid out in a clear pattern.

One place where the land cannot be described as marginal (though it took some ingenuity to make it productive) is East Anglia, notably in the Fens. Archaeological excavations at Fengate near Peterborough in Cambridgeshire have revealed remnants of what may have been a massive system of coaxial fields which were used for cattle. Their use has been confidently inferred by the high levels of phosphates in the drove roads that serve the fields, phosphates being sure evidence of the passing of many thousands of nervous cattle over the centuries.[5] Other similar finds on the Fens also show a coaxial arrangement that suggests an extensive field system. A reasonable body of evidence indicates that the Fenland system is in fact Neolithic in origin, though it was used throughout the Bronze Age until the climate suffered one of its periodic deteriorations, with an already wet area became unsustainably wetter.

A great deal of detective work has been done to discover ancient fields in likely or unlikely locations using a variety of techniques. Archaeology received an enormous boost from the development of aerial photography; the photographs taken during the Second World War, in particular, have transformed the discipline. Field systems need to be seen from a distance, preferably from above. If you have ever looked at a banked outline of a field system on a distant hill, you will have noticed how it disappears almost completely when you stand within it. For the casual, armchair archaeologist, the good offices of Google Maps have made aerial surveillance open to all, and I, for one, have spent hundreds of hours pondering mysterious rectangular shapes in Dorset, which I didn't know were there, and wondering if I was the first to spot them.

Today's archaeologists minutely scrutinise aerial photographs looking for the patterns of lost fields. These may appear as linear or rectilinear marks in ploughed soil or as crop marks, where the soil quality is slightly different and causes differential growth in corn which in turn casts a revealing shadow of long forgotten fields. It is even possible to discover the latest possible date for the establishment of a field almost entirely from an aerial photograph or even a map. Enter the wonderfully named Flinders Petrie, the distinguished nineteenth-century Egyptologist and archaeological pioneer. Petrie pointed out what in retrospect seems perfectly obvious, that if, for example, a road diagonally bisects a rectangular field, then the field almost certainly predates the road. This was the beginning of what became known as 'topographical analysis'.

For example, the A140 runs for most of its length from Norwich in the north to Colchester in the south. It would be as accurate to say that it once ran from Venta Icenorum to Camulodunum, for it is a Roman road known as the Pye Road. In the area of the villages of Scole and Dickleburgh, as Professor Tom Williamson of the University of East Anglia has observed, the existing fields were crossed by the Pye Road, cutting many of them in two, decisively marking them as pre-Roman or, at the latest, early Roman. It is thought that they date from the Iron Age as the difficult soils in that area required a more mature technology to plough them.[6] The field system extended over fourteen square miles, making it among the largest discovered in Britain. Since then further field systems of a similar nature have been found in other parts of East Anglia.

A large area north of the Thames in Essex was once covered by coaxial fields which, for the most part, follow the north-west/south-east orientation seen in Dorset and elsewhere. The soil is fertile, but again, difficult to work and most likely required the improved ploughing technology of the Iron Age to make a field system viable. The heavy London clay has been described as 'three horse' land, compared to 'two horse' of boulder clay and 'one horse' of gravel soils.[7]

It is worth mentioning the mysterious north-west/south-east orientation of many of these fields. Not all fields are laid out this way, but a glance at a reasonably detailed map or an aerial photograph will show that this orientation is the most prevalent. I have found no explanation for this in the literature, but the only one that makes sense to me is that when laying out a field it is a good idea to protect corn and stock from the prevailing wind. One of the main reasons for having a hedge is to provide such a 'wind shadow', which can slow the wind for a distance of five times the height of the hedge. Most ancient fields are long and thin, and a hedge two yards high will protect most of the width of the average ancient field from what in Britain is almost always a south-westerly wind. Any hedge orientated north-east/south-west would turn a field into a wind tunnel.

Such fields as those discovered in East Anglia and the south are for the most part absent in the Midlands, where long agricultural usage has wiped the topographical slate clean, though a few have been discovered by the observation of crop marks.[8] In the north of England, however, they can be found in several places, the best preserved being at Grassington in Yorkshire, where traces of an ancient field system, together with the field cairns of collected,

The traces of ancient field boundaries at Grassington, overlaid a by much later stone-walled field system.

cleared stone, can be seen north of the town. Here, the fields are arranged in a north-east/south-west direction (unhelpfully contradicting my hypothesis above) and are narrower than their southern counterparts, perhaps indicating arable rather than pastoral use, as long fields suit ploughing much better. They have been assigned, unequivocally, to the Bronze Age.

Coaxial systems appear to dominate Britain in this period. They are characteristically defined by linear, parallel boundaries which form long fields, divided crossways into smaller fields, or what may more helpfully be called plots, at irregular intervals. It is conceivable that these were formed organically by adding one field to another. Much more likely, however, is that they were the result of planning. As mentioned already, a look at a map or aerial photograph of such fields shows a general disregard of topography, suggesting that someone simply divided the land, though whether through the authority of some chieftain or by agreement of the community is unknown. The balance of scholarly opinion is firmly on the side of the chieftain. But whoever organised the field systems, it is a major achievement and, as we have seen, one which extends almost countrywide.

While coaxial field systems dominated the countryside in pre-history, it is worth mentioning that they were not the only form of field found in the Bronze and Iron Ages. To be 'Celtic' a field must be fairly small and with four more or less straight sides, but it does not have to be arranged in a coaxial pattern. Irregular enclosures, associated with a single small group of dwellings, are found all over Britain. Cornwall provides particularly fine examples of these, such as the fields at West Penwith, which are formed from a beautiful pattern of distinctively irregular stone walls (though not Cornish hedges, see pp. 311–14); some mere shadows on the ground, but many forming the boundaries of existing fields.[9] Eschewing straight lines completely are the fields at Burton Moor in the Yorkshire Dales, where hut circles are scattered within fourteen overlapping circular fields, forty or fifty yards in diameter.[10]

Having established that there were indeed fields to hedge in Bronze and Iron Age Britain, what about the hedges themselves? There is more speculation than fact about the type of hedges or walls used, and even, in some cases, if they were used at all. However, as we have seen, some have survived to this day, and evidence of others has been discovered as a result of archaeological digs. Dartmoor's now famous reaves are constructed from granite pieces no larger than what could be carried. They appear to be better constructed than the walls at Céide Fields and show signs of having been laid fairly neatly, with the core made of smaller stones and the outside surfaces faced with larger stones. They are a land-hungry two yards wide, but land was unlikely to be at a premium at that time, and rocks have never been in short supply on Dartmoor. There is the possibility that the stone walls of the reaves had a previous incarnation as a ditch and bank (probably hedged), as many of the reaves were built on top of banks. In at least one place the new stone wall fills in a gap in the bank (presumably a gateway of some sort), demonstrating that the stone reaves and bank were not contemporary.

The reaves as they are now – tumbled and spread by the travails of time – were never particularly tall, standing perhaps at a yard. At this height they would be little more than notional boundaries, and Andrew Fleming argues that they were hedged directly on top as some still are in Wales and Cornwall, or were planted with hedging trees after being covered entirely in earth. In his engaging book, *The Dartmoor Reaves*, Fleming notes the charming fact that in some places where the reaves meet, the different styles of the workers who made them are plain to see. The reaves appear to have been used primarily for cattle, but both cereals and beans were also grown there.

Lacking a wealth of granite or other stone, the fields near my old home in Dorset are visible only as the fields themselves, unbounded by anything but shadows. The only reason they are visible is because they appear to have shallow banks and ditches on at least two edges and every field seems to have slid down the hill a little bit. They had 'slumped'. The fields were ploughed many times over the years and the soil, loosened by the plough, tended to gradually move downhill. I have seen entire modern Dorset fields washed into the surrounding roads after an untimely downpour of rain, so we must assume that such disasters also afflicted early peoples.

The lower edge of any slumped field shows the accumulation of soil from ploughing. The ploughman clearly ploughed up to that boundary line and it is conceivable that the soil simply accumulated there, perhaps up to a narrow baulk – a strip of uncultivated land dividing the fields. However, it is more likely that he ploughed up to a bank and ditched hedge, or just a hedge or a wall, and the soil was deposited at, or even over, this boundary. A study by the University of Exeter describes such a field on a chalky part of the Blackdown Hills which evidently stopped moving downhill once it levelled out. The presence of pollen from elm, whitebeam, beech and ivy suggests that it was a hedge that caused the halt.[11]

These slumped field systems should not be confused with the medieval lynchets, which are usually steeper, distinctly terraced and seldom divided into fields. These were laboriously constructed to provide extra land, almost certainly arable, in times of land-famine. The slumped fields on the hill near my old home and those at Valley of Stones just happened. The word 'lynchet' has a chequered and moveable history, at one time referring to a strip of green between two areas of ploughed land, a usage that applies in the case of medieval lynchets to the up-slope between two ploughed terraces. It is now used for the up-slope and the flat part as a whole.

More evidence for hedges or, at least, fences has been gathered from digs all over Britain: fence post holes, the preserved, water-

Strip lynchets in West Dorset.

logged posts themselves and, in one case, the remains of a few twigs that might have formed part of a hedge. The latter sounds highly unconvincing, but Francis Pryor relates how he and his wife discovered such material in a field boundary ditch at Fengate. There, among well-preserved leaves, were blackthorn, the earliest carbon-dated to 2500 BCE with, crucially, a right-angled bend at one end.[12] This bend, he points out, is likely to have been caused by hedge trimming. If Pryor is right, this would be the oldest bit of hedge in the world. In Oxfordshire, a row of post holes alongside a ditch clearly marked out a fence, with the remains of thorny vegetation found nearby suggesting that it might have been accompanied by a hedge.[13]

The hedge remnants discovered by Pryor are matched in variety, if not in age, by finds in a Warwickshire ditch dig. At a site in Alcester, excavated in preparation for a redevelopment, Roman town defences were found, along with a pre-Roman watercourse, though whether the latter was a natural stream or a dug ditch was not clear. The filled in watercourse was found to contain a treasure. Not gold or a burial (although ditch burials were common at the time) but an unprepossessing collection of woody material which only an archaeologist could love. Careful analysis revealed an enormous variety of species of a distinctly agricultural nature. Did these plants indicate a ditched hedge? That it was a watercourse was evident from the large number of aquatic and bankside species identified, such as water crowfoot, watercress, duckweed, meadowsweet, fool's watercress and water parsnip. Typical crop weeds were also present – black bindweed, parsley piert and wild radish, along with signs of wheat. Grassland species were represented by ribwort plantain and yellow-rattle. Most indicative of a hedge was the abundance of tree species that are found in hedges to this day: hawthorn, blackthorn, field maple, purging buckthorn (the Latin name is *Rhamnus cathartica*, leaving one in no doubt of its effects if consumed) and spindle. There were also the typical plants that climb over or nestle under a hedgerow: rose, ivy, cranesbill and campion. Of particular note was *Ranunculus parviflorus*, a now rare buttercup associated with dry sunny banks, which might suggest such a bank above a ditch. Of course, a hedge is effectively nothing more than a long piece of scrubland and the plant remains could have been washed there from a nearby area of waste ground, but there seems little doubt that this was, indeed, a hedge.[14]

Ditches and banks (they are usually found together for obvious reasons) are long-lived structures, which is why so many still exist today. Alone, they are all but useless as they are rarely stock-proof. Speculation is a dangerous pastime, but it seems almost certain that if you find a ditch and bank, there was once a hedge (or fence) perched on the top. Digging a ditch and raising it to a bank is a time-consuming and energetic endeavour; one which I have had the pleasure of avoiding; hedge planting, in contrast, is something that requires little effort and no strength.

Chapter 4

THE IMPACT OF
THE ROMANS

Famously, the Romans did a great many things for us. However, one thing they did not do was transform their new colony's field systems. Agriculture in Britain was working well enough when they arrived, so the Romans took it on as a going concern and put up an 'under new management' sign. They may not have reorganised the Iron Age field systems, but they brought with them a shopping trolley of crops that had not existed in Britain before. They appear to have viewed Britain as little more than an enormous cornfield, so better bread wheat varieties duly arrived. But it is to the Romans that we also owe such things as oats, cabbage, cherries, wine grapes, apples (a much better species than the native crab apple, which is barely edible), plums (better than sloes, except in gin), several familiar herbs and, perhaps less welcome, the cucumber. Definitely less welcome was an entire catalogue of weeds and, for reasons we can only guess at, most of our deadly wild plants. The remarkable total is fifty food plants. Chickens also made the boat trip to these islands and improved stocks of sheep arrived. Important in a bad way, for agriculture in general and hedges in particular, was the introduction of the rabbit, a long-eared delicacy which arrived here in the first century CE.

The Romans wanted Britain to produce as much food as possible, so extensive improvements to agricultural technology were made. Iron ploughs were hardly unknown when the Romans arrived (it was, after all, the Iron Age), but the invader's heavy plough sported a 'coulter' which cut the soil vertically, a 'share' to cut underneath and a 'mould board' which turned the resulting sod over completely. This was a great improvement on the primitive, light native model, and was able to plough heavier soils.

Much effort has been expended in trying to find fields of truly Roman character, but with limited success. The standard model of land division throughout much of the empire was that of centuriation, this involved marking out the land for distribution in a grid of rectangular plots separated by walls or paths acting as boundaries (*limites*). Despite a great deal of research, no truly convincing example of centuriation has been found in Britain. As well as land division – often used to allocate land to veteran soldiers – centuriation was also the basis of taxation. Since much of Iron Age Britain came neatly parcelled up, no doubt the Roman civil service used existing systems rather than impose a disruptive new one. The population increased rapidly during the period and this, plus the requirements of the Romans for exportable grain and material support for their garrisons, necessitated an improvement in production, which meant more land under the plough. Land that Britons thought too much trouble to use, or hadn't got round to using, was taken under cultivation. It is these new fields that can be called Roman, but only by their period of construction, not from their centuriated layout.

The improvement in ploughing techniques made larger fields more economical, and two or more existing 'Celtic' fields were often joined together by the removal of dividing hedges or walls – a process that continued for hundreds of years after the Romans left. This could mean a block of several fields was used to produce one large rectangular field or – and this is a Roman innovation – one long, narrow field. Examples of these 'long fields' exist in scattered locations throughout Britain, such as at Martin Down in Hampshire, and alongside Housesteads Fort in Northumberland. The long fields at Overton Hill in Wiltshire indicate something slightly different. Built to the north of a

Roman road, they overlay earlier Bronze Age fields. Whether existing fields were abandoned and their outlines lost or whether they were destroyed to make way for the new arrangement is not known. They are, however, very distinctly 'long', being about seventy metres in length and only fifteen metres wide. Longer fields were better suited to the heavy plough, because tiresome turning is minimised. At Housestead, plough strips went up and down hills, contrasting with the later strip lynchets which traversed the hills horizontally. Their presence became known due to an accumulation of stones on the baulks between the strips, which means that they were unhedged, except perhaps around the strips as a whole. In the process of enlarging fields by removing boundaries and creating more fields from uncultivated land, the Romans both added hedges and walls and took some away.

There is evidence of at least one Roman hedge at Farmoor in Oxfordshire, where a field system was laid out in the form of small fields and paddocks, sometime in the second century AD. That these came complete with a hedge is indicated by the existence of blackthorn or hawthorn remains discovered during excavation.[1]

Roman villas, or at least their remains, are found all over Britain, and it is these that indicate the Romans' one lasting impact on how the countryside was organised. Villas were salubrious establishments nestling within an arrangement of stone-walled enclosures where the farming activities, such as threshing and storage, were accommodated. Beyond the immediate vicinity of such a villa, at Ditchley in Oxfordshire, there are two enclosures (amounting to 2 hectares) now visible only as dark marks in the soil, within which are a few small patches of even darker soil. Not large enough to be cornfields, these enclosures were orchards, with the darker marks indicating the ancient hedge that enclosed them.[2] Rural villas such as this one functioned as more than usually bountiful subsistence farming, and would have controlled large areas of fields. They were either run directly using hired hands and slaves or indirectly by tenant farmers. This model of a large house with a large agricultural estate would become dominant for most of the next 1,500 years and has not entirely disappeared even now, although whether or not the later manorial estates were their direct descendants is still a matter of debate.

Chapter 5

THE ANGLO-SAXONS

Although the Romans had been edging towards the exit door for nearly twenty years, the accepted end of Roman rule is 410 CE, the year that Honorius, the Western Roman Emperor, wrote what can best be described as a 'Dear John' letter to the *civitas* of Britain. Suddenly, the vast agricultural resources of Britain, brought about by the occupation, belonged to the British alone and one can imagine them waving goodbye to their guests with more of a cheer than a tear. The British already administered much of Roman Britain by then, but a unifying leadership was missing, as was a market for all that food and, worst of all, defence. A mere thirty or so years after one lot of uninvited guests left, another lot knocked on the door, then kicked it down. They were, of course, the Saxons and, unlike the Romans, they stayed.

In fact, over the next two centuries not just Saxons but Jutes, Angles, Mercians and other peoples from western Europe arrived and settled. Unfortunately, knowledge of the agricultural systems at the time is limited. According to Christopher Taylor, 'The fields and field systems of Anglo-Saxon England are the most difficult of all not only to explain, but even to find." Despite the difficulty, this

Charter from the Saxon king Edgar c.965 AD, granting land in Cheselbourne.

is the first time that fields and even hedges are mentioned in what then passed for English law. Just as their predecessors had done, the Saxons took on the country as a going concern. The field system that they were used to in what is now northern Germany was much the same as the one they found in Britain, so they felt immediately at home.

For the most part, land ownership was then quite different from what it is now, existing either as folkland or bookland. In the former, land was owned by a family group all of whom would need to agree before it was sold. Bookland, on the other hand, was much nearer to our own freehold, with ownership conferred by a charter (or book) which could be sold by the holder. This arrangement was first made as a concession to the Church for whom conventional inheritance was a problem, as all clergy were supposedly celibate. Being a more flexible arrangement, bookland was also taken up with enthusiasm by the laity.

The earliest bookland charters were written in Latin, the later ones in Old English and some in a rather bizarre mixture of the two. Around 1,500 of these revealing treasures are preserved; 200 as originals, the rest as copies made after the Norman Conquest when they were used to settle (or extend) arguments over land ownership. That these land charters were taken very seriously is indicated by the decidedly post-mortem penalty awaiting anyone who did not: 'He that casts this aside. Cast him aside, God, from heaven's riches into hell's torment unless repents he this deeply before his last day.'[2]

The charters are of particular interest here because any document that confers ownership of land must define its limits, which in this case was done with a description rather than a map. This may seem a far from accurate method (and a potentially dry read), but the charter descriptions are very evocative, taking the reader on a walk around the Saxon countryside while describing the view. Here is a brief passage from one referring to land near Iwerne in Dorset: '… thence to crane pool, thence to þung [probably the poisonous hemlock water dropwort] pool, thence to king hill, thence to slender thorns, thence to swylles [probably a stream] … thence along the stream as far as sand ford, thence to arse marsh's head, thence to the stump …'[3]

As well as painting a tantalising word picture of rural life, the charters reveal a great deal about Saxon farming methods. It is the vocabulary itself that is revealing, most notably the specialist words revealing farming methods. For example, the name for a stubble field, *ersc*, shows that such an esoteric matter was important to them – a stubble field being a useful source of grazing. Similarly, the Saxon word *wudubær* refers to woodland pasture, and *steorf* means poor pasture. Particularly intriguing is *utlæs*, which means out-pasture and rather suggests that there was an in-pasture, a reminder perhaps of the infield-outfield system of farming. Meadow makes an appearance as *mæd*, and open pasture is indicated by the word *feldlæs*.

The charters also tell us much about boundaries as that, after all, is what they were written to describe. The following, dated c.950, gives a good idea of the importance ascribed to hedges in establishing boundaries, but also that of rivers and banks. It also shows us that not all land was enclosed by its mention of 'open land'. This time the Old English is given in all its glory.

Ðis sindon þa land gemæro
Ærest on hunda leage on grægsole burnan lang burnan on grægsole hagan
lang hagan to hagena gemyðum of þen gemyþun on tichanstedes hagan lang
hagan ut to felda þæt a be ꝑyrtꝑalan oþ hit cymð ut on fulan riþe lang riþe
ut on doccena ford of þan forda ꝑest be more oþ hit cymð on þoneɪ licgendan
stoc of þan stocce lang hagan ut to heað felda to beorhfeldinga gemære to
þen hagan · lang hagan bur...

These are the land-boundaries [of Weonfeld — probably Wokefield]
First to hounds' wood to Grazeley's bourn, along the bourn to Grazeley
hedge, along the hedge to the hedge's junction, from the junction to kid
place's hedge, along the hedge out to open land, thence always by the
woodbank until it comes out to foul stream, along the stream out to dock's
ford, from the ford, west by the marsh until it comes to the fallen post, from
the post along the hedge out to heath field, to Burghfield [open land with a
barrow in it] people's boundary to the hedge, along the hedge ...[4]

As one would expect, numerous words refer to boundaries, with
the word for hedge appearing in a rich variety of spellings due to its
importance in Saxon agriculture. The most common to be found is
haga, but there is also hecg, hege, heg, haeg, hega and hay. Hega, and perhaps
hege, refers more precisely to a living boundary; haeg is, again more
precisely, a hurdle and hecg a territorial boundary. Haga can also mean
enclosure, and there is a related word, hagga for haw, the fruit of the
hawthorn (though haw is a still current word for a hedge and it is
not always clear which meaning is appropriate). The famous Dorset
philologist William Barnes has the Old English word hag to mean
a hedge, but also to chop, cut or hack. Armchair etymologies are
almost invariably wrong, but it seems possible that the two uses are
directly related, as the only way to maintain a hedge is to cut it. The
hawthorn itself is rendered hagu-þorn (þ is the Saxon 'th') and live
hedges (also called quick hedges) are called cwichege.

The Saxons also had a compound word for hedgerow in hegeræw
or heggeræw, nicely refuting the occasionally expressed notion that
the modern word is a tautological affectation. If there is a difference in meaning between hedge and hedgerow, it is not entirely

clear from the charters. One example mentions a hedgerow apple tree, which fits in with the OED definition that a hedgerow is a hedge which includes trees (presumably standard trees) other than those of the hedge itself. *Rah hege* is a rough hedge, and may be either the overgrown strips of woodland left by careful assarting or simply an example of neglect by the farmer.

Fences are also mentioned in the words *hæcce, gehæg, gearde* (the origin of garden) and *glind*. All but *hæcce* also have the meaning of enclosure. *Scidweall* is a palisade, possibly with a hedge alongside, and is likely to have been the sort of fence used when one was seriously worried about the neighbours. Ditches and, more often, dykes (both frequent companions to a hedge) appear on many occasions as *dic*, *dices* and *dyche*. A ditch is just a channel and a dyke is a long channel with the soil piled up (usually) along one side, and often with a hedge on top, but it is impossible to determine which is meant in Old English.

That enclosure was essential to Saxon farming practice can be inferred from the number of names for it, including *hægen, clūse, scēad, tēag* and *worþ*. The last appears in many place names, for example Emsworth which means 'the enclosure of Æmele'. It seems likely that these enclosures were permanent (or semi-permanent) structures that were hedged or otherwise bounded; the Saxons used the word *fyld* for the fold used to contain sheep and *penn* for an enclosure where they kept a variety of animals.

Some years ago my friend Reuben was driving his small herd of rare-breed cattle along one of the back roads of our village from one field to another. They ambled aromatically but harmlessly past a few front gardens until they came to one where the attractions of fresh young grass proved irresistible. A single cow can make a mess of a lawn in a few minutes, so the attentions of Reuben's herd quickly turned this one into a muddy disaster. A good deal of shouting and stick waving by their master encouraged the cows back on the road, but the damage was done. The owner of the land was not sympathetic to the bovine invasion and demanded compensation. The whole matter became something of a *cause célèbre* in the village for a week or so. Fortunately for Reuben, but not for the irate owner of the lawn, the law was on the side of the drover. There are modern laws which govern such matters but there are also old ones, very old ones – in this case, the oldest of them all.

Ine, King of Wessex from 688 to 726, is mostly remembered for his laws (sensibly known as 'The Laws of Ine'), which are among the earliest Saxon laws to survive, mainly because they were appended to the legal code of the better-known Alfred the Great. The law that saved Reuben a few quid is as follows: 'A commoner's premises shall be fenced both winter and summer. If they are not enclosed, and a beast belong to his neighbour strays in through the opening he himself has left. He shall have no claim on that beast, but he shall drive it out and suffer the damage.'[5] The devastated front lawn in question had no fence of any kind, not even a flower border, so its owner had to 'suffer the damage', if not in silence, at least in regret. King Ine had another thing to say about protecting enclosures:

> If commoners have a common meadow or other land divided into strips to fence, and some have fenced their portion and some have not. And cattle get in and eat up their common crops or their grass, then those who are responsible for the opening shall go and pay compensation for the damage which has been done to the others who have enclosed their portion. The latter shall demand from the owners of the cattle such amends as are fitting. If, however, any beast breaks hedges and wanders at large within, since its owner will not or cannot keep it under control, he who finds it on his cornland shall take it and kill it. The owner of the beast shall take its hide and flesh and suffer the loss of the remainder.[6]

This gives the other side of the coin. In short, if someone owns, or has an interest in, (common) land, they must fence it to keep their animals in. The fact that two of the mere seventy-six Laws of Ine concern hedges, demonstrates their central importance to rural Saxon life, and Saxon life was almost entirely rural.

The pattern of the countryside in at least the early- to mid-Saxon period was one of scattered settlements. Many or even most of these were likely to have used the infield-outfield method of cultivation. Fields near a settlement (the infield) were farmed intensively and continuously for crops, with livestock brought in from the outer fields, perhaps at night, to maintain fertility, or manure was collected and carried to the infield in pots. Animals were frequently housed with their owners, and the manure and used straw deposited on the infield.

Outfields were used for occasional arable; ploughed, sowed and stubble-grazed each year until soil fertility gave out. They would then be left for years as rough grazing before being returned to the plough. That such a system was used is known from digs, where evidence of intensively manured areas in the form of high phosphate levels and broken pots have been found. This seems like scant evidence and it would be good to discover some relict system in which the infield-outfield system is clear. Unfortunately, almost all have been destroyed by later agriculture. What little physical evidence exists is, however, convincing.

Driving through the Somerset Levels a few years ago, I remember finding them both beautiful and frightening. The narrow reed-edged roads seemed very vulnerable to a landscape that wanted to be sea and which felt as if it might physically engulf me. Areas such as this – the Fens being the other obvious example – have attracted land-hungry farmers for millennia, and indeed the Romans reclaimed land from the sea, only for the sea to claim it all back again. The Saxons' attempts were more successful and are, more or less, still with us.

The typical Somerset Levels pattern of fields can be seen around the villages of East and West Huntspill, just north of Bridgwater and the River Parrett, as infamous for its propensity to flood then as now. Among the familiar straight-edged field boundaries are some that are distinctly curved. Viewed on a map or an aerial photograph, these curved field edges resolve into ovals, about 750 by 250 metres. Many have been truncated or bisected by later additions (one has the end nipped off by the M5) but they are very clear, once recognised for what they are. How could oval-shaped field systems find their way into an irregular rectilinear pattern? In fact, it is the other way round. The ovals appear to be the first areas drained for settlement and the more regular fields around them a later development.

The Somerset Levels in benign mood.

Stephen Rippon, Professor of Landscape Archaeology at Exeter University, points out that digging ditches is hard work and a circular (or oval) ditch provides a larger area of drained land than any other for the same amount of effort. These oval areas were once surrounded by a ditch and a bank (now it is just a ditch, a hedge or both), the bank having been removed once the coastal embankment, built to protect the entire area, was established.[7]

Oval enclosures appear in several other places in Britain, near Newport in Wales, in East Anglia and also elsewhere on the Somerset Levels. Stephen Rippon suggests that these structures were the first areas to be colonised by draining, and that they were the infield, complemented by the outfield of the surrounding marsh. The latter would have proved to be good grazing ground in the summer months although too wet for anything during the winter. He goes on to suggest that this system, surviving as a relict of the establishment of agriculture on virgin land, forms a model for many if not all Saxon infield-outfield systems built on virgin or reverted land.[8]

The Saxons did not have England entirely to themselves; there were numerous visits by the Vikings over a period of about 300

Even when trimmed, this four-metre-wide hawthorn and blackthorn hedge in West Dorset is completely impenetrable.

years. Despite the *Anglo-Saxon Chronicle* informing us that the Vikings moved from a life of crime and 'proceeded to plough and support themselves', almost nothing of their agricultural methods is known, and it is generally thought that they changed the rural landscape but little.[9]

Whether or not any Saxons were protected from the invaders by their hedges is also not known, but lacking the substantial defensive structures surrounding some European settlements, hedges could have been used as defensive barriers. The average country hedge in Britain today is a poor thing, unlikely to deter even Sunday afternoon strollers, but there are a few hedges in Dorset that are four yards thick and impenetrably dense. A Saxon village community may well have been protected from the odd ruffian or band of marauders by a continuous hedge of similar sturdiness, and in perilous times the hedge boundary would have been patrolled.

If the picture of early medieval agricultural practice in England is murky, then in Scotland and Wales it is almost completely obscure and historians have had to resort to guesswork. In Scotland culti-vated oval 'islands', found particularly in Galloway, may be infields surrounded by unbounded outfields of rough pasture and occa-sional arable, but they may also be second millennium field systems. Clearly agriculture was a way of life in Wales and Scotland, but there appears to have been no overarching planning as in England. Isolated homesteads worked the land as best they could in a climate that had deteriorated since Roman times. Field systems, such as they were, were bounded by whatever came most easily to hand, and many of the stone walls that lie scattered across upland Wales and Scotland could easily date from this time.

The open-field system which was introduced into much of England and Wales was a major break with the agricultural practices of the past and, despite one of its most notable aspects being a lack of hedges, it is central to our subject (see Chapter 6). The system did not become established until towards the end of Saxon ascendancy in the ninth century, and was not brought to its peak until after the Norman Conquest. Although the Roman and 'Celtic' fields inherited by the Saxons continued in use, overall land use declined and many fields were simply abandoned, their walls and hedges left to fall or grow into scrub and woodland. Archaeology has discovered no new Saxon fields, but this is unsurprising since the population dropped dramatically in the early years of colonisation. It has also been suggested that in time the Saxons came to prefer a more open countryside, dispensing with boundaries, even when the land was used for crops. This in itself would suggest a forerunner of the open-field system which, as its name makes clear, required large fields without boundaries. Where enclosed fields continued under cultivation they were lengthened to accommodate the heavy plough, and there is a distinct move from the square or short rectangular 'Celtic' fields.

There is one form of enclosure that began life in Saxon times and has lived on until today, the deer park. Clearly, this was meant as an enclosure for the holding of deer for the hunt, but it is an unusual sort of enclosure in that it also functions as a large and elaborate trap. The existence of deer parks in Britain dates from the late-Saxon period, though their global history goes back millennia. They were granted to those with land and enough money to pay for the expensive fencing. That right was by royal assent only and was known as a 'right to empark'. The land was usually a wood, but one opened up to provide lawns and cover. The fence itself was a park pale of cleft oak usually placed atop a bank. There would be a ditch on the inside to increase the effective height of the fence, as deer are known for their ability to jump. The height on the outside was sometimes sufficient to jump in, however, effectively forming a trap. Owning a deer park was the medieval equivalent of owning a private jet and Oliver Rackham estimates that by 1300 there were 3,200 such parks in England.[10]

Gerald, who still lives in the same parish as me, was my predecessor in Snowy Eyre's farmhouse and he too had once gazed at those same prehistoric fields on the hill opposite. Apart from the fields and an abundance of undisturbed downland, the farm also boasts the largest number of rabbits one is ever likely to see anywhere. If you walk over the brow of Camel Hill to surprise them, the ground itself seems to move as hundreds leap for their burrows. In addition to its use for a little arable and a lot of stock rearing, the farm had once been a warren, an area of land in which rabbits are encouraged make their home. A warren, like a deer park, is a trap.

In Gerald's day the rabbits had a deal with the devil, who in this case was Gerald's father. To keep the population high, he used to hedge and fence the warren with a relatively fine mesh wire, with a little door placed at strategic intervals to let rabbits pass. This may sound counter-productive, but the door only opened into the warren not out, ensuring high stock levels and preventing an inbred population.

A 'free warren' was a medieval licence, provided by the Crown, a permit to catch certain animals in specified areas without fear of punishment. The licensee would care for both the animals and the land – free in this context meaning free to catch animals without being fined, while the word warren implies caring for (it shares a common root with the words warden and guardian). Warrens could be specialist enclosures like the one just described (if not so fiendish), but more often they were areas of woodland. Rabbits were not the only animals that were warrenable; hare, pheasant, partridge and, possibly, roe deer are also of the warren, though foxes, red squirrels and other furry creatures are sometimes added to the list.

Chapter 6

THE OPEN-FIELD SYSTEM

The open-field system had been operating for a couple of hundred years in England by the time the Normans arrived with their winning ways, but so had another institution, intimately tied to this agricultural innovation – the manorial system. In Northern France a clear continuity can be drawn from the Roman villa to the medieval manor. In Britain it is rather more complicated, with the Saxon invaders deserting the villas that existed and gradually setting up their own seats of localised power. Although not directly descended from the Roman villa, the idea of a ruling, military class living the high life off the bent backs of a peasantry who were little more than slaves continued in Britain until the end of the Middle Ages and arguably beyond. It was, however, only in late-Saxon Britain that a recognisable manorial system as we understand it was formed, and only after the Norman Conquest that it reached its full flowering. It was with the manor that the open-field system came into being, and it was chiefly the open-field system that was to determine the fate of agricultural boundaries for the next thousand years.

The history of the manorial and open-field systems and the lives of those who experienced them are worth examining, if only briefly, in order to explain what was to come next – enclosures. The manors and open fields came into being first under the stewardship of tribal Saxon lords before being taken over by their Norman successors. Manors did not necessarily only support open fields, they also existed in 'wooded' countryside (see p. 56) where the open-field system was not employed (see below). Nor were they scattered around the countryside for they *were* the countryside, with nearly the whole of the Norman realm divided into manors within counties. Feudalism and the manorial system were dependent not so much on a moneyed economy as one of service. The king, who possessed allodial rights (ownership of the land outright), provided tenure to the nobility in return for financial reward and service of arms. The lords gave tenure to lesser lords or to individual tenants (serfs) in return for service. The lesser lords did not farm by their own hand but had their own serfs. The Church too received substantial amounts of land from the king, this time in return for salvation – a seller's market in those days.

Serfs, who were the basic class among a nomenclatural menagerie of agricultural workers, were not tied to the lord but to the land, which they could not leave. They possessed rights to farm certain amounts of land, whether as strips in the open field or in enclosed fields in wooded areas, and had access to the common fields and common meadows proportionate to their holdings of land. Their service was to work the demesne – land held directly by the lord. This was called 'day work' because it amounted to two, three or four days of the week. A serf may also have had to supply the lord with payment in kind. They had certain duties with regard to the general upkeep of the land, one of which was the maintenance of hedges, a relatively minor task on open land, but onerous where the land was enclosed.

The open-field system largely dispensed with hedges, walls and boundaries, dividing what might well become a parish into two or three fields, plus a meadow and some waste ground. The large fields would be farmed in rotation, one of them in any year being left fallow. Most of it would be held in common, with each tenant or owner holding a number of selions (small pieces of land) scattered

Ridges of a relict open field in Somerset.

among the large fields, and enjoying rights over the meadow and waste. Waste ground is far from as useless as it sounds as it formed an important part of the common grazing and was the source of wood and wild foods for the villagers. The arable land was 'commonable', which meant that despite being held for the growing of crops by an individual, there was a common right to graze the stubble and, every three years or so, the fallow. Overall, however, the land was 'in common'.

How this radically different open-field system was developed from the field systems that preceded it has been the cause of much academic speculation. In their book *Fields* (1989), Richard and Nina Muir suggest the new system grew from the fairly primitive infield-outfield system to which post-Roman Britain may have been reduced. The Muirs note that more land was needed as the population eventually rose, and the area of intensively farmed fields was gradually extended until rough grazing was reduced to the bare minimum. Some control of who had access to rough grazing (the common) and the fallow was now required and this, they argue, provided elements for the open-field system. A further factor, which must have contributed, was the increasing use of the heavy plough, a remarkable device which could require as many as four pairs of oxen – animals not known for their steerability. The problem of having to constantly turn the plough around in small fields could be alleviated by converting short fields into long fields and then several long fields into one big field. The use of large teams of oxen was achieved by the invention of the rigid collar and tandem harness, allowing the much put-upon creatures to pull equally. Oxen and their complex harnessing arrangements and mould-board ploughs constitute expensive capital investments and would have required cooperation and sharing between farmers and a move towards commonality. Partible inheritance, where land was repeatedly divided, resulting in small strips being allocated among heirs, may also have been instrumental.

Even with all these pressures, such a dramatic change as that from isolated farmsteads individually held, to open fields, where the holdings were dispersed and the use of common rights communally agreed, could only have happened by broad agreement or by the organising hand of someone in power. While the individual tenant or small landowner might literally reap little reward from the change and suffer great disruption to his way of life, the large landowner – be it the lord of the manor or the Church – would enjoy substantial benefit at little inconvenience. The change, where it occurred, was sudden rather than incremental and once a large landowner had established the open-field system on one of his holdings he was likely to establish it on others. Thus the idea spread rapidly.

Whatever way they came about, open fields were a disaster for hedges, as most of those that existed on land where open fields were established were uprooted to make way for extremely large fields. The loss of hedges at that time is comparable to their loss during the agricultural revolution that followed the Second World War.

The open-field system was not established throughout Britain, even under the Normans, but chiefly in a broad swathe through the fertile regions of lowland England. It is easier to say where it was not used than where it was. Nowhere in Cornwall, only in scattered parts of Devon and Dorset, and in Wales, where it was found mostly in the more Anglicised south. The south-east, including around the London area and in Kent and Essex, kept the earlier, enclosed countryside.

Generally, the country was divided into 'wooded' (meaning lots of hedges, rather than woods) and 'champion' (which derives from the Old French word *champaign* meaning 'open country').

The open-field system developed alongside an increasingly nucleated settlement pattern, or, in other words, villages replaced isolated farmsteads. That nearly all of our villages and towns are of Saxon origin is clear from the fact that all but a handful have Saxon names. But which came first – open field or settlement? Whether one is a natural result of the other or whether they both arrived at the same time as a result of planning are yet more questions for academics to discuss quietly over a pint. However, at least some villages are known to have been built on well-established open-field systems and thus post-date them, and villages are not exactly rare where no open-field system has ever existed, so the two can only be loosely connected.

A little to the east of the M1 in Nottinghamshire lies one of the last living vestiges of the once common open-field system. But for a few quirks of history, Laxton too would have gone, as other instances disappeared over a hundred years ago (with the exception of Braunton in Devon, which is rather less extensive). Its survival was a combination of the very human matter of landowners not being able to agree on how to enclose the open fields, financial issues and, more recently, a desire to preserve the past. Gilbert Slater, writing in the early twentieth century, was among the first to spot that Laxton was a living relict landscape which preserved a method of agriculture and a way of life that had existed for a thousand years. Its preservation continued, first through the efforts of individuals, then that of the Crown Estate and a stewardship arrangement. Students of British history should celebrate the fact that it has survived at all, so it is perhaps churlish to suggest that those who performed such a fine service to posterity should have tried a little harder and retained more. When Slater wrote his appraisal, *The English Peasantry and the Enclosure of Common Fields* (1907), peasants still ploughed their neat strips of land and grazed their stock on common pasture and stubble, and it is a pleasing fantasy to think that perhaps (with the benefit of a generous EU subsidy) they could be doing so still. Nevertheless, parts of the ancient system and at least some of its social and legal constituents continue, administered, as it has always been, by local manorial jurisdiction (known as the Court Leet).

Laxton is a strange place to visit, for as one enters the parish from the west through a small wood (once upon a time there would have been a gate), the flat landscape opens out into a near hedge-free vista, with not even a roadside hedge to be seen. There are hedges, of course, but they are generally distant and sparse. Apart from this conspicuous lack and a more than usual agricultural aspect to many of the houses in the village, there is nothing obvious that speaks of its history, but this is indeed visible in the landscape and in detailed records going back to the Domesday Book.

An aerial view reveals the familiar patchwork of arable fields, but a closer inspection shows something considerably less familiar. What hedges there are come to abrupt terminations, seldom completely enclosing a field at all. Within what appears to be a single field, several smaller 'fields' appear to exist with what seem to be different ploughing and planting regimes. These small, often narrowly rectangular, fields usually lie alongside, or at right angles to, one another, but are seldom separated by a hedge or fence. Finally, the houses in the village itself appear to have long, narrow paddocks behind them.

It is impossible to describe a typical instance of an open-field system and its accompanying social, political and practical institutions as they varied greatly according to who owned them, geographical and geological considerations, local custom and many other factors. No truly typical open-field system has ever existed, but Laxton is a good and well-recorded example. Variously called Laxington, Lexington, Lessington and Laxintone, it was originally a Saxon settlement. At the time of the Norman invasion, the Domesday Book records it as having been held by a noble called Tochi, the son of Outi, nobles of decidedly Danish descent. As was to happen throughout Norman Britain, these incumbents were unceremoniously evicted and replaced by more suitable Norman nobles. In this case it was Geoffrey Alselin, a particularly notable noble who also received lands elsewhere. Geoffrey's only offspring was a daughter.

She married another Norman, one Robert de Caux, and their descendants retained the manor continuously until 1618 when it was sold as a result of debts and an unpleasant mix-up over inheritance.

Laxton was later acquired by Sir William Courten, a merchant of great wealth but who never lived there. He did, however, install a steward to manage the estate, Samuel Stanford, who, in 1635, commissioned the production of two of the most useful and impressive historical documents in English history: a 'terrier', listing the holdings, acreages and boundaries of the estate, and a remarkable map, drawn by a Mark Pierce. Sir William's son, also William, managed to spend his large inheritance and Laxton was sold to Robert Pierrepoint in 1640 whose descendants owned the estate until the 1950s.[1]

Nothing in history is simple, of course, and this very brief tale, which suggests 'one estate, one lord', omits to mention that part of Laxton became a 'sub manor' quite early on, when one of the de Caux family made a grant of land to Richard, soon to become Richard de Lexington. Even land under the control of the lord could be sub-contracted and Domesday records 'a man of Geoffrey Alselin' who had one plough, twenty-two villeins and seven bordars having five ploughs, and five serfs, one female serf and forty acres of meadow. This sort of sub-division was common, as was having more than one manor for a single village (what we might now call a parish), it being more a matter of whose land a worker 'held' rather than where he lived.

From Domesday to the records of Mark Pierce, there is very little information on how the estate was run or the lives of those who lived there. There is a hint that they suffered like everyone else from the ruination of the Black Death in the fourteenth century and records of an argument over a fine for brewing and selling beer outside the monopoly of the manor. Records of court hearings would have been made but almost none survive for Laxton, depriving us of the knowledge of the day-to-day problems and tittle-tattle found in some manorial records. All this can be forgiven as there still exist — lovingly and rather jealously cared for at the Bodleian Library — the magnificent efforts of Mark Pierce.

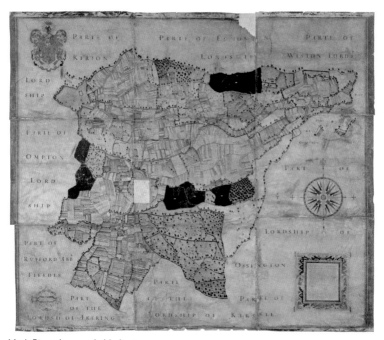

Mark Pierce's remarkable Laxton map.

Artistic licence is seldom a virtue in a map, but the Laxton map is as much a history as a geography. Scattered around the woods and fields are figures at work or play (no one appears to be at home with their feet up). To the south-west of the deserted motte-and-bailey castle is a meadow where two women and a man turn the hay, while two men in a field to the east cut hay with a scythe as a woman looks on. Further east two men lead a pair of oxen pulling a plough led by a trace horse, an activity represented many times in different parts of the map. In several fields carts can be seen, drawn by two or three horses, one of them being loaded with sheaves of hay or straw, and in another a flock of sheep is tended by a shepherd and his dog. Horsemen are everywhere and, on the northern boundary, they appear to be engaged in a hunt, while elsewhere men with pikes are following hounds chasing a hare. Even the lost sport of partridge hawking is depicted. There is no attempt, however, to restrict the activities portrayed to a particular season.

The long 'paddocks' behind the houses in Laxton village are

Detail from the Laxton map, north-west corner.

clearly visible, as is the village of Kneesall to the south-west, a few scattered houses, some windmills, woods, parks, enclosures and many, many selions. The selion was the basic unit of the open field but not the smallest. Barely visible in the open arable fields of Laxton, but surviving in pasture near the village, are present day parallel ridges. These ridges are the result of ploughing the selions into several narrow strips, the soil being built up in the middle by ploughing up one side and down the other. As the plough turns the soil, it is turned towards the middle and the result is 'ridge and furrow'.

The beauty of Pierce's Laxton map, beyond aesthetics and its extraordinary attention to detail, is that the selions are numbered and the numbers linked to the terrier which tells us who has rights over which particular selion. There were one hundred families in Laxton at the time of the map's production, ninety of which held land. Many of these were small at merely an acre or two, while the largest holding was eighty acres. The right to hold even a single selion was important because with it came other rights of common.

For those readers who missed out on rods, poles, perches at school (mine was probably the last generation to be informed of these agricultural delights), an acre is the area encompassed by a rectangle one furlong long (220 yards or about 200 metres) by one chain wide (22 yards or about 20 metres). This area is, famously, that which may be ploughed with a team of oxen in one day. However, the acre of the past, on which this definition was based, was smaller than the acre we know today. This was sometimes the area of a selion, though variation was the rule and they could easily be less than a quarter of an acre. The length of the selion would be around a furlong, but this wasn't fixed and could be less than half that to half as much again; selions had to fit with each other and any existing geographical features. Indeed, selions could be several hundred yards long, as the longer they were the fewer awkward turns of the plough were required.

The selions of any individual tenant are distributed around the two or three great fields (see pp. 53–4), and sometimes some of these may be side by side without a noticeable gap between them. In many parts of the country, a neighbour in the field would be a neighbour in the village. If, as was usual, adjacent selions were held by different families, a deeper than usual furrow was cut, marked out by a post at each end. The marking of this furrow is still performed with due ceremony at Laxton to this day. In the past there would probably have been a narrow strip of unploughed land, known as a baulk, which was dispensed with as land became more valuable. A baulk would seldom, if ever, be hedged, but both it and the deep furrow fit my catholic definition of a hedge as an agricultural boundary. In Laxton the dividing furrow was, and still is, marked with a carefully positioned stake at each end (in the other extant open-field system at Braunton, it is a large stone). While actual hedges between selions would be rare, fences or hurdles were occasionally employed if the holder wanted stock to be kept in or out.

Dividing furrows between selions, or baulks if they were used (their existence is a contentious issue), must have been a matter of endless argument over the years. I once took possession of an allotment in my village and cultivated it for several years until the parish clerk took exception to my laissez-faire attitude to weeds and duly evicted me. Allotments, or allotment gardens to give them their proper title, are direct descendants of selions, though their dimensions are measured in perches rather than furlongs and chains. Allotments have baulks between them rather than furrows, to provide access as well as a defining border. I was horrified one day to find that my neighbour, who had always seemed like an honest sort of a fellow, had encroached upon the already perilously narrow baulk by digging some of it away and incorporating it into his allotment. Such taking of liberties was evidently common, as it is recorded in the fourteenth-century poem, *The Vision of Piers Ploughman*:

> If I yede [went] to the plowgh,
> I pynched so narwe,
> That a foot lond or a forow
> Fecchen I wolde
> Of my nexte neghebore,
> And nymen [seize] of his erthe.[2]

These ridges dominated the countryside for a thousand years wherever the open-field system was used, but remain only in lightly ploughed or pastured fields. Most of those that survive are near to habitation where the land is used for pasture or keeping horses. They are the length of the strip in which they are ploughed, but vary enormously in width.

At the end of each strip there would once have been a 'headland'. This too formed a boundary of sorts, but was used as access and to give room to turn the plough, though never ploughed itself. It also formed part of the common grazing. These can amount to substantial banks due to the raised plough depositing soil on them, and can often survive the loss of the ridges themselves. There were penalties imposed on anyone ploughing these headlands and those at Laxton still exist. Speaking to a member of the Court Leet at Laxton, I learned that these headlands are renowned for their rich flora, having been left undisturbed for a thousand years.

Going west along the main road through Laxton and over to the right, is a path along the eastern edge of one of the large fields that make up the modern open-field system. This immediately

This photograph, taken near the village, show a trackway which on most farms would have been bordered by a hedge.

seems odd as there is no hedge bordering the field. Well there is, but, unusually, it is the hedge to the right of the path; there is none on the left alongside the field itself. The hedges that bound the 'gardens' behind the houses, one of which is the hedge just mentioned, are among the oldest in Britain. Apart from these, there are relatively few hedges around Laxton, though many more than there once were, due to enclosure of a large part of the parish between the seven-teenth and nineteenth centuries. To see what hedges existed when the open-field system dominated the area, we need to look at Mark Pierce's map where every inch of hedge is recorded.

The first thing to note is that a hedge surrounds the parish entirely. Even the woodlands at the border are drawn with a hedge, and a hedge (which still exists today) follows a meandering stream south of Kneesall. The second thing is that all the hedges are, in truth, hedgerows. They are represented as rows of bushes, punc-tuated frequently by standard trees, which fits with the dictionary definition of hedgerow. There are four great fields, which – given the typical three-year rotation – might seem awkward, but two fields can be treated as one, even if they are not contiguous. These fields are hedged all round. There are a few meadows, all of which had disappeared beyond the memory of those interviewed by Gilbert Slater. These too were hedged, as was the relatively small amount of waste, which survived until fairly recently before falling to the plough. A few oddities exist, including a dwelling standing in the middle of what looks like a part of the waste, in front of which is an orchard, the whole being enclosed by a fence. This may have been an authorised enclosure or the result of someone 'squatting'. Such incursions were fairly common and the trespasser would sometimes earn acceptance and pay rent to the lord. There is evidence of early enclosure to the north-east, all of it hedged apart from some particularly small fields which are enclosed by walls. This particular enclosed area is known as Moorhouse.

Although the map is extremely well drawn, it is too much to expect any indication of which tree species made up the hedges. However, from studies on both old and relatively new hedges, it is likely that they were a mixture of those woodland species suitable for the soil and climate of the area. The Laxton hedges certainly qualify as old and most of them would have been in existence when the open-field system was laid out. Those that were not there would have been planted anew, and a very straight piece of hedge which encloses an irregular area of pasture to the north-west is clearly a later enclosure. Even some of the 'new' hedges would effectively be old, because they were not truly planted but created by clearing a piece of woodland up to the boundary during the establishment of an open-field estate, in other words by assarting.

Lowland Wales would eventually adopt the open-field system of lowland England. In 1603, George Owen wrote: 'The saied Lords marchers being Englishe lords ... brought the most parte of the lands of the saied Lordshipe to be of English tenure.'[3] The historical records and physical evidence of open fields can be seen all over Wales, though obviously little exists in the mountainous north. Some are quite obvious, such as that at Rhossili on the Gower Peninsula. This followed the English pattern in having open fields, meadows and common grazing. The latter remains virtually unchanged, perched above half the length of the magnificent Rhossili Beach. Many of the strips are also intact and perfectly visible, and the baulks that have been dismissed as the figments of a researcher's imagination are in full view, though many are now adorned with a hedge. There is also a good illustration of the fact that open fields do not need to be open. On the mainland cliffs overlooking Worm's Head, where most surviving strips can be found, those standing a little back from the cliff are enclosed by hawthorn-topped banks, while several near the cliff edge are surrounded by stone walls built from material dug on the spot. If you have ever been to Rhossili on a windy day you will understand why; it is a matter of protecting crops from a battering and salty wind. Exactly the same arrangement is found at perhaps the most southerly of all open-field systems, Portland Bill in Dorset. In my experience, it is windy here every day of the year, and a couple of dozen strips have been provided with defending stone walls.

The manorial system and open-field system worked well enough, for the lords at least, but over the centuries they were undermined by the change to an entirely moneyed economy. The seeds of this change were sown with the manorial system itself because not all workers were serfs, some were 'socmen' who had the right to sell their tenure, though they were serfs in all other respects, and there were already freemen who held land at a rent but owed no service. The lords too were not above selling land when they needed a bit of cash. The most sudden change came in the terrible form of the Black Death which began in 1348 and destroyed a third of the population over the next century or so. With many of the workers gone to a better place, those that were left found themselves in great demand. The legal ties that bound serf to land and to a master loosened as labourers moved to the manor offering the highest bid, and the very idea of a serf who owed work was abandoned as service was commuted to rent. With labour in short supply, land was cheap and available to any with the money to buy it. Although the manor lived on, feudalism died, and a rising class of yeoman farmers who owned substantial holdings appeared; a class, moreover, which wished to consolidate its fields by dispensing with its associated common rights and enclosing it.

The Scots have never been as enthusiastic about boundaries as the English, who are keen to surround anything they own with hedge, wall or barbed wire and preferably all three. Anyone in England unlucky enough to be caught harmlessly walking on another's land will, at the very least, have to suffer a lecture on property rights delivered in a voice brimming with indignation and hurt, followed

A relict run-rig in the north of England.

by a completely hollow threat to prosecute should hide or hair be seen trespassing again.

Scotland was largely devoid of boundaries up until the various enclosure periods and even now the Scots enjoy a right to roam much envied by the English and Welsh. The poet, Anne Grant, in her *Superstitions of the Highlands* of 1811 tells us: 'The ground being all unenclosed, it depended entirely on the good faith and good herding of his neighbour … The sheep and cattle too, wandering promiscuously on the hills, the integrity of a man's neighbours was all he had to depend on for their return.'

Run-rig was a system of tenure used almost universally in Scotland until the close of the eighteenth century. It is similar in many ways to that of the open-field system of England and Wales, but individual ridges were periodically allocated to tenants instead of permanently. They formed the in-bye of an infield-outfield system.[4] Those few permanent boundaries that were needed consisted of a ditch, with any stones that were removed piled alongside, perhaps supplemented by stones from elsewhere and the whole thing covered in turf. Slightly less permanent stock enclosures, 'folds', were built on parts of the outfields made entirely from thick turfs, piled one above the other.

While agricultural boundaries were rare, head-dykes (or

A head dyke in the Lake District.

hill-dykes) are an exception in being ubiquitous in upland areas of Scotland (and in upland England and Wales). These are stone walls that form the division between rough common hill pasture and infield-outfield. Their purpose was fourfold: to define the arable areas, exclude grazing stock from growing crops during the summer months when they were taken to roam the hills, mark the drove roads that were once used for stock movement, and provide shelter for stock in the bleakest areas. A typical location is at the point where a slope becomes too steep and the soil too thin for cultivation. Such walls can stretch for miles, forming a feature of upland even today. Many of them are ancient, and Scottish Natural Heritage encourages their care with advice and grants. Some old, neglected head-dykes look like long piles of overgrown rocks and early writers thought them to be natural, but they were all carefully and laboriously laid over many years. A further related feature are the stone gathering-pens found above the head-dykes. They are generally called 'stone fanks' (or 'stells' or 'buchts') and mostly used for holding sheep. They can be neatly circular, triangular or square, the latter often subdivided into four sections. They are impossible to date, but are known to have been used up until the early nineteenth century and some find occasional use even today. As with head-dykes, their preservation is encouraged. Such stone folds are not confined to Scotland; the one in the photograph hails from Dorset, on the southern slope of the Purbeck Hills.

Chapter 7

INCLOSURE AND ENCLOSURES

Slowly at first, from the thirteenth century to the close of the nineteenth, thousands of miles of hedge were planted and walls erected, enclosing common fields and common waste. Subsistence farming as a communal way of life was gradually being replaced by enterprise farming and individualism. For this to happen it was necessary for common land to be taken into private ownership, so, in its various guises, common land died, slowly and painfully.

The words 'enclosure' and 'inclosure' are frequently used interchangeably, but, although they are connected, there is a fundamental difference between them. An enclosure is a physical boundary and the land enclosed within it, and to enclose denotes the act of placing a boundary around a piece of land. Inclosure is a legal term that refers to the conversion of common land into private land. When land is inclosed the rights of the commoner are 'severed', a term that also occurs in the very different context of shellfish collection when the common right to fish in delimited areas of tidal waters is severed by a 'several order'. Once common ownership is lost, it tends to stay lost and several orders that inclosed, or severed, oyster beds not long after the Normans arrived are still in force.

This is straightforward enough and it enables one to discuss these two different matters without confusing them, but one can still run into conceptual difficulties. For example, if a common open field, area of waste or meadow was acquired outright by one person this means that the field was inclosed because rights of common have been removed. If (and this rarely happened) it had no surrounding hedge or wall, it would still be inclosed, but it would not be enclosed. It is even possible to inclose an area of land while removing its hedges so that it is no longer enclosed. For the purposes of this book I intend to follow the modern convention and dispense almost entirely with the word inclosure and use enclosure for both meanings, trusting that context will make the usage clear. It is also true that enclosure and inclosure often occurred at the same time, so any distinction between them is usually moot.

The enclosure period is a long one, divided roughly into 'early enclosure' and 'parliamentary enclosure', the former beginning in the thirteenth century, the latter in the eighteenth century. As Graeme J. White points out: '… having taken some seven centuries to evolve, the open fields were by now embarked upon seven centuries of enclosure'.[1] The effect of enclosure was much more deeply felt in champion country because so much more of the land was commonable. In 'woodland' areas holdings were not in common, they were individual, already enclosed fields. It was only common pasture and common waste in such areas that could fall to enclosure.

Enclosures were to have an enormous effect on the overall length of hedges adorning the countryside because 'inclosure' usually, if not always, meant enclosure. Early enclosure and parliamentary enclosure can be divided into further stages, but they were all going the same way – towards an agricultural countryside of enclosed fields and attendant hedges.

The old manorial system of tenure, which was dependent on service, gradually became a matter of paying fees or rents. Tenure itself changed, with various confusing forms emerging: freehold, where the land had been purchased outright by an enterprising peasant (or anyone else); leasehold where the lease was bought for the duration of a number of lives, for example, the life of the holder, his wife and his son; copyhold which was an echo of the early forms of feudal tenure, based on a copy of part of the court rolls that declared the holding. The latter was very near to freehold as it was inalienable, but it did come with rent. Rather late in the day, in 1923, all remaining copyhold land was deemed to be freehold. All these tenurial arrangements could be bought and sold.

Once fields could be sold there was pressure towards consolidation. If a farmer had several strips in one field, it may be much better to have them joined together in one part of that field. This could be done by agreement with the other farmers and the lord of the manor. The various holdings may be any or all of the above mentioned varieties of tenure, so more negotiations will take place with the lord and various payments made. If any part of the land is commonable, the farmer could still enclose it, but would lose commonable rights to what was left of the open field, that is, he would not be able to graze the stubble or use the fallow.

Many references to changes in boundaries and ownership occur in rentals, charters and court rolls. An example found in the Leche family deeds speaks of 'Jankyn Williamson of Stretton leased to Jankyn Leche of Carden certain parcels of ground … As heretofore been open fields.'[2] As soon as this shuffling begins, physical enclosure of the resultant larger holding becomes almost inevitable as stock both inside the field and outside will need to be controlled, even on arable land where stock was put to fallow. A lord of the manor might have strips in the open fields too, so he also would begin consolidation. This buying, selling and swapping occurred in woodland areas too, but here the consolidation was just as likely to involve the removal of hedges to join two or more fields in a single enclosure.

The English judge, Sir Anthony Fitzherbert, Lord of the Manor of Norbury, wrote his *Boke of Husbandry* in or around 1534. It is one of the earliest of the many books that were to trouble the farmer with heartfelt and rather random advice over the next few centuries. Fitzherbert has much to say about the planting and laying of hedges, but he also argues for the virtue of enclosure. Much land was still left unenclosed so there was an onus on drovers, shepherds and swineherds to keep their charges well behaved and safe. Hedged enclosures, so Fitzherbert argues, will save the farmer money by disposing of the services of these rustics. Furthermore, he advocates the rearrangement of holdings by agreement:

> *And by the assente of the lordes and the tenauntes, every neyghbour may exchaunge landes with other. And then shall his farme be twyse so good in profytte to the tenaunte as it was before, and as moche lande kepte in tyllage, and then shall not the ryche man ouer eate the poore man with his cattell.*[3]

Much enclosure of land during the early centuries was pragmatic and piecemeal and for the most part by agreement. Until 1235, the common waste, woodland and pasture – though deemed to belong to the lord – could not be taken out of common by him. As demand for land increased, the waste became a temptation to both landless sons of farmers and to lords sympathetic to their pleas and the prospect of more rent. A certain amount of encroachment took place, with small enclosures springing up here and there, which became semi-regularised in time after a fine was paid. You could get away with almost anything, if you were prepared to pay the fine; in this case the fine was paid annually and became indistinguishable from rent. The blame for at least some of the irregularity of our present fields and their boundaries can be laid at the feet of these one-time trespassers. However, a formal path to enclose parts of the waste was made clear in the Statute of Merton of 1235. The statute may have been liberal and progressive in intent but the risk it presented – that the lord could enclose the waste for himself – was obvious even then. To ensure that the waste on which the peasants relied so heavily to pasture their oxen and stock did not disappear completely, a provision was made that parts could only be enclosed if the commoners were left with sufficient for their needs. Making sure such a clause was enforced would be difficult for an illiterate and immobile peasantry and, as circumstances changed, it became honoured only in its breach. Considered to be the first English statute, the Statute of Merton was not an auspicious start, heralding as it did the opening shots in a long war which the English and

Welsh peoples would eventually lose – the war of access to their own countryside.

A darker period was to follow during which land was enclosed by force, a period sometimes known as the Tudor Clearances. Like just about everything in history (and particularly enclosure), there is disagreement about just how hard the times were. But it is a matter of historical record that many of those who suffered loss of land rights were vocal and sometimes active in their own defence. There was also a contemporary literary genre of polemicism decrying the actions and low motives of the enclosers.

Economic and political reasons made enclosure attractive – if not always necessary – for those who might gain by it. What drove it during this period was, famously, sheep. A declining population meant there were now relatively few people to till the soil and as a result land became cheap. With wool at a premium and sheep (even a large flock) needing relatively little labour, sheep farming on a massive scale became both viable and attractive. The Statute of Merton was a further spur, enabling lords and large landowners

Typical small field of a Tudor enclosure at Okeford Fitzpaine, Dorset.

to remove the rights of the peasantry to common land making it available for sheep.

There is a contrary view that claims Tudor enclosure wasn't as bad as was once thought. Because of the drop in population, so the argument goes, villages and settlements became unsustainable due to lack of facilities. While the loss of the miller would mean having to journey for milled grain, the final straw, in some cases, appears to have been the loss of the brewer (almost invariably a woman). The British can tolerate many hardships but not a lack of beer. Thus villages were deserted and with few to work the land, sheep farming was the only possibility. While such situations may well have arisen, the well-recorded views of those who opposed enclosure suggest that the main motivation for privatising common land was greed. The methods were certainly underhand, if for the most part legal: rents would be racked up to force eviction and appalling penalties applied to anyone who continued to use their lost common rights.

The hardship and suffering that many endured resulted in the one thing that monarchs fear above all other – rebellion. There were doubtless many localised acts of violence and destruction, but the period is notable for several organised rebellions. Each of these has been honoured with a name, providing a sorry roll-call of doomed fights against repression and theft: Jack Cade's Rebellion of 1459, Kett's Rebellion of 1549, the Midland Revolt of 1607 and the Diggers' actions forty-two years later. These, and many more, are reminders of the iniquities of the past and of an alienation from the land that we suffer even today.

Robert Kett, a Norfolk yeoman farmer, was initially the target of locals rebelling against enclosure. Seeing the justice of their cause, this 'gamekeeper turned poacher' joined and then led what was to become one of the largest and bloodiest rebellions in England (though the blood was shed mostly by his followers). Despite his ultimate failure – he was hanged from the walls of Norwich Castle in 1549 – his legacy remains, as do his words: 'The common pastures left by our predecessors for our relief and our children are taken away. The lands which in the memory of our fathers were common, those are ditched and hedged in and made several; the pastures are enclosed, and we shut out.' Kett presented twenty-nine demands to the authorities, only one of which mentions enclosure directly: 'We pray your grace that where it is enacted for inclosyng that it be not hurtfull to suche as have enclosed saffren [sovereign] grounds for they be gretly chargeablye to them, and that frome hensforth noman shall enclose any more.'

It was not just rebels who objected. The most distinguished person to express a contrary opinion was Thomas More who, in his dystopian satire Utopia (1516), railed against enclosure and the greed of those wishing to cash in on the wool trade:

> Your sheep that were wont to be so meek and tame, and so small eaters,
> now, as I heard say, be become so great devourers and so wild, that they eat
> up, and swallow down the very men themselves. They consume, destroy,
> and devour whole fields, houses, and cities. For look in what parts of the
> realm doth grow the finest, and therefore dearest wool, there noble men,
> and gentlemen, yea and certain Abbots, holy men no doubt, not contenting
> themselves with the yearly revenues and profits ... leave no ground for
> tillage: they inclose all into pastures, they throw down houses, they pluck
> down towns, and leave nothing standing, but only the church to be made a
> sheephouse.[4]

Fearing lower revenues, loss of a source of military conscripts and general unrest, various monarchs passed eleven Acts of Parliament to prevent wholesale enclosure, the first in 1489 and the last one hundred and fifty years later. All of them were ineffective. Homelessness became the crime of vagrancy and for a brief period, recidivists could become enslaved. In 1607 came the Midland Revolt in which thousands of angry men and women began pulling down hedges and fences and levelling ditches, the latter causing them to be termed 'levellers'. In the mid-seventeenth century the religiously inspired 'Diggers' (who also called themselves 'The True Levellers') fought against enclosure by simply ignoring it, digging and planting where they would. They did not pull down hedges and fences but were opposed to enclosure nevertheless. In the words of their manifesto:

> The earth (which was made to be a common treasury of relief for all, both beasts and men) was hedged into enclosures by the teachers and rulers, and the others were made servants and slaves; and that earth, that is within this creation made a common storehouse for all, is bought and sold and kept in the hands of a few, whereby the great creator is mightily dishonoured.[5]

These various rebels had nothing against hedges, fences, walls and ditches as such, it was 'inclosure' they hated rather than 'enclosures', though the former would almost invariably require an increase or decrease of the latter. The innocent hedge was merely caught up in a battle for the land it enclosed.

Chapter 8

THE ENCLOSURE
OF THE FENS

Another act of 'inclosure', but not so much 'enclosure' as few hedges were gained, was the attempt to drain the Fens that began at the beginning of the seventeenth century. Unlike all the other protestors, those who objected to these drainage schemes were successful – at least for a while. Before wholesale drainage, this enormous wetland common provided a livelihood for many. Small, more amenable areas of the Fens had been drained piecemeal in the twelfth and thirteenth centuries, and a few of these fields are still visible, such as those to the south of Wiggenhall St Mary Magdalen in Norfolk. The long, narrow and rectangular layout of field, dyke and (much reduced) 'wall' or bank is clearly of some age as they are clipped by the prosaically named Middle Level Main Drain built in the middle of the nineteenth century, and bisected by the Magdalen High Road. Such fields as these were not the cause of rural strife, it was the plan to drain a much larger area and remove the common rights they embodied that provoked indignant protest and sometimes direct action.

The Lincolnshire aristocrat Lord Willoughby had made a plea against drainage as early as 1597 claiming that '… instead of helping

There are many enclosures in this view of the modern Norfolk fenland, all enclosed by dykes.

the gennerall pore, it would undo them and make those that are allreddye ritch farr more ritch'.[1] Nevertheless, the plans progressed and were supported by Willoughby's son, the Earl of Lindsey, by the Earl of Lincoln and no less a personage than King Charles I. An anonymous pamphlet of c.1646, entitled 'The Anti-Projector, or the History of the Fen Project', continued the opposition: 'The Undertakers have always vilified the Fens and misinformed many parliamentary men that all the Fen is a mere quagmire, and that it is a level hurtfully surrounded, and of little or no value. But those who live in the Fens and are neighbours to it know the contrary.'[2] The writer goes on to mention the cattle and sheep that thrived there (it was effectively an outfield) before detailing the specialties of the Fens: '... we have a great store of osier, reed and sedge which are such necessaries as the countries cannot want them for many uses, and sets many poor on work. Lastly we have many thousand cottagers, which live in our fens, which otherwise must go abegging.'[3]

Despite the protests, the drainage scheme went ahead, but ultimately it was to fail. The floodwaters rolled back in and the commoners returned to their land in 1649 when both project and king were cut short. The Fens were eventually drained in the eighteenth and nineteenth centuries and became a land enclosed by ditch and bank, and sometimes hedgerow.

The Fens now make up a remarkable landscape in which any area of land more than five feet above average is considered to be a hill. I once spent a few days there with my friend Charlie who looked after the extensive RSPB Fenland reserves. The first thing that became clear was the high level of anxiety suffered by anyone who takes responsibility for the welfare of birds. If a mushroom fails to make an appearance in its usual spot for ten or twenty years, a mycologist will presume that it is just resting; if a godwit goes missing for a day, then it is missing presumed dead. In the Fens a mere 5 cm increase or decrease in the water lying at the bottom of a ditch is a matter of concern, or at least comment, as it is likely to forebode a disaster for the population of reed warblers or some other wetland bird.

The second lesson was an appreciation of the supreme intricacy of the landscape. Understanding the landscape of any area of high and dry land does not prepare you for an understanding of that of the Fens. The history of this dynamic and challenging countryside is written in palimpsest; visible only from maps and aerial photographs. Its interpretation is a puzzle that has, for the most part, been solved by geologists and historians. An example of a feature

Blasted willows on the Fens, the road curved slightly at this point, following a 'roddon'.

Part of an Aussie gate, guarding the path over a large pipe. The 'berms' can be seen either side of the water.

that does not seem to have a ready explanation is the shape of the roads that sit a metre or more above the surrounding land. They are mostly straight, but frequently become dangerously, and notoriously, sinuous. Here, the winding stretches follow the ancient 'roddons', fingers of raised ground built from the silts of ancient riverbeds. Quite why a riverbed should be raised rather than sunken seems

79

puzzling – but it is not that the bed rose, rather that the drained, peaty land on either side sank as it dried out.

Like the roads, the field boundaries (which consist of dykes) are straight lines across the landscape; most of them arranged radially to drain into a larger waterway. However, also like the roads, they sometimes follow a snake-like path, matching still existing rivers and streams, or, more often, those that were lost as the land was drained. The dykes are fascinating entities in themselves. As well as drainage, they perform the function of hedgerow or wall in providing a stock-proof enclosure. The cattle will go down into the dyke to drink or to graze on the lush vegetation that springs up on the 'berms' – the flat ground at the bottom of a dyke on either side of the water. However, they will not cross, as they know the way to be treacherous and impassable. There are breaks in the dykes where the water disappears below pathways through a pipe or tunnel and these are made stock-proof by the 'Aussie gates' (lengths of barbed wire hooked between two posts) that stand incongruously, unattached to any hedge, wall or fence.

One dyke that Charlie showed me drained into a small river; unlike most of the other dykes, this one was dry, with its mouth a yard or so above the river surface. It was an old dyke that no longer served the land, or, more precisely, the water table, that had sunk around it. Much was learned from this visit, but one thing stood out above all else – that the dykes forming the network of drainage and field boundaries are sometimes known as 'wet hedges'.

Chapter 9

PARLIAMENTARY ENCLOSURE

Enclosure brought with it thousands of miles of new hedge, wall, ditch and dyke. Such boundaries were frequently in places that had never seen them before – the waste. This happened less in champion country, which had little waste to lose, as most that existed had already been incorporated into the open fields. However, in the woodland countryside much was lost, replaced by the hedgerows that we now value so highly.

To the west of Poole in Dorset, skirting a section of Poole Harbour, lies Lytchett Minster. It never possessed open fields, but instead had a handful of small fields in the village itself. The poor quality of the soil meant that there were extensive areas of common waste, so this appears to be a rough-and-ready form of infield-outfield. It is a fairly late settlement – the first record dates from the thirteenth century – probably because it was considered marginal land of wood and heath. In this respect it is a little atypical, but a great deal can be learned from the history of its enclosures. Fortunately, this history has been well recorded in contemporary maps that provide information back to 1584. By a complex series of events, a surveyor detailing late enclosure used the same numbering system as that employed by an early surveyor. Over 800 individual enclosures are recorded, all of them numbered, those numbered below 650 being the enclosures made before parliamentary enclosure began in earnest in 1750. (Such a large number is explained by the fact that the records also include the village of Lytchett Matravers to the north.)

Looking solely at the records for Lytchett Minster reveals that the whole of the parish was originally common land, save for a few small fields near the village. The pre-parliamentary enclosures cover approximately 60 per cent of the area, with a large wasteland to the east, two slightly smaller areas to the west and two small patches handily close to the village. One of the western wastes (an inverted triangle to the south-west) is odd in that it is detached from the main body of the parish, although in those days non-contiguous parishes were more common. While most of the new fields are roughly rectangular (few with completely straight edges) and laid out in a coaxial pattern, those which adjoin the remaining wastes have the typical appearance of assarting in that the leading edge of the field system is rounded. Where, in one place, an assarted enclosure is next

Map of Lytchett Minster, showing enclosures.

to a road, it is semi-circular; in another, at the top of the same area of former waste, it appears that a small, circular area of woodland has been hollowed out, leaving a thick hedge all around it. In the east, two areas of enclosure are separated by a very narrow strip of woodland (about 20 yards wide and 340 yards long), which also suggests assarting, though whether or not this counts as a hedge it is difficult to say. In total about 60 miles of hedgerow was established prior to parliamentary enclosure.

It was the parliamentary enclosures that claimed what remained of the waste, save all but a few small fields in the detached section (which evidently no one could be bothered with). The new enclosures are, without exception, rectilinear and with distinctly straight hedges. The straight lines of parliamentary enclosure hedges make them easily recognisable everywhere. There are rows of small enclosures, mostly near to roads and paths or in the small areas of former waste near the village, with larger enclosures on the periphery of the parish; some much larger at up to 170 hectares. One of these larger fields appears not to have been taken completely out of commons as it is marked as 'Turbary Allotment', indicating that it was reserved in order that the right to cut turfs for roofing could continue. The great length of many of the hedges (up to 1,000 yards long) means that there are fewer of them in number as a result of parliamentary enclosure in Lytchett Minster. Their overall length is about 12 miles.

Parliamentary enclosure saw the ultimate demise of open-field and other forms of common agriculture and most common land had disappeared by the end of the nineteenth century. The very first Act was passed in 1604 to enclose land at Radipole, Dorset, but the heyday of parliamentary enclosure began around 1750, then ebbed and flowed until its work was done. The aim was to modernise agriculture in Britain by sweeping away the persistent and troublesome trappings of a manorial past. As we have seen, much had already been accomplished in reordering the land by this time; perhaps as much as 75 per cent of it was already enclosed.[1] The main area affected by parliamentary enclosure was the champion country where the open-field system still continued, even though depleted by occasional, piecemeal enclosure. The Acts affected only England and Wales.

The tiny fields and massive hedges at Kingcombe, West Dorset.

While the former open-field land now needed thousands of miles of hedges and walls to enclose it, the extensive woodland countryside was frequently troubled by a different problem – not too few hedges, but too many and too big. In places such as Devon, Dorset, Sussex and even parts of Norfolk, hedges had taken over the countryside to a remarkable extent. In many places 10 per cent or more of agricultural land was occupied by hedges. Some of these hedges were three yards wide and, worse, many of the fields were truly tiny at only a rod (five metres) wide. In areas with high rainfall, such as Devon, the narrow fields and wide hedges kept the soil permanently wet, crops failed to thrive and, no doubt, stock suffered. Such a landscape was disastrous for the tenant farmer, but not for the landlord who – assured of his rent – could use the tenant's holding as a subsidised rough shoot, the tenant himself not being permitted to hunt under pain of imprisonment or worse.

Such fields are now considered national treasures (for example, the fields at Kingcombe in Dorset), but at the time they were a dreadful drain on the resources of the much put-upon tenant farmer. Early- to mid-nineteenth-century agriculturalists campaigned against them with articles and pamphlets, such as J. H. Turner's 'On the Necessity for the Reduction or Abolition of Hedges' printed in 1845.

The impact of similar pamphlets and the general movement towards agricultural improvement precipitated the end of many of these tiny fields and big hedges. We think of hedgerow loss as being a post-war disaster, but it began long ago.

The enclosures of the preceding centuries had progressed apace and were even speeded up by 'enclosure by agreement'. This was a process whereby an entire parish could be enclosed after negotiations between the interested parties, mediated by an official Enclosure Commissioner who guided proceedings and attempted to settle the inevitable disputes. However, the history of land usage and ownership needed the sharp axe that only Parliament could wield to cut through the tangle. The complex arrangements of tenure which had developed during the ascendency of the manor – copyhold, freehold, leases, customary rights, common rights and so on, each with the added complication of heritability – were a great barrier to consolidation. Similarly, rights of access to existing enclosures, waste or open field could drive a coach and horses through any attempt to enclose an entire parish. Enclosures by agreement were also open to challenge years later when someone decided that it was they who owned a particular part of the land after all. The local courts could adjudicate in individual cases, but only Parliament had the power to sweep aside these obstacles in their entirety. This was done mostly through private enclosure Bills, instigated by members of the public and examined by bands of itinerant Commissioners and surveyors who met as a committee at public meetings in the parish concerned (almost invariably in the pub). Private Bills became Acts only after approval by Parliament.

Those concerned were chiefly the large landowners, but also small farmers who saw advantage in the reordering of the countryside. The whole process of reaching agreement, allotting land fairly, making maps, marking out the enclosures on the maps and, not least, marking out of new roads (one reason why country roads are so winding), was one of the largest undertakings in British history. Although some of the Acts were tidying-up exercises, by 1914, when the last straggler was brought into the fold, 5,200 enclosure Bills had been enacted into law, transforming 6.8 million acres of land in England alone and another 1.7 million acres in Wales.[2]

Rectilinear enclosure walls in the Peak District.

Parliamentary enclosures, at least those after the mid-eighteenth century, are central to the recent history of hedges and walls because they reconfigured the countryside on a massive scale, creating new ownership boundaries, all of which needed to be enclosed externally and internally. The enclosures, established on what was effectively a blank slate, were arranged with geometrical precision and required straight hedges and walls – miles of them. The generally accepted figure for the main period of enclosure is 200,000 miles (322,000 km).[3]

Of course, not everyone agreed that a complete removal of the open-field system, with its associated rights of common, was a good thing. Those against and those for fell, inevitably, into who would lose and who would gain. There were, however, cheerleaders for both sides, ready to offer their opinions, canvassed or not. The often extreme passions that are still roused by enclosure revolve around issues of justice and political rights, countered by arguments about agricultural utility and social utilitarianism. Numerous fiercely argued pamphlets and newspaper articles for each side can be found from the very start of the parliamentary enclosure period.

The open-field system was criticised for being unwieldy and conservative; unable to easily adopt modern farming methods and new crops (such as turnips which could transform stock levels, and legumes with their talent for fixing nitrogen) and institutionally resistant to change. Others pointed to the fact that it had lasted for a thousand years and had served well, and noted that open fields had, in fact, embraced new methods, adapting them to their special situation. Although much ink was used in the defence of the relative practicalities of one agricultural system over another, most of it was spilt in arguments over justice. But even if it was admitted that enclosure improved agricultural yields and profits, who was it who benefitted? Not those who were dispossessed of common access to the waste and effectively thrown from their villages.

The frequently smug assertions of those promoting wholesale enclosure make uncomfortable reading. In the mid-nineteenth century, Lord Worsley, the MP for North Lincolnshire, spoke of the poor as squatters upon the commons, rather forgetting that they had every right to do as they pleased upon the commons, since it was they who owned them. Even the normally sensible agriculturalist, Thomas Hale, writing in 1758 at the start of the period of extensive parliamentary enclosure, took the questionable stance of suggesting that the tenant farmer would benefit from enclosure, even while admitting that rent would increase 'to three or four, and sometimes to ten times its former price'.[4] He also repeats the commonly expressed sentiment that as far as the poor were concerned, it was all for their own good:

> The advantage that a poor man has by keeping two or three sad creatures
> of cattle, of any kind, upon the common land, are not nearly equal to what
> he and his family would find, by being sure to know where to get constant
> employment as labourers. The privilege is Indeed a source of idleness: and
> that can never be for private nor publick advantage.[5]

Defenders of the poor were equally vocal. Writing in objection to the General Enclosure Act of 1801, which made enclosure much easier, a correspondent of the *Windsor and Eton Express* argued:

> This iniquitous scheme for augmenting the wealth of the rich by the robbery
> of the poor, so far transcends all former acts of spoliation of a similar
> kind, in extent and in recklessness of general and individual rights, but it
> comprehends not merely wild and sterile heaths, but lands which have been
> rendered productive by the labour of the occupiers.[6]

Riots were a regular occurrence throughout much of the parliamentary enclosure period as were attacks on hedges and ditches; as Thomas Hale was keen to point out, 'Dry hedges are easily laid flat, and quicksets pulled up.'[7] To prevent this, he advised the farmer to,

> ... make his fence by a ditch seven feet deep, and as many wide, and
> prevent their throwing in the earth, by spreading it as it is thrown out, upon
> his land. This will serve as a manure to the soil, and though passion might
> have led the mob to throw in the bank if it had been left, they will not be
> at the pains of digging for that purpose ... Thus the effects of malice will

be prevented … and the benefit of the expence and labour assured to the
proprietor; if water can be got into the ditch, the better.[8]

The dispossessed also attempted redress by simply ignoring an act
of inclosure. In 1849 the *Exeter and Plymouth Gazetteer* reported how
commoners were excluded from common land on which they had
enjoyed rights to winter pasturage, after its enclosure by the lord
of the manor. When they put their sheep to pasture regardless, the
sheep were duly impounded. At this point a Mr Landwick decided
that he had suffered enough and: '… congregated together some 40
or 50 men at one of the public houses on the eastern side of the
town. Having given them drink he led them in a tumultuous manner
through the town, joined every step by similarly disorderly persons,
hurraing, using threats, and some with sticks; and when they found
the gates too strong, they got ladders …'[9]

Mr Landwick succeeded in retrieving his sheep, but quickly
found himself in court. A preliminary hearing suggested that he
would have been better advised to have requested from the Commissioner a revision of the order suspending the common rights,
to which he replied that, 'When men attempted to maintain their
rights, it could not be done in drawing-room style.'[10] This assertion
poignantly encapsulates the powerless predicament of the working
man.'

Academics argue to this day about the pros and cons of enclosure.
Those lined up against include J. L. and Barbara Hammond whose
minutely researched *The Village Labourer 1760–1832*, published in 1911,
is a sustained polemic against the oppression of a largely defenceless
rural poor by the wealthy and well placed. Those who see enclosure
as essentially beneficial argue that most of those who lost their
rights did not actually have those rights in the first place, but simply
used the commons for grazing even though they had no customary
right to do so. More generally, many regard enclosure as an inevitable result of the rise of industry. Indeed, it is hard to imagine how
modern farming would work if bits and pieces of open fields and
wasteland were in the possession of those who had inherited them
from their eighteenth-century rural ancestors (effectively, a large

proportion of the population). Perhaps the answer would have been to give them all shares in agri-businesses.

The Enclosure Commissioners were required to take into account everyone who had an interest in the land and apportion it as best they could, according to the size and quality of the various holdings. For some recipients, the holding they were awarded did not compensate for what they had lost and many found it impossible to make a living. This was exacerbated by the cost of erecting hedges or walls to enclose the land, a task and cost that was forced on all who received holdings through enclosure. The most seriously affected were those who had no formal right to any land – such as the cottagers and labourers – but may have used common pasture anyway.

By the time of the parliamentary enclosures, the yeoman farmer was largely a character of the past, replaced, for the most part, by people who owned land but did not farm it themselves. Be they lord, a distant financial company or a local man, most landowners were landlords. Hale's estimate of how much rents would increase proved exaggerated; but it was still large at around 50 to 100 per cent. Optimism about the benefits of enclosure to agricultural productivity proved even more ill-founded as the increased yields – though they varied dramatically from area to area – improved by little more than 10 per cent. How a rent increase could be sustained for so little improvement in production is a puzzle even now. But, since farmers could not easily leave their land for pastures new, it seems likely to be a simple matter of the rich landlord getting richer and the poor farmer getting poorer. It would be a generation before rents sensibly matched production." The tenant farmer, it seems, fared little better than those with no claim to land at all.

Whatever the effect on the poor and the unfortunate, enclosure had a profound and usually devastating impact on the land (not to mention the rights of the Welsh and English to walk without hindrance in their own country). Forests, which had been held at least in part in common, were cleared for agriculture. These included the vast ancient woodlands of the Blackmore Vale in Dorset, Charnwood Forest in Leicestershire and Needwood Forest in Staffordshire, almost all of which were completely lost. The Blackmore

Vale is an example of how it was not only open-field areas that suffered enclosure. Woodland was also cleared to provide the vast number of fences, posts and gates required for the new enclosures, although some trees would have been coppiced (cut back to ground level to encourage multiple stem growth) to produce a supply of fencing timber. Heathland and wetland, now so fiercely and rightly defended by conservationists, were dispensed with in favour of agriculture and 200,000 plus miles of neat and straight hedge, wall, fence, bank and ditch were planted, built and dug.

The reason for 'inclosure' is clear enough – it consolidated land holdings and opened up common land for agricultural exploitation at a time when subsistence farming had mostly disappeared and food was needed for the cities and townships. The advantages of 'enclosure' are not so clear. Certainly, boundaries need defining, but beyond that, why enclose more than is strictly necessary? Agriculturalists of the time had much to say about the practical benefits of hedges and walls, some of it true, some of it hopelessly optimistic. There are, it appears, many good reasons for planting a hedge, not least in terms of protecting breeding stock, as the *Chester Chronicle* of 1809 makes clear:

> Should an enlightened breeder wish to improve his sheep, how is he to effect it, while his ewes mix promiscuously with his neighbours flocks? … when he can confine ewes within his own enclosure, he can make whatever experiment he pleases, by putting a few, or many ewes, to any particular tup without any fear of having a spurious breed, by the interference of his neighbours: he is also enabled to keep his flock from many disorders: few commons but have some tracts of land liable to the rot: how are they to be prevented from depasturing upon it?[12]

This is a serious point. I have friends who keep pure or rare breed herds and find the prospect of random genes making their way into their stock quite appalling. Before enclosures became the norm it was difficult to improve flocks or herds as there was no way of breeding selectively. The risk of disease spreading through stock of mixed ownership was high and without enclosure to defend against it, a sickness could quickly spread to most of the sheep or cattle in a parish.

Thomas Hale, who, as already noted, was a great enthusiast for enclosure, mentions another advantage of hedges, that of protection: 'They are of great service to the crop, of whatsoever kind. They defend it from winds, and from those cold and nipping blasts which are so mischievous in the early part of the spring. An inclosed piece of land is always warmer than a piece in an open field of the same soil and condition.'[3] Hale's *A Compleat Body of Husbandry*, which has much on enclosure and hedges, is a valuable resource for anyone wishing to understand the agricultural attitudes of the time, and he provides plenty of good advice. The following is particularly dear to my heart: 'The hedges also, if rightly managed, are, in themselves, a great profit, and supply wood for all necessary purposes; and they may be made in many places to yield valuable fruit.'[4]

Hale's opinion of the open-field system was correspondingly low and he writes colourfully about the advantage enclosure gave the farmer in terms of privacy and the freedom to do what he wanted: 'It [enclosure] gives a liberty also of making whatsoever alterations or improvements he shall choose: he may plant and sow what he pleases, and in what manner he pleases which he cannot do without a thousand insults, interruptions, and inconveniences, from the malice, envy, or folly of his neighbours, while it lies open.'[5]

The well-rehearsed contrary view, that hedges could be more of a nuisance than an aid to the farmer, was also expressed. For example, hedgerows came in for criticism for the excessive shade beneath the many trees they contained. This can be observed in British landscape paintings and prints from the period in which hedgerows are usually shown standing dense with substantial trees. Even Thomas Hale thought that hedges could sometimes be too much of a good thing, noting that: 'In meadow land there is sometimes a loss by too many hedges, from the quantity of grass they spoil by their shade.'[6] Though he thought the problem was actually down to bad management.

Elihu Burritt, an American philanthropist and pacifist who spent many years in Britain, provides an interesting outsider's perspective. In 1863 he walked from London to John O'Groats in

A hedged and walled landscape in Yorkshire showing signs of neglect and the dreaded barbed wire.

Scotland, publishing an account of his journey a year later in which he recorded his observations on the countryside, including the following on hedgerows:

> Though trees are the most sacred things the earth begets in England …
> the farmer here looks at them with an evil eye, as horse-leeches that bleed
> to death long stretches of the land he pays £2 per acre for annually to his
> landlord. The hedge, however wide-bottomed, is his fence; and fencing he
> must have. But these trees, arising at narrow intervals from the hedge, and
> spreading out their deadening shades upon his wheat fields on either side, are
> not useful nor ornamental to him. They may look prettily and make a nice
> picture in the eyes of the sentimental tourist or traveller, but he grudges the
> ground they cover.[17]

The enthusiasm for relatively small enclosures waned with time, in part because the disappointingly small increase in yields did not make up for the poor ratio of hedge area to field area, but also because farm machinery began to require larger and larger fields. Even at the height of the Parliamentary Enclosure Acts, complaints were made about the small sizes of the resultant fields. Many such fields were enlarged dramatically by the simple expedient of removing a single, dividing hedge that had been planted only a few years earlier. We imagine that the late nineteenth century to be the heyday of the hedgerow, but many were already being dispensed with soon after the close of the parliamentary enclosure period.

Elihu Burritt concludes his observations on hedges in prescient mood: 'If, therefore, the hedges of England disappear before the noiseless and furtive progress of utilitarian science, the trees that rise above them in such picturesque ranks will be almost certain to go with them. Then, indeed, a change will come over the face of the country, which will make it difficult for one to recognise it …'[18]

PART II

THE PRESENT

Chapter 10

HEDGEROW LOSS

Post-war Britain saw a period when approximately the same amount of hedge that had been so industriously created during the period of the Enclosure Acts was, notoriously, torn down. There had already been a certain amount of pre-war hedge loss, but the evidence for this is confusing. Between 1875 and 1937, arable land declined by around 25 per cent after government support was removed for domestic grain in the mid-nineteenth century, allowing cheap imports from North America.[1] This suggests that pasture was increasing, though there is no reason to assume that more enclosure would have been needed to accommodate stock.

Pre-war hedge loss is indicated by a contributor to the *Northampton Mercury* in 1937 who writes proudly of the short work his 14hp Fowler traction engine, four-furrow plough and seven-tined cultivator made of 570 acres of arable land and 400 acres of pasture: 'A good many hedgerows had been cleared to make fields of about 30 acres, and one of 65 acres had been made out of six small enclosures.'[2]

From 1937 to the end of the war, arable land doubled in area to its highest ever level. This increase is hardly surprising as, without much in the way of imports, it was necessary to grow as much food

A hedge-free vista in East Anglia.

as possible at home. What is surprising is that 1944/5 was the peak for arable land, which has been steadily declining ever since.[3] We naturally assume that it has gone up and up, but Britain now imports vast quantities of food, and much of the land – of which there is famously a limited amount – has been taken out of agriculture altogether for urban and industrial development, road building and a thousand other purposes. This is area of land, not yields which have increased to spectacular levels due to post-war developments in crop varieties, fertilisers, machinery and general management.

After the privations of the war years – privations that continued well into the 1950s – food independence became a central political goal, and successive governments set about achieving self-sufficiency with ruthless determination and not a little recklessness. The Labour government, which came into power in 1945 under Clement Atlee, introduced the Agriculture Act of 1947. Back in the 1950s, my erstwhile landlord, Snowy Eyre, was told by a man from the Ministry of Agriculture to take his plough around his newly acquired farm. This was merely a continuation of what had been happening throughout the war, and much of the increase of arable in the war years was due to an official knocking on a farmer's door to tell him

A relatively rare sight now, the once common herb-rich meadow.

to plough up his pasture. Every last scrap of land that could be made more productive by planting corn or potatoes was duly ploughed. The great-uncle of my friend Bryan was forced to plough up his favourite meadow. Among the dozens of wild flowers growing there was one he called the scented orchid, also known as the butterfly orchid. Despite his extreme reluctance to lose this treasure, Bryan's great-uncle ploughed away because had no choice. The farm was in Somerset where the butterfly orchid is now near to extinction.

Such vandalism seems appalling to us today (though rural vandalism is still in fine fettle), but it must be seen in the context of the time. During the war years Britain knew hunger and anxiety over food availability continued into the 1950s. In 1952 the *Portsmouth Evening News* covered a lecture given by the agricultural writer L. F. Easterbrook in Petersfield, Hampshire. Under the headline 'Famine Threat to Britain?' it reported Easterbrook's view that starvation was 'a greater danger to-day than the atom bomb or international war' and his recommendation that food should be grown wherever possible.[4] He was aware of the potential impact on the landscape, however, suggesting 'that the grubbing out of hedges and trees to provide very large fields was a policy that could be taken too far'.[5]

The public's concern for hedgerow destruction has waxed and waned over the last seventy years, but it began very early on. In the following year the same newspaper stated that:

> Ever since the new farming came into being during the war and hedges began to go under planned schemes of development, there has been a considerable outcry against the loss of this familiar feature of the English scene in so many areas. Hedges suddenly became a bone of contention. Townsmen, hitherto not conspicuous for their concern about farming affairs, cried 'shame' when derelict hedges disappeared and many people grew alarmed at the apparent prospect of a countryside devoid of all its characteristic hedgerows through the action of heartlessly progressive farmers.[6]

The aim of the 1947 Act was to banish food shortages in Britain for ever and in time it achieved its goal. Its rationale was expressed thus: 'The twin pillars upon which the Government's agricultural policy rests are stability and efficiency. The method of providing stability is through guaranteed prices and assured markets.'[7] The Act introduced subsidies (which have steadfastly refused to die), grants for capital expenditure and price maintenance (known more bluntly as price fixing). 'Assured markets' were established by already existing public bodies such as the Milk Marketing Board and part of the Act permitted the wholesale interference with the running of private farms:

> Where it appears to the Minister necessary so to do in the interest of the national supply of food or other agricultural products, he may by order direct that all or any of the powers conferred on him by the next following subsection shall be exercisable by him for a period of one year from the coming into operation of the order.[8]

This was followed by a list of things that farmers could and could not do, most notably the restriction on the amount of land used for pasture and meadow, thus increasing arable. For the humble farmer, resistance was futile, unless he was content to part with £100 or spend three months at His Majesty's pleasure or both. Mercifully, this clause was repealed in 1958.

I do not think that Snowy took down many hedges, as that counted as hard work, but he did plough up some interesting downland, while leaving much of the farm to his beloved foxes. However, in many parts of the country, the plough was allowed to go where it would and the hedge became a memory. Or did it? A comparison between maps made at the turn of the twentieth century and recent aerial photographs shows, superficially, surprisingly little difference in the extent of hedgerows. There has certainly been a massive loss of hedges, but our perception of the extent of that loss is sometimes faulty. Many people assume that the large fields in their local area are the result of government sponsored rural vandalism; this is not necessarily so.

Measuring hedgerow extent (usually expressed simply in terms of their length) and making comparisons over time are notoriously difficult tasks and not to be taken on lightly. To do so involves hours, if not days, pouring over aerial photographs and maps, with magnifying glass and wheeled map measurer in hand and a notebook and bottle of headache pills at the ready. In addition to the perils of accidentally including footpaths and contour marks, there are problems of deciding what to count. For example, does a road count as being likely to possess one hedge, two or none? Should you measure overall lengths or just count the number of hedges, or both?

The potential pitfalls can be illustrated by the conceptual error that the renowned geographer Sir Dudley Stamp fell into in his 1955 book, *Man and the Land*. Stamp estimated that the average field was five acres, worked out the length of the hedge boundary it required (a bit over a third of a mile), multiplied it by the number of five-acre fields that would fit into the agricultural areas of Britain and came up with the answer – 1.7 million miles.[9] This is much too high a figure for a number of reasons, the most egregious error being that he forgot that adjacent fields share hedges. In an infinite landscape of rectangular fields there will be two hedges to every field, not four. However, simply dividing the result by two will fail to get the correct answer, as real hedges are not so well behaved. For example, a single length of hedge may be the eastern boundary of a single large field, while also being the western boundary of three or four.

Anyone who dips their toe into the muddy waters of measuring hedges will notice one thing above all others: how very different fields are in size and character in one part of the country compared to another. A map showing four square miles of Norfolk placed next to a map of the same area of Devon will have you wondering if you have the scale all wrong. The Norfolk map may have a hundred fields in it, while on the Devon map there may be six or seven hundred. If you count up the hedges there will be a similar difference in number.

The point of considering the two extremes of Norfolk and Devon is that the Norfolk fields were never as small as those of Devon, at least not for a couple of hundred years. For example, the 1903 map of fields north-east of Kings Lynn shows field sizes very similar to those of today. An area here of four square miles has ninety fields, the majority of which are large at around 25 hectares (61 acres), but with ten relatively tiny fields on the western edge of the village of Great Bircham. Since 1903, fifteen lengths of hedgerow have been removed out of 180. Half a dozen of these are from the small fields near the village and the rest are typical consolidation exercises where hedges of two to three hundred yards have been grubbed up to make two

The small fields of East Devon.

fields into one. Four or five new hedges, averaging about 100 yards, have been planted. The total loss is about 2 km out of a 1903 length of 80 km, which is 2.5 per cent. This is a very long way from the popular estimate of hedgerow loss as around 50 per cent. Certainly, if you were on holiday in Norfolk driving past these enormous fields you might well shake your head at the barren monoculture these fields present and imagine that it was loss of hedgerow that created it, but you might well be wrong. Is this example from Norfolk exceptional? Yes, but not as much as one would expect.

Let us take a look at the opposite extreme, Devon. Near Stockland (where I have done a bit of hedge laying myself), the same area of four square miles contained no less than 660 fields on the 1903 map. Most were small and some were truly tiny at an acre or even less. Counting a length of hedge as being any stretch between two nodes (that is where one hedge meets another), there were 880 of them. Looking at a modern aerial view, 260 have been lost, which is a substantial reduction, representing 34 km out of an original 114 km, or 30 per cent. It is also a greater loss because of the age and character of the hedges removed. Much of the area shows signs of ancient assarting (see pp. 15–16), where the 'leading edge' of woodland clearance for fields is curved. The old, lost hedges were remnants of ancient woodland which would have harboured thousands of species of plant, animal and fungus.

The south-east of England is often considered to be particularly bad for hedgerow loss, an accusation that has some merit. Kentish fields in 1900 were large, certainly compared to those in Devon, with sizes sometimes in excess of 25 hectares. However, many fields have been enlarged to 60 or 70 hectares by the removal of dividing hedges. Sometimes the resulting field is used as a whole, but often the old fields, despite no longer being hedged, continue to be used individually. One must suspect that the hedges between them have been uprooted for no reason other than the moderate convenience of the farmer. Kent was singled out many years ago for its cavalier attitude to hedgerows, and I recall watching a Kentish farmer defend his position in a television interview in the 1980s. He was both defiant and proud of what had been done, characterising the Kent

An enclosure wall south of St Andrews, surrounded by large fields.

countryside as having been transformed from second-rate to first-rate. First-rate it may have been for agriculture, but as countryside it is now, in a few places, a desert. However, Kent is still a fairly well-wooded county, more so than my own West Dorset, so I hesitate to criticise.

In lowland Scotland, enclosures were created a little later than in England and Wales. In the arable lands of the east lowlands, many of these enclosure hedges (or walls) have been lost, usually by the removal of a single hedge, though here too gratuitous hedge removal is sometimes seen. A typical Scottish lowland landscape can be found south of St Andrews, though these are bounded mostly by stone walls, not hedges. In a four square mile sample, nineteen out of 142 lengths of wall or hedge had been lost, amounting to 4.9 km out of the 45.5 km that existed around 1900, a loss of approximately 11 per cent.

What about the home of enclosure Britain, the former open fields? Just to the north of Hook Norton in Oxfordshire is a fairly typical chessboard arrangement of fields. A map of c.1900 shows about 220 fields, whereas today there are 130 fields showing the inevitable rationalisations of fields too small to fit modern agricultural practice. This does not, however, amount to a great loss; 16 km out of 76.7 km, or 21 per cent, and of course most of these will be enclosure hedges of less value as habitats than ancient hedges.

Finally, another piece of enclosure England: an area near Peterborough that is distinctly 'barley baron' country. It was across 4,000 acres of this landscape that N. W. Moore and his colleagues traced the history of the hedges scattered over three manors.[10] They found that in 1364 there was just 20 miles of hedge; by 1780 this had risen to 58 miles through private enclosure; and to 76 miles by the end of parliamentary enclosure. In 1946 it stood at 71 miles, dropping dramatically to 46 miles by 1963 and ending up back where it started at 20 miles by 1965. This represented a total loss of around 70 per cent since its peak.

After surveying four square miles of this area myself in 2014, I concluded that of the 58 km of hedge recorded in 1900, 12 km had been lost – only a 21 per cent loss. Many of the surviving hedges are poor things, but they are still hedges. The Local Action Plan for Cambridgeshire, published in 2003, states that between two surveys carried out in 1969 and 1988 there was a hedge loss of 33 per cent for the whole county. Perhaps my selection had been particularly lucky or, more likely, the surveyors took a narrower view of what constituted a hedge.

Such back-of-the-envelope surveys as my own may be imprecise but they do give a sense of how varied the situation is in different parts of the countryside. Even taking my starting point of c.1900, the figures obtained from this quick, random survey show a smaller loss than has been estimated by those who have taken more time and more care. In selecting specific areas I chose decidedly rural locations, ones where hedgerows have not been destroyed by

Few would consider this to be a hedge, but it certainly once was (complete with ditch), and is still beautiful and species-rich.

habitation expansion. This partly accounts for my low figures, but perhaps more relevant is *what* has been counted. If a hedge, or indeed wall, appears to have been removed entirely or almost entirely, then I count it as lost. However, others have considered a hedge to be lost if it is still extant but severely neglected, thus raising the figures accordingly. In their 1974 book *Hedges*, Pollard, Hooper and Moore, mention that some surveys fail to count hedges that have been cut level with the ground (a drastic but fairly normal method of keeping them under control) because they are not clearly visible from aerial photographs and easily missed if viewed from the ground. This too would mean reporting a higher loss than truly exists. While I must bow to the professional researchers, it is possible that we have been unduly gloomy in our assessments of hedgerow loss over the last hundred years.

I console myself that although my rough figures do not support professional assessments of hedgerow loss, these professional assessments fail to agree with each other by a considerable margin. For example, taking two independent figures for the total length of British hedgerows in the late 1940s and two independent figures for the total length of British hedgerows obtained in the mid-1980s and performing the necessary subtractions, one finds a total loss of hedgerow over this thirty-five year period to be 174,000 km at best and 460,000 km at worst." This discrepancy illustrates the difficulties encountered by researchers when attempting to perform the seemingly simple, if tedious, task of measuring hedge lengths on maps and photographs. Sampling errors, systematic errors, differing definitions and the difficulties of reading the source material all contribute to a confusing picture.

The debate about how much hedge we had in Britain in 1945 and how the situation has changed continues. The classic assessment was undertaken by Pollard, Hooper and Moore and appeared in their New Naturalist book, *Hedges*, of 1974. They discuss the problems in detail and suggest an annual loss of 3,000 miles (4,828 km) of hedgerow lost each year from 1946/7 to 1963 in England and Wales.

We do have a figure for the total length of hedgerow in the mid-1950s, courtesy of the Forestry Commission, which had been tasked with assessing the trees and forests of Britain in general. The figure they arrived at was 620,000 miles, which is nearly 1 million km. If we subtract the 477,000 km of hedges reported by the Countryside Survey in 2007, we seem to have lost about 520,000 km or 52 per cent. This is a high figure and 50 per cent, or thereabouts, is often quoted in articles fretting over the fate of the countryside. However, what the Countryside Survey regards as a hedge is something that actually works as a hedge and is managed as a hedge, not something that was one once or looks a bit like one now. The table helpfully supplied in the report gives two other values which make for more encouraging reading: 114,000 km for relict hedges which still form part of a boundary because they are accompanied by a stock-proof fence, and another 114,000 km for relict hedges which no longer form a stock-proof boundary. These generally take the form of rows of mature or maturing trees, spanned perhaps by untidy and gappy bits of hedge and scrub, the whole not necessarily joining with other hedges to form a coherent hedge boundary in itself. While quite useless for agricultural purposes, beyond a little soil control and shelter, these relict hedges may well be both pleasing to the eye and of biological interest. If we include these wounded survivors, then only 300,000 km or 30 per cent of hedges were completely lost in the fifty years to 2007.

Hedgerow extent did not start declining after the Second World War and continue at a steady rate until the present day, nor was the decline consistent throughout the countryside. Immediately post-war, relatively few hedges were disturbed, but in the 1960s and subsequently in the 1980s there was a rapid decline, whereas since the early 1990s there has been a period of relative stability and even an increase.

Comparisons between the three countries of Britain are difficult because it may well be more a comparison between methodologies of the researchers rather than hedge lengths. However, reports suggest that in Scotland hedge length has declined from around 42,000 km in 1947 to around 20,000 km by 1988, a loss of over 50 per cent.[12] There appears to be no systematic survey of Wales, though it is estimated that about 49,000 km still exist; we can only assume that the decline follows that of England.[13]

Bringing matters almost up to date, the Natural Environment Research Council published the latest of its Countryside Surveys in 2008. The figures are worth mentioning because they show the situation as it is now and how it changed over the period 1984 to 2007. Apart from dismissing ditches, the council takes the same catholic view of boundaries as I do, including walls, hedges, fences and banks. Hedges are divided into useable ones and remnant or relict hedges. Hedges in whatever condition are lumped together as 'woody linear features'.

Woody linear features (as one feels they must now be called) have changed barely at all in the near quarter century covered by the survey, merely dipping around 1990 to rise again to a total of 700,000 km by 2007. Well-managed hedges (those that are not remnants) have declined, while remnant hedges have, of course, increased. The big change came between 1984 and 1990 when hedges in good condition decreased markedly and those in poor condition increased by around the same amount. Hedges in Wales appear to have suffered proportionally more than those in England and Scotland during this period.

The survey also covered walls, where a similar pattern was found. There were 198,000 km in 1984, dropping to 173,000 km by 1990 and staying at that level. There are marked regional differences. Scottish walls barely change throughout the period, remaining at about 80,000 km. English walls drop suddenly to 82,000 km from 98,000 km and Welsh walls to 14,000 km from 22,000 km, respectively 16 per cent and 36 per cent losses. Apart from indicating gains and losses and showing how these have stabilised in recent years, the figures pose an interesting question: what happened in the mid 1980s to cause so rapid a loss of hedges? Once again, food policy – this time dictated by Europe – seems to be the answer.

The Common Agricultural Policy (CAP) was devised as a central policy of the European Common Market (later the EU) in the late 1950s. It shared the same aims as Britain's home-grown policy of ten years earlier – to produce enough food to feed the people. It also used the same techniques: subsidies, price maintenance and a guaranteed market. Britain joined the Common Market in 1973 and by the early 1980s a feeding frenzy had taken place in agriculture. Assured of both a market and a very good price and with little to hold them back, farmers across Europe produced food like never before and the infamous butter mountains and wine lakes became an expensive problem. In order to produce so much food, pasture had to be ploughed, heathland cultivated and hedgerows uprooted.

At the height of the agricultural bonanza in the mid 1980s, a farm not far from my home received a grant to remove an attractive wood so that the land could be opened up for arable farming. Two or three years later the same farm was sold and the new owner promptly applied for, and received, a grant to replant the wood.

This agricultural excess became an embarrassment to those in authority and a great annoyance to taxpayers who were witnessing the countryside being turned into a factory at their considerable expense. Since then, reform has taken place, notably a reduction in the prices paid for agricultural produce. The option of simply taking away the subsidy was rejected because, it was argued, it would put farmers out of business completely. Instead, it was replaced by direct payments, and while this means that farmers can sometimes get paid for just being there, at least they don't get paid for producing mountains of food no one wants and levelling the countryside flat in the process. If you think this is all completely insane, welcome to a club with a large membership.

As is clear from the Countryside Survey and the comparatively low levels of hedgerow loss found in my half dozen samples, the complete removal of hedges is not the whole problem, nor even the main problem, it is neglect. I take a very sanguine view of neglect. The small lawn in my neglected back garden is also neglected. In April it turns yellow with dandelions, in May white and yellow with daisies; half of it is green only because of the moss and in the autumn random fungi make guest appearances. Twenty-five years ago, in a fit of tidiness that shames me to this day, I applied weed and moss killer plus some fertiliser. The lawn became green, lush and profoundly boring. It took fifteen years to recover from my misguided attention. I had gone from neglect to over-management; now I mow it with more regularity than before, dig up the odd dandelion that seems to be too pleased with itself, and feel it is just right.

Whether a neglected hedge is a good or a bad thing is down to how well it matches expectations. If it is essential for stock-proofing, then it is clear where laissez-faire ends and dereliction of duty begins – the moment when the sheep get out. If stock-proofing is not the issue, then neglect is not always bad.

The natural inclination of a hedge is to become a wood, so if no management is carried out at all the hedge will just keep growing; the shrub layer will be lost and the entire hedge will become leggy and thus gappy too. Apologies for such technical language but these are the terms used by hedge-layers; Old Dick, who had laid hedges in Dorset for over sixty years, once talked to me about a hedge, noting: 'T'was as gappy as m'teeth, mind.'

An uncared for hedgerow will eventually turn into a row of well-spaced, standard trees with intervening patches of scrub. This can be both beautiful to look at and an ecosystem of its own, but it is no longer a hedgerow. A similar situation occurs in a neglected, tra-ditional hedge. Left untended for years, it may transform itself into a linear coppice with gaps between dense hazel stools or standard

There are clear signs that this was once a laid hedge. It has now retired into its dotage.

hawthorns. Lovely and ecologically interesting as these may be, they too have lost their status and are no longer hedges despite how they look from a distance. They will need to rely on a trusty barbed wire fence to make them stock-proof.

Roadside hedges tend to be substantial and dense affairs, even though they are usually (though not always) cut mechanically rather than laid. It is the internal hedges that have suffered most from neglect or poor management. On arable land one frequently sees machine-trimmed hedges cut regularly to a height of one metre every year or two. Such hedges are distinctly hedges, though generally they are neither stock-proof nor intended to be so; they are mere field markers, of little use beyond defining a boundary, perhaps protecting the fields from soil erosion and maybe a place for birds to perch. They can be attractive in their way, looking like rows of bonsai trees, but they have little biological interest. Even if the machinery is used to trim a hedge to a more respectable height, after a few years at a particular height the surviving stems, prevented from branching by the repeated cutting back of their new growth, will become gnarled and twisted and the hedge gappy.

On a solely arable farm the hedge is almost superfluous, as indeed

The bank and shape of the hawthorns make it clear that this was once a laid hedge.

it has always been; what remains is often just a gappy remnant or low-cut and sparse scrub with maybe a standard tree here and there. Even if more or less intact, internal hedges on arable land often fail to join up, giving them an aspect of isolation and disappointment.

In between the two extremes of under- and over-management comes the well-managed traditional hedge. What constitutes a traditional hedge will be considered later, but briefly it is a living, linear boundary, managed is such a way as to keep it functioning as a boundary, which will, over time, become a home for many species of plant, fungus and animal.

On pastoral land the well-managed hedge may well be the romantic ideal, but barbed wire fencing has become the quick option for stock-proofing. Many, indeed most, pastoral hedges will be fortified by a wire fence, allowing the hedge to lose any purpose and ultimately, perhaps, to deteriorate. The presence of barbed wire makes traditional hedge laying difficult and an untidy mess can ensue. Wire, however, can reduce 'gapping' in pastoral hedges as it prevents grazing within the hedge, though this is hardly an elegant solution.

One cause of hedge loss that is not often commented on arises

A 'lost' hedge in Dorset, now surrounded by a wood.

from those hedges that are subsumed within newly planted woodland. Hundreds, perhaps thousands, of miles of hedge have disappeared when woods have been established alongside them or around them. They are certainly no longer hedges but it cannot entirely be said that they are lost. They can be beautiful in their own way and will often support many more species than the new wood, at least in the early stages of its growth. In this they can 'seed' the new wood, fulfilling an essential function.

Chapter 11

PROTECTING THE HEDGEROW

The variable fortunes of the British hedgerow follow the winding path set by government policy (both domestic and European), agricultural technologies and the price farmers obtain for their goods. Apart from a desire by enlightened farmers to retain a countryside that is both attractive and productive it is, sadly, down to government to provide a more substantial incentive. Since the mid 1980s numerous schemes have been developed to do just this and, on the whole, they have been successful. Not paying farmers to trash the countryside was an excellent start, but paying them to care for it instead is considerably more positive. The incentives to make improvements are matched by disincentives to cause harm.

The Environment Act of 1995 gave hedgerows a mention in section 97, but it specified nothing beyond giving ministers the power to make regulations. However, the hedgerow acquired legislation of its own in the Hedgerow Regulations Act of 1997. It is worth noting that this is indeed about hedgerows – stone walls do not get a mention – and that it applies only to England and Wales. Scottish hedges had suffered too, but they were mostly of a later date and thus less important biologically. They were also regarded as less of an integral part of the Scottish landscape where stone is king.

The very many pages and provisions of the Act boil down to this: if you want to remove a hedge, you need to get permission. The rest of the Act fills in the details – lots of them. For permission to be required the hedge must be at least 20 m long or, if less than 20 m, it must join to another hedge; gaps of up to 20 m in a hedge still count as part of the hedge; the hedge must be 'important'.

Several characteristics can raise the status of a hedge to important. It could incorporate a scheduled monument; exist on a site of archaeological interest; mark the boundary of a pre-1600 estate; be an integral part of a field system that existed before the Enclosure Acts. It could also tick any one of a large number of boxes relating to the species from which it is made or any that it harbours. Any hedgerow with seven woody species in a central 30-metre length is automatically important, though six or five will also be enough provided it has certain other desirable characters. It is interesting to note that in the climatically challenged northern counties of England, where trees struggle to rise from the ground, the number of species required is reduced to six, five and four. The woody species which qualify are helpfully listed. There are over fifty of them and they include most of the familiar hedgerow trees and shrubs, plus a few you would see but rarely (such as wild pear and wild service) and a few you would not wish to see at all (such as immigrant cotoneaster). There are a few missing which are fairly common in hedges – redcurrant, cherry plum and the feral apples which grow from discarded apple cores. Only two species of oak are listed, while the bewilderingly large number of willow species and rose species are lumped, with a sense of resignation, under 'Salix species' and 'Rosa species'. The presence of several 'woodland' species of herbaceous plants alongside the hedge may stay the hand of the farmer, as will any of a large number of the plants on 'The Vascular Plant Red Data List for Great Britain'. The Act includes a list of the woodland plants consisting of such species as bugle, wood anemone, dog violet and the remarkable, parasitic toothwort. Grasses and ferns also receive an honourable mention, and in total there are fifty-seven species of plant which give the hedge a stay of execution. Anyone intent on uprooting a hedge had better be an accomplished botanist.

The 1997 Act was unpopular even before it came into effect. The MP for Lewisham and Deptford, Joan Ruddock tore into the government of the day with a long speech, declaring that: 'The regulations are fundamentally flawed – a weak and timid attempt that will leave almost 80 per cent of hedgerows unprotected.'[1]

Ms Ruddock was well informed, as few parliamentary enclosure hedges would fall under the protection of the Act. Farmers, on the other hand, considered it another piece of bureaucracy sent to try their patience. In the same debate Peter Atkinson, the MP for Hexham, riposted with: 'The hon. Member for Deptford has forgotten the important fact that farmers have to make a living.'[2]

The Act came into force on the 1 June 1997 and the honour of being the first person refused permission to remove a hedge went to a Mr Porter, a Suffolk farmer. In fact, refusals are fairly rare, permission being the rule rather than the exception. A quick look at my own District Council record over the last eighteen years revealed twelve applications, only one of which – an application to remove a hedge that ran across a field – was refused. Among those permitted was one to remove 150 metres of hedge to enable two fields to be farmed more efficiently. Permission is granted on a number of grounds, but they must be truly pressing, such as that refusal would be detrimental to a business or that removal is necessary for essential drainage work. What is striking is that in so rural an area as mine in Dorset so few applications have been made under the Act. Whether one should be reassured by this or dismayed, I simply do not know.

Prosecutions under the Act are extremely rare, partly because they are difficult to pursue and councils are reluctant to involve themselves in expensive court proceedings over a hedge. Rutland County Council abandoned what the casual observer, indeed any observer, might have considered to be an open and shut case. Their main reason for throwing in the towel was that: 'Details as to the status of the hedgerow cannot be established because the hedgerow has already been removed and destroyed.'[3]

Of the two hedges concerned, one appeared to be a parish

boundary and marked on a map from the eighteenth century and thus protected under the legislation. Examination of the debris left over found several species indicative of a hedge of importance. Nevertheless, the Act is very complex and the council felt that it provided too many avenues for the defence to explore for a successful prosecution to be certain. Instead, and as usually happens in such circumstances, the council issued a Hedgerow Replacement Notice. Serious doubts should be harboured about the application of a slapped wrist and a Replacement Notice.[4] It is simply impossible to replace a hedge by planting half a dozen suitable woody species in a row. Yes, it will, if looked after, form a hedge, but not the hedge that was there before, which may have been the product of many centuries and will include an array of species which cannot be replaced in a few days' planting. Mosses, lichens, fungi and fungal associations, insects, nematode worms and many other 'insignificant' organisms develop in a hedge, but only with time, a lot of time.

After an admittedly brief search I can find only one prosecution under the 1997 Act. It was brought by an enthusiastic Epping Forest District Council against someone who owned a strip of land along a roadside on which there was a 100-year-old hedge. The hedge shielded some houses from the road, so its removal caused consternation. The defendant had removed the hedge, upset the neighbours and ended up with a bill for £11,000.[5]

Has the Act been successful? Ignoring the fact that it was a clear case of stable door and bolting horse, it seems that it has. The low level of prosecutions and refusals may seem odd or worrying, but the point of having a law is to ensure good behaviour, not bring prosecutions. The Act is very well known in farming circles and elsewhere, as a translation of it is provided by every organisation with even the remotest connection to the countryside. Local councils, nature conservation bodies and farming organisations all warn of the consequences of unauthorised hedge removal. That it is illegal to remove certain hedges without permission is certainly well known to everyone involved in agriculture and this alone prevents hedgerows being uprooted on a whim.

So much for the stick, now to the carrot. Various schemes have

A hedged landscape in Dorset, supported by AES. Note the 'set-aside' strip in the foreground.

been devised to address the problem of lost hedges and walls by helping farmers with the task of replanting or rebuilding, or, more usually, just fixing them. They fall under what must be one of the most inelegant of terms, agri-environment schemes (AES). Their general remit is to wind back the clock to a time when not every last corner of a farm was used to grow crops. They encourage the planting of sensible woodlands, the reintroduction of meadows and old pasture, the establishing of wildlife corridors (they are very keen on these) and, of course, hedges and walls. On the whole, these efforts are made in the direction of what is known in the conservation trade as an 'integrated model', which incorporates wildlife into the existing farming landscape, as opposed to the 'segregation model' in which wildlife is confined to reserves, while elsewhere agriculture is allowed to do its worst or best as it sees fit. For hedges, walls and ditches – which are, after all, agricultural entities – the integrated model does, or should, fit very well indeed.

The Countryside Stewardship Scheme of 2015 (not to be confused with the 1991 scheme of the same name) is only the latest in a fairly long line of such initiatives. Much of its funding comes via the EU, along with an entire acronym-heavy industry of government bodies, pan-government bodies, quasi-government committees, charities, researchers and foot-soldier administrators. A lot of good work is done, but, overall, not really good enough to justify the vast expense.

A paper from 2006, which examined the benefits of several schemes under the AES umbrella, informs us that a cool €24·3 billion had been spent throughout the EU since 1994, and then goes on to condemn the benefits thus accrued with the faintest of praise.[6] The UK example cited involved strips around fields, usually next to a hedge, which were left unploughed. This is a favourite conservation measure, neatly taking surplus arable land out of cultivation while purportedly improving biodiversity. It would, perhaps, be worthwhile if the strips were left for fifty years or 500, but not for the five of the scheme. The paper shows that small improvements in species numbers were found, mostly fairly common species, but virtually no ingress of any occupants of a Red Data list. The isolation of some of the fields which 'benefitted' from the interventions was held to be the reason for this – you cannot expect a bee-orchid to appear in a field if the nearest potential parent plant is forty miles away: 'The poor effectiveness of the evaluated agri-environment schemes to promote endangered species was therefore largely because of the schemes being implemented in areas where these species simply did not occur.'[7]

There is nothing wrong with throwing huge sums of money at a huge problem, especially if the problem is the destruction of our fellow species, but they must be thrown with a good aim. Hedges are sometimes planted or maintained at great cost under these schemes with little reference to their actual utility. A Midland style hedge, for example, may be appropriately established in one of the home counties, Oxford for example, but if it is on what is now entirely arable land it will be an absurdity, as it was designed for pastoral or mixed farming country.

Another fault, identified in a more recent report, was the ongoing nature of many of the payments, rather than payments made for capital expenditure on specific projects such as hedges and walls.[8] Nevertheless, while some of the schemes are ill conceived, those relating to boundaries are considerably more successful. Natural England reported in 2009 that 24 per cent of stone walls were maintained, 41 per cent of hedgerows in England were actively managed and 6 per cent restored – all under AES. These figures are perfectly believable because farmers and hedge enthusiasts tell me that much of what they do comes under the auspices of one AES or another. My friend James, who owns a particularly beautiful farm of mixed arable and pasture in the neighbouring valley, told me that he certainly would not have done as much work on his hedgerows had he not enjoyed the 40 per cent or so support from the EU. His one criticism was the absurd amount of paperwork involved. Once you enter into any of these schemes, putting in a new hedge or planting up a field corner for bird or deer cover becomes impossible without a whole new stack of paperwork, even when it is done without a request for financial support.

Sticks and carrots have their place, but a great deal of the work of government agencies and charitable organisations, such as the Wildlife Trusts and the RSPB, is about convincing those who have a responsibility for the countryside that caring for it is worthwhile. There is now much information available on how to manage boundaries sensitively and the benefits of so doing. Most of the many farmers I know are countrymen and women who are proud to own fields that grow more than just wheat and barley, who speak excitedly about the buzzards that circle above their farms like the aircraft stacked above Heathrow, or who look forward to picking sloes and plums from their hedgerow. To the true farmer the countryside is not a factory floor, it is home.

PART III

NATURAL HISTORY

The 'green lane', with hedges both sides, is among the best of hedgerow habitats.

Chapter 12

HABITAT

A walk along a hedgerow is always full of delight for anyone who takes time to walk slowly and observe. No two stretches of hedge are ever quite the same, though they tend to fall into types based on their soil, soil pH, moisture levels, climate and age, what was originally planted and whether or not it has a ditch and bank. There is no typical hedgerow flora, fauna or mycota, as the hedgerow is not a natural system that has developed its own specialist species. As far as such things are known, there is only one species confined entirely to the hedgerow – the vanishingly scarce Plymouth pear, *Pyrus cordata*. If we were to call a hedgerow anything more specific, it would be a woodland edge habitat, as it is indeed an edge and the plant species found in hedges are a closer match to those at the edge of a wood than those at the centre.

However, it is not exactly a woodland edge as it lacks the potential for any interaction between the hedge itself and the woodland depths. For example, a deer grazing on the fresh growth of the edge cannot dart to safety inside a hedge at the first sign of a predator as it could in a wood. A hedge is an edge habitat that has two sides or, in other words, a hedge is all edge. This brings us to a second reason that a hedge is different from a woodland edge – it is more exposed and thus often drier than a true woodland edge. Hedges are also known to be more nutrient rich than woodlands and with a generally lower acidity.

Edge habitats are interesting, complex and – before the intervention of man – relatively rare. They provide a vantage point for birds, a navigation beacon to bats, a sunlit protection to plants, cover for mammals and footholds for introduced plants trying to make a home. Many trees only fruit reliably in edge habitats, their blossoms available and easily accessible to bees and other insects, and their berries providing food for birds. Because some hedges are laid periodically, they are also slightly stressed habitats, making them dynamic and cyclic in a way not seen in meadow or woodland. Plants and animals come and go as the environment changes and as the hedge progresses from initial planting to maturity. The hedgerow habitat also changes with the various cycles and methods of management.

A particular instance of edge habitat 'behaviour' is found in fungi. Fungal mycelia often produce their 'fruiting' bodies (mushrooms) on the undisturbed strip of land beside a hedgerow when they will not do so within dense woodland – a process known as 'stress fruiting'. The mycelium – the mass of fine fibres that make up the underground and main part of many fungi – responds to the lack of sustenance it detects as it grows away from the trees that support it. Lack of food causes stress and the fungus changes its strategy from vegetative reproduction to sexual reproduction in a perceived last-ditch attempt to continue the existence of the species, if not the individual. In addition, fungi require light in order to produce their fruiting bodies (mushrooms) as they equate light with moving air, and it is this that they need to disperse the spores they produce. Taken together, these two effects make many hedgerows excellent habitats for fungi.

Another aspect of an edge habitat, which certainly applies to hedges, is that it permits an interaction between two habitats. For example, the cirl bunting nests and sings in hedgerows, but feeds on seeds lying on the ground in fields. The corollary is that a change in management of the adjoining fields will be as damaging to the cirl bunting (or to rabbit or bee), as would the loss of the hedge itself. Edge habitats, like those formed by hedges, are integrated environments that must have all their components in place to support the species that live there. Furthermore, although a single hedge is an ecosystem in itself, if there were no other hedges, woods and reasonably herb-rich fields to support them, they might still survive as a hedge, but the species they support would diminish.

As we have seen in Part I, some hedges are derived directly from ancient woodland and are thus species-rich from the start. Later (but still ancient) hedges will have accumulated a large biota over the centuries and are important for this alone. In either case, the ancient hedge, of which thousands of miles still exist, provides a reservoir of species set in a landscape that has been despoiled of them. It is a tragedy of our own making that we must rely on them to do this, but we should be grateful that in many places they are still able to do so.

Finally, it is often said that hedges provide a corridor for organisms between more extensive woodland habitats. This is true, though perhaps not as true as one would like. Estimates of the movement of woodland plants along a hedgerow have given them an unimpressive top speed of 5.5 metres per year, with a slothful 1 metre per year being much more likely. At these speeds, a plant would take an absurdly long time to travel even from one side of the average farm to the other. Several woodland species, often those that have been in the hedge from when it was first created by assarting, are reproductively challenged and refuse to move at all. Insects will obviously do much better but, since most of them fly, the hedge is more of a linear reservoir than a corridor. Small mammals that use hedgerows could, in principle, use a hedge as a corridor, but most of them leave the hedge every day to forage and must be viewed in the same light as the insects. In as much as hedgerows act as links between woodland habitats at all, it is generally accepted that wide hedges are considerably more obliging.

A more literal consideration of the corridor comparison is slightly more encouraging. Hedge shrubs are frequently planted in two rows, providing a generally rather narrow path down the centre. It is common to see a well-worn path traversed by rabbits, foxes and badgers, and no doubt other mammals. However, these corridors are used by animals going about their daily business, not moving house. Fungi need no corridors as their spore dispersal mechanisms are more than adequate. No doubt snails and other non-flying invertebrates can use hedges as dispersal corridors, but for most organisms the hedge is a reservoir and refuge.

Hedges do not, of course, consist of only a single type of edge habitat. They may be dense hawthorn and blackthorn and little else, or they could have five different species of hedgerow tree, several climbing plants and a few well-spaced standard oaks. Hedges vary greatly in height and there is much variation in the level of management they enjoy. Those accompanied by ditches may support water-loving plants such as sedges, watermint or watercress. Combine these variations with the inevitable differences that there will be between, say, a hedge growing on chalk in Wiltshire and one growing on rocky clay in West Lothian, or between a hedge dividing arable fields and one separating a country lane from pastoral land, and we have a vast range of habitats, each attracting and supporting a different biota. It is therefore impossible to give a list of species that are typical of hedges, as it begs the question which hedge? A comprehensive natural history of the British hedge would effectively be a reduced natural history of Britain, with some rather random species – such as marsh samphire, water crowfoot and oystercatcher – missing. In fact, about around a third of British plants have been recorded in hedgerows, which is probably an underestimate.[1] If a wide verge is included, then there is little limit to the number of species that may be found.

However, some species have a strong association with hedges and hedgerows, not because that is the only place they are found, but because a hedge is the first place you would look for them. About two hundred British plants appear sufficiently often in a hedge to be afforded the status of hedgerow plant.

Natural history today displays something of a siege mentality, understandably so. No television programme, newspaper article or press release from a wildlife trust or charity can say anything about

This Devon hedge has a central wildlife corridor sufficiently large to accommodate *Homo sapiens*.

the natural world without mentioning that something terrible has happened or is about to happen. Concerns about the state of British biodiversity prompted the setting up, in 1994, of the UK Biodiversity Action Plan (UK BAP), now superseded by a Strategic Plan for Biodiversity. Among the many efforts made by the UK BAP was an attempt to protect species associated with hedges and hedgerows. In 2009 Dr Rob Wolton produced a report, 'Priority species linked to hedgerows', listing and discussing 130 species significantly associated with hedges and hedgerows.[2] This, of course, does not give a complete list of species found in hedges, only those for which there is some concern or which are so dependent on the habitat provided by hedges that any loss of hedgerow would seriously compromise their existence. For example, no trees are included except the very rare Plymouth pear (*Pyrus cordata*) and each of the four species of fungi listed are rare everywhere; however, also on the list is a familiar bird, the yellowhammer. All these species – rare and not so rare – are associated primarily with hedges and at least some of these, as well the more common species, will be mentioned below.

A hedge can be divided into a handful of habitats. There is the habitat created by the main shrubs that form the bulk of the hedge and there is that created by any standard trees that live there. Directly below the hedge shrubs is a strip of land, sometimes termed the hedge bottom, which supports its own species. These can be narrow and open to light, dense, wide and dark, or wide and with a rabbit or badger run hidden inside. If a hedge has a bank, there will almost certainly be a ditch. Either side of the hedge, or hedge bank and ditch, there will likely be a narrow strip: the hedge verge. This will be quite different from the hedge itself, or the hedge bank and ditch, but I include it here because it is a habitat that is entirely dependent on the hedge beside which it lies. These verges vary greatly, depending on all previously mentioned considerations, but also on whether the adjoining land is arable, pastoral or a highway. How a verge is managed is also crucial – cut roadside verges differ from uncut roadside verges, fallow verges from grazed, and arable verges sprayed with fertiliser from unsprayed.

These separate habitats – standard tree, hedge shrub, hedge

bottom, hedge bank, ditch and verge – cannot be seen in isolation. Some species, a fungus, say, may do nothing more than consume the woody parts of blackthorn, but most species will require more than one habitat and some will require all of them. For example, an insect may feed on the leaves of a shrub but pupate in the leaf litter of the hedge bottom. Rob Wolton's report cites the example of the yellowhammer which feeds in the verge, nests in the hedge bottom, hides from predators in the shrubs and uses the trees to perch and sing. This is an important consideration in conservation efforts and in hedgerow management.

Nevertheless, species are generally associated with particular zones of the hedge habitat, even though they may visit or experience stages in their life cycle elsewhere. Seventy-nine of the priority species determined in Rob Wolton's report were each allocated to their main part or parts of the hedgerow. Moths were excluded because their behaviour was insufficiently well understood. The results give some indication of how life is distributed in the hedgerow habitats. In the standard trees there were 45 species that merited action; in the shrubs that make up the bulk of a hedge there were 33; the hedge bottom had 32; and the verge 27. This is interesting, but cannot necessarily be extrapolated to hedge species in general. It is to some extent a self-selecting group with 'under threat' being the criterion, and may misrepresent the proportions of species found in each zone.

The relatively large number of species that, at some time or other, used the standard trees (45 out of 79, or 57 per cent) shows the increased importance of hedgerows with such trees compared to hedges which by definition do not have them. This has clear implications for hedge management, as it demonstrates that hedges without standard trees are considerably less species-rich. The extent of the benefit to wildlife varies with the species of the trees concerned, but, perhaps more crucially, their age. It takes decades and centuries to establish fungal associations and a broad range of lichens, and only old trees will support wood-rotting fungi and many insect species rely on rotten wood for their existence.

Despite being unable to provide a comprehensive list of the

This recently restored roadside hedgerow has standard trees, ditch, bank and verge. It is in a pastoral location.

component species of a hedge habitat, there are a number of species which can be said to form the backbone of hedges. These are the shrubs and trees which make up a hedge; the trees which form standards; the accompanying shrubby plants which use the hedge as support (such as dog rose, black bryony and honeysuckle) and those herbaceous plants that fill the verge so prettily in spring and summer. These, and the animals that live among and upon them, form the basis of my natural history of the hedgerow. But there are also those species that almost invariably get overlooked: the fungi, the lichens, the mosses and the galls. Many of these are specific to familiar hedge trees and plants, and it is to these that I give pride of place.

A machine-trimmed roadside hedge with no ditch or bank, but a road verge one side and mixed farming the other.

A rather dull enclosure period hedge and ditch in Oxfordshire.

Chapter 13

SPECIES

I like to think that I walk along a hedge with my eyes open and that I will be able to name most of the species of plant, and note with shame those whose names are a mystery to me. But there is so very much more to a hedge than meets the eye. The majority of species occupying a hedge are tiny or even microscopic. Most, by a very long way, are insects.

The reasonably knowledge-able naturalist would be pleased to identify or note a hundred or so species of plant, animal, lichen and fungus in an average hedgerow. But how many species might there actually be? Certainly, one hundred species is a gross underestimate; so maybe three hundred, five hundred is more the mark?

The road side of Rob Wolton's hedgerow.

The slightly overgrown pastoral side of the hedgerow.

Just how large an underestimate was revealed in an inspiring article published in 2015 in British Wildlife.[1] Dr Rob Wolton knew that there was more to a hedge than was evident to casual observation and was determined to find out how much more. He chose the ninety accessible metres of the hedge which happened to border the lane to his house, and followed its fortunes over a period of two years. It was a Devon hedge in that it was, well, in Devon, and consisted of an earth and turf bank on which the hedgerow trees were planted, and it had a single ditch (see p. 302). In other words an average Devon hedge, though considerably above average compared to most hedges in Britain.

Dr Wolton recorded everything he could identify and sent off specimens to friends and colleagues whose specialism lay in arcana such as the Curculionoidea (weevils) who could put names to those things he could not. An organism counted as a species belonging to the hedgerow if it was within two metres either side of the tips of the branches of the main hedgerow trees. Birds were included if they nested, fed or merely perched and sang there, though not if they simply flew over the top (swallows and passing cormorants did not count, for example). Sensibly, no microscopic organisms were included.

A mildew, not counted in the survey, infecting several plants.

The significant revelation is that he found 2,070 species of plant, animal, lichen and fungus, with many species still awaiting identification (there are several hundred parasitoid Hymenoptera currently languishing in the Natural History Museum). As identities are determined, more species are added to the list. Insects predominate with 1,718 species, followed by nearly one hundred other invertebrates, including thirteen slugs and snails, and fifty spiders, harvestmen and pseudoscorpions. There were one hundred and twenty-five plants, eighty fungi and lichens, and fifty vertebrates including, obviously, birds. Regardless of the details, this is a remarkable list for its length alone and one hopes that it might give pause to anyone inclined to destroy a hedge.

When I walked the same hedge with Dr Wolton he suggested that 2,070 species, plus all those waiting in bottles and cardboard boxes, was actually a conservative estimate and that 3,000 might be nearer the mark. For example, many more fungi species may be present but did not feel inclined to produce their visible fruiting bodies during the course of the study. I commented on a serious downy mildew infection which coated the leaves of several of the herbaceous plants, but he had decided not to bother with mildews and had also ignored rust and smut fungi.

In 1985 I attended the launch of B. E. and J. P. Ellis's *Microfungi on Land Plants* (this is a small claim to fame, the mycological equivalent of having been at the Marquee Club when the Rolling Stones played their first gig). This now classic work lists 3,500 species within its 900 pages, all of which are microscopic or at least very small. Their impact, however, is not so small, showing up as massed individuals, or as lesions or other deformities on their hosts. Many of these will have been in that Devon hedge. Others missing from the list are soil organisms such as nematode worms, bacteria and various species that find themselves on odd branches of the tree of life but bear no common name, even as a group. No doubt there were also myriad parasites on the various vertebrates and invertebrates.

There is a great temptation to look at the natural world with a superficial eye – to most people a hedge is nothing more than a line of stunted trees, and even a well-versed naturalist will miss most of what is there. But, as Dr Wolton's survey powerfully reminds us, a hedge is very much more. It would not surprise me if the 2,000 or so species that he found and named could be doubled or even trebled.

Estimates of the number of species, of this or that group, found in a hedge are sometimes published by charities and other organisations intent on impressing us with the bounty that hedgerows provide. The Derbyshire Wildlife Trust, for example, suggests 'Over 1,500 species of insect can be found in hedgerows', but as Dr Wolton found 1,700 (and still counting) in a *single* hedge, such estimates may need revising.

Why so many species in this particular Devon hedge? Well, why not? Wherever a large organism exists, there will be many attendant species which go along for the ride, using it as shelter (this can apply to plants as much as animals), a perch, a home or as a food source. Even the dullest hawthorn enclosure hedge will be found to have a large head count, should anyone take the time to do the counting. But there is more to it than this. No one could deny that this was a good hedgerow, in that it began life as a Devon hedge – complete with turf bank, productive ditch, hedge shrubs and substantial trees – and had suffered neither too much attention nor too little. This, no doubt, is the main reason. If, however, a cereal baron had bought the surrounding land, removed all the hedges for half a mile, felled all the woodland and ploughed up all the pasture, it would not have had such a large biota because it would not have been integrated into a large ecosystem. Instead, it would have been isolated, incapable of restoring lost species from nearby populations and devoid of those species for which a hedge is just a perch or a place of retreat after feeding in nearby trees or pasture.

Having established that hedgerows form rich and varied eco-systems, how great is their total extent across Britain? A reasonable estimate might be around 700,000 km. This is approximately the distance to the moon and back, seventeen times the circumference of the Earth and twenty times the length of the British coastline (if the larger islands are included). It would take you sixteen years to walk (if you never rested) and ten months by car (if you drove that distance at 60 miles per hour without stopping). If we take the average hedgerow to be two metres wide, that gives a total area of 1,400 square kilometres or 140,000 hectares or 540 square miles: an area larger than Greater Manchester or three Isles of Wight and equivalent to the combined areas of the Queen Elizabeth Forest Park at Stirling, the Brechfa Forest in Carmarthenshire, the New Forest in Hampshire, Sherwood Forest in Nottinghamshire, the massive Kielder Forest in Northumberland and Thetford Forest in Suffolk. As you will imagine, I have had fun working this out, but it is always good to get things into perspective.

The area, although large, is a square with each side only 24 miles long. It would fit into Devon nearly five times over. It is not, though, the area that truly counts, it is the fact that hedges are distributed over most of Britain and that they form so great a length of edge habitat. In fact, if a dictator decided to plant six hundred square miles of wood, the most visually compelling and environmentally positive way for him or her to do so would be to plant it in the form of extensive hedges.

Chapter 14

WHAT CAN BE FOUND IN A HEDGE?

There is nothing like going for a walk with someone who knows what they are talking about and when it comes to identifying species, my friend Bryan is more a master than a jack-of-all-trades. We often go plant or mushroom hunting together, carrying cameras and loupes rather than baskets. While I can more or less hold my own with the fungi, I fall down when it comes to some of the flowering plants, ferns, mosses and lichens. In a typical hedgerow I can usually identify about twenty or so species of plant in a thirty-metre stretch, but most grasses, any mosses and all but four lichens are a mystery to me. Bryan is made of more erudite stuff and in two visits to a seventy-metre length of hedgerow he managed to name ninety-nine species of plant – there was nothing that foxed him. In total there were four ferns, fourteen grasses, rushes and sedges, five shrubs, ten trees and sixty-six other plants which come under the folk category of herb. Here is Bryan's impressive list:

| Hart's tongue fern | *Asplenium scolopendrium* | Fern |
| Male fern | *Dryopteris filix-mas* | Fern |

Soft shield fern	Polystichum setiferum	Fern
Western polypody	Polypodium interjectum	Fern
Bearded couch	Elymus caninus	Poales
Cocksfoot grass	Dactylis glomerata	Poales
False brome	Brachypodium sylvaticum	Poales
False fox sedge	Carex otrubae	Poales
False oat grass	Arrhenatherum elatius	Poales
Grey sedge	Carex divulsa	Poales
Hairy brome grass	Bromopsis ramosa	Poales
Hairy sedge	Carex hirta	Poales
Remote sedge	Carex remota	Poales
Rough meadow grass	Poa trivialis	Poales
Soft rush	Juncus effuses	Poales
Timothy	Phleum pratense	Poales
Tufted hair grass	Deschampsia cespitosa	Poales
Yorkshire fog	Holcus lanatus	Poales
Barren strawberry	Potentilla sterilis	Herb
Bittersweet	Solanum dulcamara	Herb
Black bryony	Dioscorea communis	Herb
Bluebell	Hyacinthoides non-scripta	Herb
Broad-leaved dock	Rumex obtusifolius	Herb
Broad-leaved willowherb	Epilobium montanum	Herb
Burdock	Arctium minus	Herb
Bush vetch	Vicia sepium	Herb
Cleavers	Galium aparine	Herb
Clustered dock	Rumex conglomeratus	Herb
Common fleabane	Pulicaria dysenterica	Herb
Common hempnettle	Galeopsis tetrahit	Herb
Common mouse-ear	Cerastium fontanum	Herb
Cow parsley	Anthriscus sylvestris	Herb
Creeping buttercup	Ranunculus repens	Herb
Creeping cinquefoil	Potentilla reptans	Herb
Creeping thistle	Cirsium arvense	Herb

Dandelion	*Taraxacum agg.*	Herb
Dog violet	*Viola viviana*	Herb
Dog's mercury	*Mercurialis perennis*	Herb
Field forget-me-not	*Myosotis arvensis*	Herb
Field horsetail	*Equisetum arvense*	Herb
Greater chickweed	*Stellaria neglecta*	Herb
Greater plantain	*Plantago major*	Herb
Greater stitchwort	*Stellaria holostea*	Herb
Greater willowherb	*Epilobium hirsutum*	Herb
Ground ivy	*Glechoma hederacea*	Herb
Hedge bedstraw	*Galium mollugo*	Herb
Hedge bindweed	*Calystegia sepium*	Herb
Hedge garlic	*Alliaria petiolata*	Herb
Hedge woundwort	*Stachys sylvatica*	Herb
Herb robert	*Geranium robertianum*	Herb
Hogweed	*Heracleum sphondylium*	Herb
Honeysuckle	*Lonicera periclymenum*	Herb
Knotgrass	*Polygonum aviculare*	Herb
Lesser celandine	*Ranunculus ficaria*	Herb
Lords and ladies	*Arum maculatum*	Herb
Marsh cudweed	*Gnaphalium uliginosum*	Herb
Marsh thistle	*Cirsium palustre*	Herb
Meadow buttercup	*Ranunculus acris*	Herb
Meadow vetchling	*Lathyrus pratensis*	Herb
Meadowsweet	*Filipendula ulmaria*	Herb
Moschatel	*Adoxa moschatellina*	Herb
Nipplewort	*Lapsana communis*	Herb
Oilseed rape	*Brassica napus*	Herb
Prickly sow thistle	*Sonchus asper*	Herb
Primrose	*Primula vulgaris*	Herb
Red campion	*Silene dioica*	Herb
Red clover	*Trifolium pratense*	Herb
Redshank	*Persicaria maculosa*	Herb

Ribwort plantain	*Plantago lanceolata*	Herb
Rough chervil	*Chaerophyllum temulum*	Herb
Silverweed	*Potentilla anserina*	Herb
Spear thistle	*Cirsium vulgare*	Herb
Square-stemmed St John's wort	*Hypericum tetrapterum*	Herb
Stinging nettle	*Urtica dioica*	Herb
Tufted vetch	*Vicia cracca*	Herb
Water figwort	*Scrophularia auriculata*	Herb
Wavy bittercress	*Cardamine flexuosa*	Herb
White clover	*Trifolium repens*	Herb
Wild angelica	*Angelica sylvestris*	Herb
Wild carrot	*Daucus carota*	Herb
Wintercress	*Barbarea vulgaris*	Herb
Wood avens	*Geum urbanum*	Herb
Wood dock	*Rumex sanguineus*	Herb
Woody nightshade	*Solanum dulcamara*	Herb
Bramble	*Rubus fruticosus agg.*	Shrub
Dewberry	*Rubus caesius*	Shrub
Dog rose	*Rosa canina*	Shrub
Field rose	*Rosa arvensis*	Shrub
Redcurrant	*Ribes rubrum*	Shrub
Ash	*Fraxinus excelsior*	Tree
Blackthorn	*Prunus spinosa*	Tree
Dogwood	*Cornus sanguinea*	Tree
Elder	*Sambucus nigra*	Tree
Field maple	*Acer campestre*	Tree
Grey willow	*Salix cinerea*	Tree
Guelder rose	*Viburnum opulus*	Tree
Hawthorn	*Crataegus monogyna*	Tree
Hazel	*Corylus avellana*	Tree
Oak	*Quercus robur*	Tree

The surveyed hedge at Kingcombe, West Dorset, with a large number of plant species.

What are we to make of this list? First of all, like the one produced by Rob Wolton, it is remarkable for its length alone, though Bryan assured me that ninety-nine species is by no means unusual and that he knows hedges with more. Second, is the large number of trees. A glance at the hedge will tell you that it is ancient and the tree species number merely confirms its age. Ten species in a length of hedge indicates – according to a formula devised by M. D. Hooper in 1965 – a hedge that is a thousand years old, and this may be close to the truth in our example. In fact, 'Hooper's rule' includes all woody plants, not just trees, so we must add the five shrub species to the list taking it well past the 1,000 years which Dr Hooper reckons to be the limit beyond which his rule fails. The rule only requires thirty metres to be taken into account, which brings it down to about ten species and back to 1,000 years.

Hooper's rule is one of the most famous pieces of modern hedgerow lore and is frequently mentioned by non-specialists eager to encourage me when I tell them of my interest in hedges (or perhaps they are just being polite). Dr Hooper himself considered it to be little more than a rough-and-ready guide which worked only under certain circumstances and which required confirmation from other sources. In general, it can help to distinguish between parliamentary enclosure hedges, those that are pre-parliamentary and ancient hedges.

Returning to the list, what is notable from the species names is that the hedgerow habitats are heterogeneous. The grey willow is a tree of wet ground (see below), as are the two plants with 'marsh' in their common name: marsh cudweed and marsh thistle. The latter's habitat being further indicated by the second half of its Latin name, *palustre*, which means marsh or swamp. Sedges too are familiar plants of wetlands and no less than four are present. Similarly, there are two species with 'wood' in their name (wood avens and wood dock) and two (cow parsley and wild angelica) with *sylvestris* (Latin for wood or forest) in their Latin name. This is unsurprising considering the trees present. What is surprising is the number of species that bear a reference to 'field' or 'meadow', either directly or through their specific epithet *pratense* or *pratensis*, *arvensis* or *arvense* and *acris*, all of which refer to field or meadow. Furthermore, there are wood or field inhabiting plants which do not give away their preferred habitat in their name, such as dog violet, dog's mercury and bluebell for the woods, and wintercress, oilseed rape, creeping buttercup and most of the grasses for the fields. Taken together, these names suggest a very mixed habitat.

The hedge concerned lies in a damp Dorset valley, not far from the River Hook and within the Kingcombe Nature Reserve; it has been periodically laid (see p. 298) and has a two-metre-wide border between it and the winding road which runs alongside. Anyone with some knowledge of the species we found would probably be able to picture in their mind what it looks like. It is exceptionally well stocked with plants, as we have seen, in a way typical of well-tended ancient hedges wherever they are found. In fact, a hedge is usually a mixed habitat, often reflecting the flora of grassland and woodland at the same time.

Bryan and I took another walk, this time even nearer to home. Here is the list of plant species we found:

Hart's tongue fern	*Asplenium scolopendrium*	Fern
Bird's foot trefoil	*Lotus corniculatus*	Herb
Black bryony	*Dioscorea communis*	Herb
Black medic	*Medicago lupulina*	Herb
Common centaury	*Centaurium erythraea*	Herb
Common knapweed	*Centaurea nigra*	Herb
Cow parsley	*Anthriscus sylvestris*	Herb
Cuckoo pint	*Arum maculatum*	Herb
Dandelion	*Taraxacum agg.*	Herb
Field bindweed	*Convolvulus arvensis*	Herb
Field scabious	*Knautia arvensis*	Herb
Germander speedwell	*Veronica chamaedrys*	Herb

Goat's-beard	Tragopogon pratensis	Herb
Greater knapweed	Centaurea scabiosa	Herb
Hairy St John's wort	Hypericum hirsutum	Herb
Hedge bedstraw	Galium mollugo	Herb
Hemp agrimony	Eupatorium cannabinum	Herb
Herb robert	Geranium robertianum	Herb
Hogweed	Rubus fruticosus agg.	Herb
Marjoram	Origanum vulgare	Herb
Meadow vetchling	Lathyrus pratensis	Herb
Oxeye daisy	Leucanthemum vulgare	Herb
Ragwort	Jacobaea vulgaris	Herb
Red campion	Silene dioica	Herb
Ribwort plantain	Plantago lanceolata	Herb
Rough chervil	Chaerophyllum temulum	Herb
Salad burnet	Sanguisorba minor	Herb
Self-heal	Prunella vulgaris	Herb
Small scabious	Scabiosa columbaria	Herb
Smooth hawksbeard	Crepis capillaris	Herb
Tall fescue	Festuca arundinacea	Herb
Wild basil	Clinopodium vulgare	Herb
Wild carrot	Daucus carota	Herb
Wild parsnip	Pastinaca sativa	Herb
Wood avens	Geum urbanum	Herb
Yarrow	Achillea millefolium	Herb
Yellow wort	Blackstonia perfoliata	Herb
False brome	Brachypodium sylvaticum	Poales
False oat grass	Arrhenatherum elatius	Poales
Glaucous sedge	Carex flacca	Poales
Hairy brome	Bromus ramosus	Poales
Red fescue	Festuca rubra	Poales
Rough meadow grass	Poa trivialis	Poales
Upright brome	Bromus erectus	Poales

Bramble	*Rubus fruticosus agg.*	Shrub
Dewberry	*Rubus caesius*	Shrub
Dog rose	*Rosa canina*	Shrub
Ivy	*Hedera helix*	Shrub
Ash	*Fraxinus excelsior*	Tree
Blackthorn	*Prunus spinosa*	Tree
Buckthorn	*Rhamnus cathartica*	Tree
Dogwood	*Cornus sanguinea*	Tree
Domestic apple	*Malus domestica*	Tree
Field maple	*Acer campestre*	Tree
Grey willow	*Salix cinerea*	Tree
Guelder rose	*Viburnum opulus*	Tree
Hawthorn	*Crataegus monogyna*	Tree
Hazel	*Corylus avellana*	Tree
Holly	*Ilex aquifolium*	Tree
Wayfaring tree	*Viburnum lantana*	Tree
Wild privet	*Ligustrum vulgare*	Tree

The list contains sixty-one species, not as numerically impressive as our first list, but still long for a stretch of roadside hedge covering one hundred and twenty metres. The most striking comparison between the two lists is the low number of plants, other than trees, that are common to both. Eighty-nine non-tree plants were found along the first hedge, compared to forty-eight along the second, but only seventeen were found in both. More than half of these seventeen were species that are hard *not* to find as they appear in very nearly every hedge in the kingdom – dog rose, hogweed, cow parsley, dandelion, rough chervil, red campion, herb robert, meadow vetchling, hedge bindweed and ivy. The hedges concerned were situated in adjacent Dorset valley bottoms and both were roadside hedges. So why was there so little overlap? The reason, of course, is the difference in soil. The first was of wet, slightly acid soil, the latter of dry chalk. This will come as no surprise to anyone familiar with the plants concerned – many of those in the second list are denizens of chalk grassland, and indeed the hedge was situated on a chalk bank that came directly down to the road edge. Around fourteen of these species are typical of chalk grassland, while wild privet is typical of chalk scrub. The two oddities are grey willow and glaucous sedge, both species, one would assume, which insist on damp soils. The first is more tolerant of variations in pH and a lower moisture level than most willows, while the second has broken the mould of the sedge tribe in being a common sedge of dry chalk grassland. The point of this comparison is to show how very different hedges can be from one soil to another – hedges are not created equal.

In 1990 a much more extensive and formal survey was undertaken by Stephen Howard Jones who studied 180 hedgerows in Yorkshire and Oxfordshire (approximately 90 from each county) all situated in entirely arable land.[1] In total he recorded 172 species of plant, consisting of 23 trees, 9 shrubs, 21 grasses and sedges, 3 non-flowering plants and 119 herbaceous plants. As might be expected, there were more plants recorded in Oxfordshire than in Yorkshire. More surprising, was that fewer than half the species (81) were common to both counties.

While 172 species of plant is a respectable number, it took 180 hedges from two counties to reach that figure. Compared to the 144 species that Bryan and I found in two stretches of hedge it seems a poor show. The reasons for this are, however, fairly straightforward. The hedges in the study were from arable land, none of which adjoined a road. Our studies were of pastoral hedgerows in heavily wooded areas next to roads. One of our hedges had a wide, undisturbed verge, while the other had a small chalk bank. Both roadside hedges and pastoral hedges can be more productive of species than those in arable countryside. In both cases, the hedge verges (or banks) are left unploughed, if not entirely undisturbed, allowing colonisation by many species of plant and subsequently other dependent species. On arable land, the field is usually cultivated right up to the hedge, reducing the width of land that escapes the plough. Sometimes, however, close grazing, trampling and browsing of a hedge can have the opposite effect and a pastoral hedge can be less species-rich than an arable hedge. For the most part, low stock levels,

An exception to pastoral hedges being more species-rich than arable hedges. Where the hedge is used as welcome shelter for livestock, the poaching destroys most of the herbaceous plants.

additional wire fencing and the use of pastoral fields for ungrazed fallow, hay and silage ensure that this is not a frequent occurrence. Hedge verges on arable farms, such as they are, are plagued with over-spray and leaching from the application of fertilisers. Nitrogen is a minor culprit here, but phosphates do a lot of damage, stimulating the growth of weed species which can outperform other, smaller or more sensitive plants. Drainage is another factor that puts species levels in pastoral land above those in arable. Pastoral land does not need to be as well drained as arable, and a poorly drained pastoral hedge will provide a good habitat for plant species that thrive in wet soils.

Hedges fall into several groups based on their primary tree-shrub constituents. In a 2001 paper by D. D. French and R. P. Cummins, published in the journal *Applied Vegetation Science*, 1,200 lengths of hedge and hedgerow were carefully selected to provide an overview of what types of hedge exist in Britain and how they are consti-tuted.[2] The authors classified them into eleven types, based on their dominant tree species or combination of tree species. Of the hedge samples taken, there were eight gorse-dominated hedges, six willow-dominated, five almost entirely of wild privet, nineteen of beech, nine of planted exotics and forty-nine of elm. These numbers are dwarfed by those of blackthorn (270) and even more so by those that were almost entirely hawthorn (552). There were another 250 or so in which hawthorn was very common, such as mixed hazel (157), elder-hawthorn (40) and rich-hawthorn – in which hawthorn is common but with a variety of other woody species also present (61). It is worth noting that even the beech-dominated hedge, as defined, can include up to 40 per cent hawthorn. There will, of course, be incidental hedgerow trees such guelder rose, spindle and dogwood as well as standard trees like ash and oak, but these do not form the basis of the classification.

The authors also classified hedge bottoms (the area underneath or near to the hedge itself) into intensive arable (562), mixed/rotational (341), grassland (162) and woodland (146). My first Dorset hedge falls firmly into the last category, despite the large number of field species found on the broad grassy verge, and my second hedge surveyed fell reasonably well into the category of grassland. Figures such as these can be very dull, but those produced by French and Cummins are truly revealing of the current state of the British hedgerow.

In what follows, distributions for many of the species described are given. There are several, very useful, online maps which provide distribution data for nearly all the species that live in Britain, of which the National Biodiversity Network's Gateway is probably the best known.[3] Unfortunately, the more obscure a species is, the less reliable the distribution map. If a weevil expert lives in Wantage and holidays in Skegness, then these two areas will be disproportionately represented for species that need a weevil expert to identify them. At worst (and taking dandelions as an example) these maps may provide data not so much on the distribution of *Taraxacum* but on the distribution of taraxacologists.

Chapter 15

TREES OF THE HEDGEROW

A hedge is, in form at least, a linear wood and you cannot have a wood without trees. The tree species counted by French and Cummins are for the most part those that were planted by the farmer, but more trees end up in hedges and hedgerows than are planted. The Dorset hedge just described had a remarkable ten trees along the short length examined, but there is no limit to which trees may be found in a hedge – almost any of Britain's native trees and many non-native specimens can find their way into a hedgerow. This book is not the place to describe in great detail the individual trees that make up a hedge or hedgerow, instead I intend to consider the trees as a component of a hedge and to describe some of the species of fungi, plant, lichen and animal which rely upon them for their livelihood.

Some of the species which make hedgerow trees their home are true generalists, while others are extremely particular about where they grow, insisting on living only on the twigs of a willow or the broken shells of hazelnuts. Overall, tree species acquire guest species with time and according to the tree species' population density. If a tree arrived just after the last Ice Age and has a reasonably large population, it will host a relatively large number of species of insects, fungi, lichens and so on. Oak, which has been in Britain for thousands of years, is noted for being the very best of hosts. Sycamore, by comparison, is something of a latecomer, and hosts little beyond sycamore blackspot and a few aphids, though it does form a reliable substratum for many lichens. Long provenance is never the whole story, some trees are naturally better at playing host than others.

Let us start with those that are usually planted intentionally; the trees that form the very basis of a hedge. The primary purpose of a hedge is as a barrier. While almost any tree could be used, a magic three are used more than any other: hawthorn, blackthorn and hazel. These possess two fundamental characteristics that make them suitable: ease of laying and impenetrability. Just how common hawthorn and blackthorn are is obvious to even the most casual observer, but if there was any doubt it is dispelled in the research paper described above. In addition to being the primary tree in nearly half of all hedges, three of the groups have hawthorn as the second most dominant tree. Hawthorn makes a dominant or sub-dominant appearance in 94 per cent of all hedges; for blackthorn it is 27 per cent. Two thirds of British hedges have hawthorn or black-thorn as their main species.

Below, I describe the practical usage of most of the common hedgerow trees. I provide examples of the many species that depend on them, concentrating on the more subtle species such as the macro and microfungi, galls and insects. The latter, of course, provide food for birds and their presence is one of the reasons why we see so many birds in hedgerows. Missing from the discussion is the insects that rely on dead wood for their livelihood. Most hedges will contain some dead wood, and in many it may form a major component. Some of the larger fungi are described and it is worth noting that while they will usually depend on the hedgerow trees and shrubs, other organisms depend on them. No one likes maggots in their mushrooms, but these are, largely, the larvae of fungal gnats, of which there are many species. These too provide sustenance for small birds, and these birds may in turn provide food for other birds or for mammals. The hedgerow habitat shows many of these chains of dependence and is part of its joy.

Hawthorn (*Crataegus monogyna*)

The use of thorn species in hedges goes back a long way, as shown by the remains found in a Peterborough ditch (p. 35). There is no doubt that they were used throughout the history of hedge planting and by the mid-eighteenth century – when the parliamentary enclosure movement got underway – hawthorn and blackthorn plants were grown commercially on a vast scale to supply the demand for new hedges. In 1778, one Richard Stone boasted a stock of 500,000 whitethorn, the two-year-old shoots going for a bargain price of four shillings per thousand. A few years later, in 1794, the *Chester Courant* advertised, 'A Large quantity of three years-old SEEDLING WHITE-THORNS – enquire of Mr Roger Lewis, at the Ring-of-bells, Daresbury, Cheshire.'

Whitethorn is an alternative name for hawthorn and a reference to its bright spring blossoms. Yet another name, quickthorn, derives not from its ability to grow quickly, but from the meaning of quick as alive – thus distinguishing it from a 'dead hedge' (see p. 21). Both terms were frequently used for hawthorn, as in the following from the *Leeds Intelligencer* of 1777 advertising: 'One Hundred and Thirty-two acres of good Land, well watered, chiefly old Meadow and Pasture, well fenced with Quick-Thorn Hedges.'

Hawthorn is certainly the most common hedge tree species and for a good reason. It is stock-proof, easy to lay and readily produces side shoots from laid stock, thus producing a dense hedge in a short amount of time. It is hardy, generally resistant to disease, content in wet soils, tolerant of dry soils and lives long. In an 1899 report published in the *Journal of the Royal Agricultural Society*, hawthorn scored higher than any other tree or shrub in ticking most of the boxes in a list of seventeen qualities most looked for in a hedge. It is notable for being the sole tree to be planted along the newly built railway lines, and the method of planting by the various railway companies was regarded as exemplary. Unless a ditch was essential for drainage and

Common hawthorn in berry.   May blossom.

a bank thus formed, they would plant them on the level, as banks are known to wash away, exposing the roots. The ground would be manured, limed and fallowed, and the young trees kept free of weeds by 'stirring' the ground.

Of the different species of hawthorn, the commonest by far is *Crataegus monogyna*, the common hawthorn. This is a native species and regarded as being an understorey woodland tree (one that does not grow very high). It has a pervasive range in Britain, being found everywhere except in some of the more challenging parts of the Scottish Highlands. The other fairly common hawthorn is *C. laevigata*, the midland or English hawthorn. This too is a native species, but confined to the south-eastern half of England, delimited by a curved line stretching from Hull over to Liverpool, then down to Bristol and across to Brighton. Like so many other plant species, it is missing from a large area around the Wash. It is thus fairly widespread, but, from my own observations, is difficult to find even in its heartland, contenting itself with odd guest appearances in hedges.

From a distance there is little to distinguish between these two species, but the leaves of C. monogyna are deeply lobed while those of C. laevigata only shallowly so, and there is only one pip in the berries of the former (hence monogyna, one womb) compared to two or three in the latter. The two are known to hybridise with each other and with several other Crataegus species that have arrived from the continent 'corrupting' the native species, much to the annoyance of ecological purists. Identifying a hawthorn precisely to a species is the job of a master botanist, but being able to tell C. monogyna from C. laevigata is sufficient for most.

Midland or English hawthorn, though the pink in what is left of the flowers suggests a cultivar or hybrid.

Unfortunately, if you wish to repair or replant a hawthorn hedge it is not always enough to simply order the correct species from the nearest nursery. Although not yet having acquired species, subspecies or even varietal status, hawthorn plants from different locations show markedly different properties, and sometimes look different, to those of the local and previously employed stock. This sort of problem pops up all the time in conservation. For example, a friend of mine, who likes to keep a professional eye on conservation measures enacted by our local council and highways agency, was appalled to find that the wildflower seeds used to plant up the chalky banks of a new by-pass were all the right species but of the wrong provenance. Subtle differences were visible to the trained eye, and not so subtle differences, such as cowslips being twice their normal size, were visible to all. The well-intentioned efforts of the authorities became a local ecological embarrassment. The next time such a planting was undertaken, my friend took no chances and insisted on collecting and supplying the seeds himself.

In 2001, a research paper in the *Journal of Applied Ecology* found that 80 per cent of the hawthorn plants supplied by the UK horticultural trade in 1997 came from continental Europe. Some seeds came all the way from Germany or Hungary where the plants are adapted to substantially different growing conditions. Even simply sourcing from within Britain is insufficient, as hawthorn varies greatly across the country. Apart from a seemingly creepy insistence on species purity, does any of this matter? Yes is the answer, because the truly local hawthorns fare much better than the poorly adapted immigrants, showing a markedly greater resistance to powdery mildew, better branching abilities and more thorns. Overall, they make a better and denser hedge, and they leaf and bud-burst at the 'correct' time of year, enabling the flowers and fruit to flourish by avoiding frost damage. The paper also suggested that local insect populations had adapted to the leafing and flowering timetable of local populations of hawthorn, something that would be disrupted if alien plants were introduced. The picture of C. *laevigata* on p. 153 is an example of an import, as is evident by its pink colouration.

Whichever species, form or sub-variety it may be, the hawthorn is a beautiful tree. The blossoms light the hedgerow in spring and the berries glow in the sunrises and sunsets of autumn. May is, of course, the month when the tree flowers and it is this that gives it the alternative name of May-tree. It also supplies the origin of the sometimes misunderstood warning to 'ne'er cast a cloot til Mey's oot'. This places the shedding of winter garments to the time when the blossom appears, half-way through the month, and not 1 June as would be the case had May referred to the month. (However, since the saying is Scottish in origin it may be that it makes no difference.)

The blossoms are glorious to the eye but an offence to the nose, smelling, as they do, of fish, and not fish in prime condition. The culprit here is trimethylamine, a chemical product of animal decomposition. The tree has long held a folk association with death – which is easily explained – but also of love. The latter association, however, requires a more delicate explanation than I am prepared to give here.

Hawthorn is a tough plant, but it suffers badly from one disease

Erwinia amylovora, fire blight, in Oxfordshire.

– a bacterial infection, accidentally imported from North America in 1957, known as fire blight. The leaves brown, as though someone has lit a bonfire nearby, and wilt prematurely. *C. laevigata* suffers most from this disfiguring if seldom fatal disease. I have seen it only once, on a walk near Port Meadow at Oxford, so it is not common in hedges. The disease becomes a serious problem if a hawthorn hedge is used around an orchard. The bacterium infects the pomaceous members of the rose family, which includes hawthorn, but also apples and pears.

Fire blight may be a disease as far as we (and the hawthorn) are concerned, but to the bacterium that causes the problem (*Erwinia amylovora*) it is just life. After the oak, birch and willow, the hawthorn is Britain's most accommodating host of other species, forming a rich ecosystem all of its own. Whether the bacteria, fungi, insects, mammals or birds associated with hawthorn are considered diseases or pests, or thought of as being beneficial, are value judgements made only by humans. We speak approvingly of many insects but to their host plant they are usually just pests. A fungal infection may not sound very pleasant but all trees are infected by fungi and most could not function easily without them. Many fungi live their lives as tree pathogens and we may despair at the sight of a tree's demise at their hand. But would we truly prefer the extinction of an entire species to the occasional loss of a tree? What, though, if the loss were not occasional but destroyed thousands or even millions of trees, as happened with the ill-fated elm? We may well wish that the offending fungal parasite, *Ophiostoma ulmi*, had not been so destructive in its behaviour, but the thoughtful naturalist would not wish an entire species consigned to Dodo-like oblivion.

Hawthorn too has its fungal parasites, though nothing as devastating as *O. ulmi*, and we can enjoy their remarkable existence with less regret. Chief among them are the rust fungi, nine species of which are known to infect hawthorn including cedar hawthorn rust (*Gymnosporangium globosum*) and quince rust (*Gymnosporangium clavipes*). The double species name of the former reflects a way of life involving two host plants, colonised in turn to complete the pathogen's life cycle. In fact, both species involve two hosts and the common names have rather confused the matter. Although these two species are, obviously, different, they both require one host in the cypress family (Cupressaceae) and another in the rose family (Rosaceae), which includes hawthorn. These rusts affect several species but in the case of the hawthorn it is usually a juniper/hawthorn or an eastern red cedar/hawthorn pairing. Both juniper and eastern red cedar are in the genus *Juniperus*. The full life cycle of these organisms is of sufficiently baroque complexity to compel one to wonder how such an arrangement could have evolved. I will not go into the details here but merely report the effects they have on infected hawthorns. Quince rust damages the fruit, green stems and petioles (leaf stalks), covering them with remarkable orange-yellow 'rust tubes'. Cedar hawthorn rust is spectacular in its own way, covering the leaves with bright yellow spots which can make the whole tree appear yellow. Unfortunately (unless you are a hawthorn), both species are rare for the simple reason that the juniper is rare.

Hawthorn, like so many other plants, suffers from the fungus known as powdery mildew (*Podosphaera oxyacanthae*). This coats the leaves with fine white 'fur', curling and discolouring the leaves in the process. The overall effect does nothing for a hawthorn tree's good looks but, when seen under a microscope, powdery mildew is a thing of complexity and beauty.

Not all fungi are parasitic, some just consume dead organic material, performing the essential task of ensuring that we do not disappear beneath a mile-thick layer of leaves and twigs. Some of these are specific to certain habitats such as fields, woods or marshes, and some will only grow with certain trees. One of these is *Tubaria dispersa*. Like most British fungi it has been saddled with a recently coined common name, the hawthorn twiglet, which does it no favours. It forms extensive and dense colonies of small, creamy-white mushrooms in the leaf-litter beneath hawthorns, growing on the seeds of the decaying haws. Another mushroom species (which is also happy to grow with blackthorn) is the very rare pinkgill, *Entoloma niphoides*. It is fairly substantial in size, growing to 12 cm in diameter and is white all over, except for its pink gills.

Anyone wishing to discover which species of insect or fungus is associated with a certain tree could do worse than search on the Latin generic name of the host tree. Faced with naming a new species of insect or fungus (or anything else) a taxonomist will often choose the new species' habitat as a basis for the specific epithet (the second part of the Latin name). This is particularly true of the hawthorn, which has lent its name to several species including the midge, *Dasineura crataegi*, that produces the hawthorn button-top gall.

Galls can be formed by insects, bacteria, fungi, nematode worms and even other plants, and are one of the most remarkable features of the natural world. Created by the invader modifying the growth pattern of the host to suit their needs, their purpose is to provide shelter and food for the invading organism. Some are impressive constructions; others merely curled up leaf edges. The gall of *D. crataegi* is formed by a gall-midge infestation which disrupts the formation of the hawthorn's terminal shoots, causing dense rosettes of stunted and deformed leaves and surrounding them with long, warty projections. The orange-red larvae feed within the protection afforded by the distorted leaves, then fall to the ground to pupate. In a nice case of 'little fleas have lesser fleas upon their backs to bite 'em', *D. crataegi* is in turn parasitised by the hymenopteran insect,

A familiar fungal infection of hawthorn (and other trees) is *Diplocarpon mespili*, otherwise unhelpfully known as *Entomosporium* leaf spot. Visible as purple/red markings with a tiny black mass in the centre which produces the spores, a serious infection will sufficiently weaken a tree to cause its death.

Aprostocetus lysippe. The latter is known as a parasitoid; a parasite with bells and whistles which is invariably fatal to its host.

Since the hawthorn is so often encountered in hedges, it is worth looking at three more of its associated galls. Formed by an aphid rather than a midge, *Dysaphis crataegi* creates brilliant red blisters on the upper surface of the leaves. The concave surface houses the aphids which in June retire to a second host, the wild carrot (or some other umbelliferous plant), before returning to lay their eggs after their summer holiday is over. Two other galls are worth a passing mention. The mite *Phyllocoptes goniothorax* forms little rolls in hawthorn leaves, and another mite, *Eriophyes crataegi*, covers them with unattractive white blisters,

A common species that also bears the specific epithet of hawthorn is the hawthorn leaf beetle, *Lochmaea crataegi*. It too is specific to hawthorn and one of the few beetles easily identified by a novice. Only four or five millimetres long, it is easily identified by its striking wing cases which are speckled and striped in bronze and black. Considerably less attractive is *Ovatus crataegarius*, an aphid found only on hawthorn.

Several hundred species of moth have been recorded in hedgerows, twenty-five of which are entirely reliant on hawthorn. One of the latter (though occasionally found on blackthorn too) is the hawthorn moth, *Scythropia crataegella*, a medium size moth whose larvae take the sensible precaution of feeding as 'leaf miners'. Leaf miners make frequent appearances in hedges as few plants are not host to at least one of the more than a thousand species of insect that spend their larval stage protected by the leaf that they are eating. The added advantage they gain is that they consume the more nutrient rich flesh of a leave, not its low nutrient cellulose skin. Many are identifiable by the shape of their track marks (mines) and knowledge of the host plant on which it is found. Most are moth, wasp, sawfly and fly species.

The hawthorn shield bug lacks any reference to the hawthorn in its Latin name, *Acanthosoma haemorrhoidale*. The slightly alarming specific epithet is merely a reference to the blood-red markings on the back of this otherwise leaf-green insect. Its favourite food is, unusually for an insect, the ripe haws. However, it is not confined to the hawthorn and is happy to consume the leaves of a number of tree species. It is common in southern Britain, less so in the north.

The complexity of relationships and dramas played out on the humble hawthorn is nicely demonstrated by the behaviour of ants which feed on the honeydew of a jumping plant louse (psyllid) called *Cacopsylla crataegi*, which feeds on the hawthorn. The louse larvae are parasitised by a tiny wasp, *Prionomitus mitratus*. This wasp, in turn, suffers from the attentions of a hyperparasitoid (a parasite of other parasites which invariably kills its host) in the form of another tiny wasp, *Pachyneuron muscarum*. In a clear case of picking on the wrong guy, the ant attacks *P. muscarum*, leaving *P. mitratus* to do its worst on their herds of psyllid larvae.

Blackthorn (*Prunus spinosa*)

I prefer blackthorn to hawthorn, on aesthetic grounds alone. It is quite beautiful at any time of the year, but particularly so in the winter when its dark brown bark stands out against the pervading browns and greens of the countryside or against the winter sky. Every year in March and April the hedgerows come alive for the first time when the strikingly white frothy blossoms appear, slightly in advance of the blackthorn's leaves. Despite its beauty it can be ominous in appearance when not in leaf; its bark nearly black, its thorns exposed, and it is this, perhaps, which explains the tree's long association with witchcraft. There is a blackthorn hedge on the hill above my village that I can see from my office window. Every tree in its one hundred and fifty yard length leans precipitously with the prevailing wind and I once told my daughters it is the remains of a goblin army, transformed by a benign witch into a row of blackthorn.

It is found throughout Britain, apart from the Scottish Highlands, and is tolerant of most soils, but will not thrive in acid conditions, hence its more frequent use in the south. Blackthorn is the main tree in over a quarter of hedges, especially in the south-west and a common tree in my own West Dorset where few hedges dispense with its services completely and some are made up of it entirely.

Famously the blackthorn produces the sloes from which so many gallons of sloe gin are made; one can only pity those who live in parts of the country where the blackthorn is a rarity. The plant's Latin

The brilliant white spring blossoms of blackthorn.

name is Prunus *spinosa*, the *Prunus* part simply meaning plum, so it is close to the wild cherry (Prunus *avium*) and the cherry plum (Prunus *cerasifera*) and may in fact be one of the ancestors of the cultivated plum (Prunus *domesticus*). The *spinosa* epithet is a reference to the blackthorn's fierce and abundant spines which make it so accomplished as a stock-proof hedge. Grazing animals are seldom damaged by them, but the relatively thin hide of Homo *sapiens* provides little defence. It was once thought that they were poisonous, but in fact the spines only leave small quantities of bacteria-laden bark in a wound, causing inflammation and discomfort.

Slightly smaller than the hawthorn, the blackthorn is a staple of the hedgerow, if not quite so popular with farmers. *The Complete Farmer* of 1777 pronounced that, 'Blackthorn is not reckoned so good for Fences as the White, because 'tis apt to run more into the Ground, and is not so certain of growing.' The phrase 'run into the ground' refers to its tendency to push up new trees from barely underground runners and make a mess of any hedge. In my limited experience of hedge laying, much of my time was taken up with removing hundreds of tiny, unwanted blackthorn trees, some of which had established themselves at a considerable distance from the hedge. Blackthorn also suffers from a disinclination to be replanted, making nursery-grown trees a relatively unreliable proposition. However, a well-laid and tended blackthorn hedge is all but impenetrable and will last for centuries.

As well as directly forming a live hedge, the blackthorn has found further employment in establishing boundaries, as William Ellis suggests in *The Timber-tree Improved* of 1742: 'This prickly tree is most serviceable for making dead Hedges to save the live ones, because this Wood will last two or three Years under this Use, when the White-thorn will last but one.'[2] It seems likely that the blackthorn has long been a first choice for dead hedges as its merits are so obvious.

It is worth mentioning one more agricultural use for blackthorn: the creation of field drains. Drainage schemes of varying quality and success have been attempted throughout history – few realise how very boggy Britain was before the introduction of agricultural drainage. Ditches are the simplest form of drainage but much of our agriculture depends on field drains (sub-surface drains) which discharge into these ditches. These used to be ceramic but are now mostly plastic. During the enclosure period, a more primitive field drain was made by digging a series of ditches across a field and filling the ditch bottoms with blackthorn and stones. The excavated soil was returned to fill the ditches level with the field.[3]

Blackthorn is near indestructible, but like the hawthorn it does bear the burden of accommodating a large number of insects, fungi and other so-called pests. As already noted, one man's pest is another man's interesting species, so I offer first of all *Taphrina pruni*, a gall-forming fungus which you may have encountered on sloe collecting expeditions. The sloes become twice their normal size, lose their colour and are frequently wrinkled. They also completely lack a stone, with just a cavity where it should have been, hence the gall's common name – pocket plum gall. The spores are ejected from the surface and all being well (for the gall) a fresh infection is begun elsewhere. The bird cherry (*Prunus padus*), which is sometimes found in hedges, also suffers from the attentions of this fungus.

No less interesting is the common bracket fungus, *Phellinus pomaceus*, which gently consumes the wood and produces large

The remarkable *Taphrina pruni* which makes a take-over bid for sloes.

brackets which situate themselves underneath the branches of mature blackthorn. Their surface is orange brown and pleasingly velvety. The spores are produced in thousands of holes on the underside of the bracket.

The flower buds of blackthorn are sometimes usurped by the gall midge, *Asphondylia pruniperda* (literally: spineless plum-loser), forming galls shaped like tear drops. These are hollow and lined with a fungus on which the midge feeds and which proceeds to consume the gall once the midge has flown. The gall of the mite *Eriophyes similis*, which appear at the edges of the leaves, is rather more visible being shiny and red.

Phellinus pomaceus.

The common rust fungus, *Tranzschelia pruni-spinosae*, attacks the leaves of blackthorn, which turn yellow then brown, before becoming covered with round pits, as though someone had used a tiny shotgun on them. Rusts and smuts have few friends as they usually make an unattractive mess of whichever plant they call home. This species has adopted as its specific epithet the entire Latin name of its host in hyphenated form, a most unusual construction. Even less appealing are the number of fungi which attack the sloes but do so inconspicuously. One of these, a brown rot fungus called *Monilinia laxa*, may have been the culprit in a particularly disappointing, indeed nasty, batch of sloe gin I made a few years ago.

Blackthorn hosts several butterflies and is the primary food plant for the following: the black hairstreak, *Satyrium pruni*; black-veined white, *Aporia crataegi* (also found on hawthorn); brown hairstreak, *Thecla betulae* (also found on birch); and the intriguingly named scarce swallowtail, *Iphiclides podalirius* (a rare visitor). Various moth species such as the lackey, magpie, common emerald, small eggar, swallow-tailed and yellow-tailed are also found on blackthorn.

The very common gall of the mite
Eriophyes similis.

Thecla betulae, the brown hairstreak.

Hazel (*Corylus avellana*)

Hazel has been important since before the dawn of agriculture, with farmers well versed in it uses and cultivation. The Roman poet Virgil mentions hazel three times in Book 2 of *The Georgics*, including the line 'Plantis edurae Coryli nascuntur' [From suckers the hard *hazels* grow].

Despite lacking thorns, the hazel makes a very good hedge, even entirely unaided by other trees: its shoots grow tall, quick and straight, and it is an extremely easy tree to lay into a hedge. Hazel stems are long and the tree naturally grows in coppiced form, with many stems growing from the base. This provides long and abundant timber for the hedge when it is laid again. As well as a hedgerow tree, it was, and still is, coppiced by man. Hazel coppices existed on most pastoral farms, mostly for making hurdles as a form of stock control (see Chapter 23 on pp. 284–5).

In West Dorset, I have noticed that a single tree will fill a twenty-foot gap, if the stems from a single coppice stool are laid in opposite directions. However, hazel is by no means as stock-proof as a thorn hedge and can only be reliably so when situated on a bank above a ditch, as William Ellis describes:

> In 1742 I had a hedge made and a ditch three feet wide, in all, from live stake, scowered so deeply up, as to raise the earth on the other side eighteen inches higher than the common surface of the ground; and though this was almost a hazel hedge, yet, by the help of such a deep scowered ditch, and laying down the plaishes thicker than ordinary, the hunters, shooters, and poachers, have not since been able to press it so much as to give any cattle of my own, or neighbours, room to go out, or into it, by any gap.[4]

Steeplechases are now confined to the relatively tame setting of a racecourse. Not so in the past, when you raced your horse across country from one church steeple to another. The *Leicester Journal* of 1838 reports breathlessly on a steeplechase over open farmland in which, 'The last fence was a good sized ditch, with a hazel hedge on the farther side, and a bad take off.' This same colourful narrative employs a name for a type of hedge that seems to have gone out of fashion, though it may still be used in hunting circles: 'Then came a tremendous bullfinch, with a ditch beyond it.' A bullfinch, in this context, is a thorn hedge complete with ditch, which has not been laid for fifty years or so, that is so high and impenetrable that no one can take a horse over it – or, to put it more accurately, be taken over it by a horse. The OED suggests it is a corruption of bull fence. It has spawned the verb to bullfinch, meaning to take a horse through such a hedge regardless.

If there is a disadvantage to hazel beyond its conspicuous lack of spines, it is the fact that the stems (though not the entire shrub) die easily and rot quickly. Unlike blackthorn and hawthorn, hazel was not cultivated in vast numbers in nurseries as it was seldom planted during the enclosure period. Nevertheless, French and Cummins (see p. 148) found 13 per cent of the hedges in their survey to be 'mixed hazel', so it is clearly a very common hedgerow tree, whether planted intentionally or not. Though not a tree of choice in the Midlands, hazel is known to have been planted during the establishment of enclosures in Essex. In West Dorset hedges in which hazel is

A recently laid hazel hedge.

dominant are very common, demonstrating its association with the woodland areas of agricultural history. It may be that its easy growth from cuttings or seeds made spending money on nursery-grown plants unnecessary

As a wildlife habitat it is excellent, in particular for its associated fungi. One of the most fundamental symbiotic relationships on the planet is the so-called mycorrhizal relationship between fungi and plants; indeed without it most life on earth would quickly grind to a halt. The fungi we see in woods and fields are merely the reproductive organs of a much larger organism which lives in the soil (or other substratum such as fallen wood). This main part of the fungus is a mass of fine fibres (hyphae) which together form a 'mycelium'. It is this mycelium which feeds and, when conditions are right, produces the familiar mushrooms and other 'fruiting' bodies. Many of these mycelia feed on dead organic matter, but many obtain their sustenance from a living plant. The mycelium produces specialised structures which either penetrate the cells of the root-hairs (arbuscular mycorrhiza) or penetrate *between* the cells of the root-hairs of the plant (ectomycorrhizal – literally, 'outside the roots'). The fine hyphae of the mycelium present an enormous surface area to the soil and so are able to readily absorb water and minerals (notably phosphates), some of which they supply to the plant via these specialist structures. In return, the plant supplies the fungus with sugars. Ectomycorrhizal fungi are the ones that will concern us here as it is they that produce the large fruiting bodies (mushrooms) we might encounter in a hedgerow. Some are symbiotic with only a single host. Hazel is one of the most productive in this regard, with several host-specific fungi to its name. Fungi sometimes find the dense, dark environment of a hedge a difficult place in which to grow their reproductive organs (mushrooms) but a walk along a hedge in autumn will nearly always find half a dozen or so, some of which will be associated with, and growing under, hazel. Foremost among these is *Lactarius pyrogalus*, also known as the fiery milkcap, a large, grey mushroom which produces copious quantities of a milky substance if fractured in any way. *Pyrogalus* means 'fire-milk' and should you taste the 'milk', you will find out just how appropriate this is.

Of greater use is one of the best of all edible fungi, the summer truffle, *Tuber aestivum*. Though it grows with other trees, such as beech and oak, it has a strong association with hazel. It is a fairly common fungus, at least it is as far as anyone knows because it grows, of course, underground. Without a dog to sniff it out it is like looking for a black thing in a dark room that probably isn't there. The only times I have found summer truffles were after gently scratching away part of the soil around a tree, or by finding a partially nibbled one that had been unearthed and discarded by a squirrel who could detect its distinct smell.

Many more mycorrhizal fungi exist under hazel, but let us content ourselves with one more – the hazel bolete, *Leccinum pseudoscabrum*. Despite its common name, it actually grows most frequently with hornbeam. It looks rather like a penny bun mushroom, *Boletus edulis*, also called a cep, but has a long, slightly scaly stem and does not taste so good.

It is worth mentioning here that many fungi, particularly the *Boletus* species, are, as anyone who has picked wild mushrooms will know, frequently host to the larvae of various invertebrates. Chief

The summer truffle under hazel.

among these are the fungal gnats of the order Diptera. These despised creatures are instrumental in breaking down organic matter and are a foodstuff for birds. I have known fifteen different species to occur in a single collection of oyster mushrooms (*Pleurotus ostreatus*), but there are several hundred of them. Having almost any large fungus in a hedgerow will increase the species count by a dozen or so.

The glue crust fungus, *Hymenochaete corrugata*, is a very common bracket-like fungus. Its odd name derives from its odd habit of growing where two hazel branches cross and effectively gluing them together with its fruiting structure.

One of the most common fungi of hazel is *Phellinus ferreus*, which appears on the underside of its branches that grow at an angle. It is quite large, forming brown velvet 'cushions' several inches long and wide, sometimes breaking into tiers. More common still is *Hypoxylon fuscum*, a small, hemispherical, black fungus (commonly called hazel woodwart), which coats the branches of hazel in dense clusters.

One fungus I am always absurdly pleased to see, as it is one of the first I learned about, is *Hymenoscyphus fructigenus*. This grows on aged, empty hazelnuts that have been languishing below the tree for a year or so. It is a pretty little thing, covering a shell with scores of pale

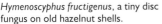

Hymenoscyphus fructigenus, a tiny disc fungus on old hazelnut shells.

Sarcoscypha austriaca, the scarlet elf cup.

orange discs, each of which is perched on the end of a short stem. The spores are created in the top surface of the disc and are ejected at high speed in their thousands.

Even prettier, and with a similar spore production method, is the scarlet elf cup, *Sarcoscypha austriaca*, a species found in the leaf litter below hazel (though it is not too fussy where it grows). The fungus forms deep, blood red cups, 1–2 inches in diameter, and appears with great reliability in January and February when it provides a startling sight at that drab time of year. It sometimes appears at the same time as snowdrops, and a friend – who has lived in my village for the best part of a century – told me that as children he and his friends used to make posies of flower and fungus for their mothers. The pretty gift came with a certain amount of religious symbolism – the snowdrops representing the purity of Christ with the elf cups as Christ's blood.

A fungal disease of the hazel leaf, rather than the wood, is another species of *Taphrina*, *T. coryli*. It is not as attractive or so obviously a gall as *T. pruni*, as it merely discolours and blisters the leaves. Also less clearly a gall is *Phytoptus avellanae*, the big bud mite. It does what its common name suggests, enlarging the buds of leaf and female flowers to make a destructive home for hundreds of the parasite. Nor do the male flowers of the hazel (the catkins) get away lightly, as they can be infected by the gall midge *Contarinia coryli*, whose jumping white larvae make a home between the scales of the young catkins, swelling them into disfigured lumps.

Insects abound on hazel, some welcome, some not. For anyone

Colocasia coryli, nut-tree tussock.

wishing to pick hazelnuts, the nut weevil, *Curculio nucum*, is firmly in the not category. The larvae feed on the nut before boring a small hole through the shell and falling to the ground to pupate. The adult is a particularly hideous monster, which looks more than usually as if it came from another planet. Not dissimilar, though slightly less frightening, is the hazel leaf-roller weevil, *Apoderus coryli*. The eggs or larvae do not form a gall, instead the adult female rolls up the edge of a leaf and lays her eggs inside. These hatch and feed on the rolled-up leaf which is where they pupate.

As with hawthorn and blackthorn, hazel is the food plant for many moths, some sixty or more of which are found in Britain. Three bear a version of the generic name of their host as a specific epithet – the nut-tree tussock, *Colocasia coryli*; the nut leaf blister moth, *Phyllonorycter coryli* (a leaf miner which forms large grey patches on the leaves); and the chequered fruit-tree tortrix, *Pandemis corylana*. The very common scalloped hazel, *Odontopera bidentata*, which sometimes feeds on hazel, probably derives its common name from its colour. These four moths are from four separate families of moth. With so many moths dependent on hazel it is surprising that there are no butterflies for which it is the primary host.

Toothwort nestling under hazel with lesser celandine.

It may seem odd to write about an herbaceous plant at this point, but it is so dependent on hazel that this is the only place to include it. Toothwort, *Lathraea squamaria*, is a member of the broomrape family (Orobanchaceae) and is completely parasitic (holoparasitic). Many members of this family have taken to parasitism as a way of life, giving up chlorophyll and leaves as wasted effort – though some others do make a small attempt at fending for themselves (hemiparasitic). Toothwort's main host is hazel, but it can also be found on elm (if you can find an elm first). It grows at the base of hazel trees parasitising its roots. Only the flowers appear – it needs no other organ to rise above ground level – and these are a dirty, pale pink all over, curling gently like a shrimp.

Ash (*Fraxinus excelsior*)

Like the other giant trees of the hedgerow – the oak and elm – ash was seldom, if ever, planted as a hedge tree, but as a standard. Ash springs up in a hedge very readily through self-seeding and is quickly incorporated into the hedge during laying, if it has not grown too thick. It can still be seen laid in many hedges today, and it lays easily without breaking. There is one ash at Kingcombe, which was laid many years ago, with a single horizontal 'plash' (a small stem, partially cut through and laid to form part of a hedge) nearly twenty inches in diameter and over twenty feet long. Ash was, and is, a very useful tree for its timber, but feelings are mixed over the advisability of planting them in hedgerows. In 1718 the garden designer and horticulturalist Stephen Switzer warned against it:

> Ash is what most People chuse to plant in Hedges; but this I cann't but mightily condemn, for 'tis a very inhospitable Plant, and whenever the Hedge comes to be a little old and thin (which Ash, being set therein, forwards very much) there is nothing but Gaps, and 'tis a hard matter ever to recover it; so pernicious is the Ash.[5]

In an 1804 edition of The Gentleman's Magazine, a correspondent (signing himself 'A Practical Farmer') writes in response to Mr L, who has sung the praises of the ash tree: 'It is a well-known fact, that all sorts of timber are injurious to crops, and especially to crops of corn; but none is so pernicious as that sort which Mr. L. most recommends: viz. Ash.'[6] He continues berating ash and ash advocate alike, before providing a little interesting historical insight into both tree and rural life:

> The tenants in this well-cultivated county formerly were encouraged to plant ash in the hedge-rows, at the request of their landlords, and also with a view to their own advantage, as they supposed; because they were then frequently allowed ash, gratis, for what they termed plough-boot, and cart-boot, i.e. to make their ploughs, waggons, and carts of, if it grew upon the farm.

The problem appears to stem from the large root structure of the ash, which absorbs both nutrients and moisture from much of the surrounding area, greatly reducing the growth of crops. Its large crown is also criticised for dripping on and shading over the crops, though many or most trees would have been pollarded, a method of pruning in which the upper branches are removed. This would

Ash keys.

reduce the problem of shade but also provide timber for carpentry and firewood.

As the idea became more widespread that ash was unsuitable as a hedgerow tree, it gradually became less frequently planted. The wood, however, was too useful to dispense with and ash was planted and coppiced instead of pollarded. Cut on a six or seven-year cycle, the poles were used for everything from walking sticks and hoops, to hurdles and wattle fences. A fourteen-year cycle produced poles with a more noble purpose – to support hops.

Although ash does not support ectomycorrhizal fungi (those with large fruiting bodies), it sports a large number of saprotrophic species, which live off dead organic matter such as leaf litter or fallen timber, digesting it from within. The most spectacular is the dryad's saddle, *Polyporus squamosus*. This splendid bracket fungus is frequently visible in hedgerow ash trees, distinctive for its foxy, speckled top combined with cream-coloured pores. Fungi too rot down, and sometimes the underside of this species becomes infected by bright orange spheres of *Nectria peziza*, a close relative of the much-hated coral spot fungus – the nemesis of many a garden tree. Another great beauty is the large bracket fungus, *Inonotus hispidus*, which has a furry,

Polyporus squamosus, the dryad's saddle. An early fruiting fungus.

reddish-brown top and beige tubes below that produce droplets of water.

The first fungus I ever identified was *Daldinia concentrica*, otherwise known as cramp balls or King Alfred's cakes (not, as has been suggested, King Alfred's balls). It is very common on ash and almost, but not quite, exclusively so. The large, round, black fruiting bodies are brittle and look completely dead, but if you take one home and are lucky enough for it to shoot its spores, it will leave a large corona of black on your table.

Thoroughly rotten, hollowed out ash trunks are a haven for certain species of the mushroom genus *Pluteus*, the most notable of which is *P. leoninus*. It is one of the most beautiful of all British fungi and quite rare, only appearing when the wood of the tree turns to near-compost; a reminder that rotten trees are fascinating habitats and should not be removed unless there is a pressing need.

Hymenoscyphus fraxineus is more beast than beauty, especially when compared to *Hymenoscyphus fructigenus* (see pp. 168–9), which benignly minds its own business living on hazelnut shells. *H. fraxineus* occasionally produces similar, tiny cup-shaped fruiting bodies from which sexual spores are released. Unfortunately, the other stages

The beautiful *Pluteus leoninus* growing inside a hollow ash.

Eupithecia innotata f. fraxinata, ash pug moth.

in its irregular lifestyle are devastating to ash trees, causing what is usually known as ash dieback. This has caused a substantial loss of ash in mainland Europe, but has only been occasionally identified with absolute certainty in Britain. Affected young trees die quickly, whereas old trees hold their own for several years before succumbing. Forecasts about the ultimate effect of ash dieback range from not too bad to the near total loss of the British ash and the fifty or so species that entirely rely on it. The populations of around another thousand species associated with ash are also possibly under threat. Is the ash going the same tragic way as the elm? No one knows, but eighty million trees is a lot to lose.

Of the thirty moths found on ash, eight rely on it exclusively. These include the barred tooth-striped moth, *Trichopteryx polycommata* (a species subject to a Biological Action Plan); lilac beauty, *Apeira syringaria*; ash pug, *Eupithecia innotata f. fraxinata* (the extended Latin name indicating a form of the species associated with ash), and the splendidly named brick and coronet moth, *Agrochola circellaris*.

The ash also has its fair share of galls: *Dasineura acrophila*, a midge gall, turns the leaflets upwards to form a distinct peapod shape, while the grubs of another midge, *D. fraxina*, settle themselves into pouches made along the midribs of the leaflets. The commonest gall on ash is *Psyllopsis fraxini*, a psyllid (jumping plant louse, in the same suborder as aphids) which blackens and turns up leaflet edges, but the most spectacular is the gall mite *Aceria fraxinovora*. This attacks the ash keys, not the leaves, covering them with unattractive brown lumps.

Beech (*Fagus sylvaticus*)

Writing in 1794, Sir George Buchan Hepburn (Scottish judge, landowner and an honorary member of the Board of Agriculture) had much to say in praise of the use of beech in hedges:

> The late Mr Brown of Coalstown, and his son, the present Mr Brown, begun, about 25 years ago, to inclose a part of their property ... These fences were made partly with the thorn and beech mixed, and partly with the beech alone; but of the three the beech is by far the best to fence. These facts seem to recommend the beech to the serious attention of the landed proprietors, who have it in their view to enclose grounds of that kind of soil.[7]

In response, Mr Brown (presumably the younger) wrote to Sir George: 'I would by no means confine the beech hedges to grounds of an inferior quality. I am convinced it is the most beneficial hedge that can be planted in every soil; I find that ... it is the soonest to fence.'[8]

Relatively few farmers have taken to beech with quite the enthusiasm of the Mr Browns, but beech hedges are by no means uncommon and are often seen as a single species hedge (or were originally planted as such). Immature beech trees are not deciduous in the same way as mature specimens; the leaves brown, but do not fall. The beech trees of hedges are kept indefinitely immature by trimming and so do not lose their leaves in winter. If a hedge beech is allowed to develop into a standard tree then the leaves will fall. As with many standard trees developed from a sapling planted and later laid as part of a hedge, the stem can take a few twists and turns

A true beech hedge.

before rising above its diminutive companions. These can be very appealing to look at, though they do nothing for the stock-proofing qualities of a hedge.

Internal beech hedges are rare, but they are frequently seen as roadside hedges and in more formal locations. Where they are planted, the result is a strong, dense hedge, but with a tendency to turn into a linear beech forest if not well tended.

It would be possible to fill the rest of this book with the fungi of beech, as it has one of the largest number of fungal associations (particularly mycorrhizal) of all British trees. Many *Boletus, Lactarius* and *Russula* species (and lots more of other mycorrhizal genera) are found with beech, though they are most likely to be encountered on the verge beneath a standard tree. A few of the fungal species that are not mushrooms, and which are commonly seen without too much searching, are worth mentioning. The most obvious and spectacular of these fungi tend to grow more on well-established standard trees.

The largest fungus of beech, and the largest fungal fruiting body in Britain, is the southern bracket fungus, *Ganoderma australe*

('australe' deriving from the Latin word for south). Mycologists are very uncomfortable with the appellation 'fruiting body', as only plants can fruit; basidiome is the correct term for the part of most of the larger fungi – such as mushrooms and brackets – that produces spores. The brackets of this impressive fungus are often a metre in diameter and frequently in tiers; brown on top and pure white on the fertile layer below. Examining the fertile layer with a lens reveals hundreds of thousands of pores, each the opening of a tube a centimetre or so long. Inside the wall of each tube are embedded the fertile cells which form and eject spores at high velocity into the middle of the tube, where they fall into the open air. This is remarkable enough, but the tubes are a fraction of a millimetre in diameter and the mechanism is precisely tuned to ensure that the spores reach the middle of the tube but do not hit the other side. In the correct light, the spores can be seen streaming from the tubes like a fine smoke. A single bracket can produce several trillion spores in a season. It is a perennial fruiting body creating a new layer of tubes each year.

Also highly productive of spores is the porcelain fungus, *Oudemansiella mucida*. It is a slimy white mushroom up to four centimetres in diameter. Hundreds of them grow high up on the dead branches and the trunks of dead beech. The slime is so prolific that it can drip on your head as you walk beneath.

Less spectacular, but more likely to grow on the dead wood of a beech hedge, is beech woodwart, *Hypoxylon fragiforme*. Having begun life in the pink, then gradually turned a reddish brown, its black colour is only arrived at with maturity. Further, related species are beech barkspot, *Diatrype disciformis*, which grows on fallen beech branches, forming black discs, and beech tarcrust, *Biscogniauxia nummularia*, which also grows on fallen beech and other trees, forming irregular flat, black patches.

Ganoderma australe, the Southern Bracket.

Ubiquitous on dead beech, *Oudemansiella mucida* or porcelain fungus.

Beech woodwart, *Hypoxylon fragiforme*.

The latter was previously known as *Hypoxylon nummularia*, but appears to have suffered a particularly nasty case of taxonomic revisionism.

Beech is host to a handful of galls. *Acalitus plicans* pleats the leaves and covers them, or part of them, with hairs. The culprit inside is a mite that feeds while protected by the folds and overwinters in the scales of the leaf buds. It is the edges of beech leaves that suffer from *A. stenapsis*, curling upwards and around to form a neat hem, with the mite feeding on a mass of hairs within the tunnel thus formed. Quite what these hairs consist of, I do not know, but it may be an example of fungal farming where the mite encourages a fungus to grow by creating the right conditions and then proceeds to consume it. The midge *Hartigiola annulipes* is slightly more interesting, forming a tiny, cylindrical gall with a rounded or pointed termination, each containing a single midge larva. The gall is yellow, darkening to a reddish brown with age.

About two dozen moths are found with beech, two of which bear the specific epithet of its host. *Cydia fagiglandana* is found on oak as well as beech, which may explain the extension to its specific epithet, as *gland* here means acorn. The specific epithet of *Parornix fagivora* means 'beech-eater'.

Beech supports its fair share of beetles. Two clear beech lovers are *Cerylon fagi* and the economically named *Cis fagi*. *Silvanus fagi* has a near-identical Latin name to the beech itself, but in reverse, no doubt because the genus is known for living in woods.

Gorse (*Ulex europaeus*)

We seldom appreciate the beauty of extremely common plants; few love the dandelion for its looks and the spectacular displays of yellow gorse go unadmired. Any spring walk along a hedge or scrub containing gorse in flower will assail the senses of sight and of smell, especially on a warm sunny day. The aroma of coconuts that gorse produces can be overwhelming. It can flower at any time of year, though it is most prolific in late April, and in winter it provides nectar for those bees that are still awake. Gorse is considered to be a seriously invasive plant worldwide and is no doubt delighted to find itself in the top 100 of such species along with the domestic cat and the cane toad. Introduced into New Zealand and Australia, it is now a serious pest there and a search is underway to discover a fungal pathogen or an insect to clear it away completely.

Gorse frequently appears in hedges and was once planted as a hedging shrub. The survey on p. 148 found eight out of 1,200 hedges to be dominated by gorse, and we must assume that these were planted intentionally. In his *Practical Agriculture; or, A Complete System of Modern Husbandry* (1805), R. W. Dickson advises: 'On those dry and sandy banks where there is not sufficient depth of soil for the support of the thorn, furze makes a tolerable fence, provided it be not suffered to grow too high, and be clipped or cut at proper seasons.'[9]

Although gorse (also called furze and whin) would seem in many ways an ideal plant for hedging, it is too short-lived at twenty-five years to form a permanent barrier. However, when cut it is a handy shrub for making a rough-and-ready dead hedge, and in the past was sometimes laid on top of newly planted hedges to protect them from being grazed. Nowadays it is sometimes used as a windbreak hedge on poor soils, often on sand near the sea. Gorse is also very good at planting itself as an impromptu hedge by colonising fences (see the photograph on p. 332).

There are two other species worth mentioning: the western gorse, U. *gallii*, which in Britain is just what it says it is, being seen occasionally topping Cornish hedges. There is also dwarf gorse, U. *minor*, which strongly favours the central southern counties of England.

As a wildlife habitat, gorse is quite splendid. Several fungi grow preferentially with gorse and some exclusively. One that is very common is *Tremella mesenterica*, the yellow brain fungus which grows from the branches at almost random times of the year and is quite startling in its appearance – a convoluted yellow jelly glued to a branch. It is normally about 5 cm in diameter, though I have seen one grow three times that size. It does not grow on the gorse itself, but on *Peniophora incarnata*, a fungus that forms smooth, rose-pink patches on the bark of the gorse.

Gorse is well known for its habit of burning to the ground, leaving nothing but a charred skeleton. It seems that this is more of a lifestyle choice than perpetual bad luck, as the seeds germinate more readily after a light toasting. Gorse's tendency to periodically burst into flames is another excellent reason for not using it as a hedge. The fungus *Daldinia fissa* is sometimes seen to grow on the burnt wood, but I have only ever seen it once, on a burnt gorse hedge in Northumberland. It is a close relative of the larger and very common fungus, D. *concentrica*, which grows on dead ash. Both are black or dark grey spheres which shoot their spores from tiny pores on the surface. It does grow on other plants but is most commonly found on gorse. It may be that the fungus bides its time peaceably inside the living gorse, fruiting only when circumstances threaten its survival. It has been suggested that this fungus (and two other European species with a similar habitat requirement) are xerophytic, that is, adapted to very dry conditions – such as burnt wood.

Gorse is an occasional host for the edible velvet shank mushroom, *Flammulina velutipes*. The Latin name means 'little flame with a velvet foot', a reference to its golden cap colour and black, velvet stem. It is surprising to find that so tough and prickly a plant allows a gall, but it does. *Asphondylia ulicis* is a midge which changes the growth habit of gorse buds, both flower and leaf. Affected buds are larger and hairier than normal and contain a single yellow-orange larva.

Daldinia fissa. An occasional inhabitant of gorse.

The grey gorse piercer, *Cydia ulicetana*, is a fairly common moth with strongholds in Wales and East Anglia, whose larvae feed on the seeds inside the pods. The gorse tip moth, *Agonopterix nervosa*, feeds on gorse, but also broom and other pea family shrubs. Like most moths, its colouring is of drab greys and browns, and one would

Exapion ulicis, the gorse weevil.

Piezodorus lituratus, the gorse shield bug.

need to love moths a great deal to find it either attractive or particularly interesting. Much more exciting is the common and rather dapper gorse weevil, *Exapion ulicis*. This is one of several species which have been tried as a biological control of gorse. The larvae feed on the young seeds and the adults bore holes into the stems with their typical long snout. Finally, there is the handsome gorse shield bug, *Piezodorus lituratus*.

Sea Buckthorn (*Hippophae rhamnoides*)

Sea buckthorn is unlikely to be found in an agricultural hedge, but it has become much more common over the last few years as a roadside tree planted by highway authorities. It grows vigorously, but never very high, and needs little attention beyond cutting back occasionally. There are one or two proper sea buckthorn hedges in existence and perhaps there were more in the past. Thomas Hale in his *A Compleat Body of Husbandry* (1758) thought it was suitable for certain conditions:

> The late lord Petre, of Thorndon in Essex, gave slips of a particular shrub, called the sallow thorn, or sea buckthorn, to an owner of some marsh land, whereupon no other hedge would grow, and it succeeds to this day very well. This is not a shrub one would chuse preferable to others for a hedge; but where the rest will not thrive, 'tis valuable.[10]

Sea buckthorn is native to Essex, as it is a plant of the eastern coast of Britain, so it is unsurprising that Lord Petre's plants did well. It is a great pity that it was not used more as a hedging plant in place of hawthorn, as its fruit is vastly more tasty and nutritious than the bland and mean haw. The highly acidic berries of sea buckthorn can be made into a juice, jelly or accompaniment to fish in place of lemon, and are considered a 'superfood' because they are packed with all the buzzword chemicals that are reputed to help you celebrate your 110th birthday. A friend once suggested to me that the planting of hawthorn during the enclosure period was a plot to further keep the peasantry off the land. Had sea buckthorn been

Sea buckthorn berries. Now seen in many roadside hedges in August and throughout the autumn.

used, every autumn field would have swarmed with local people, intent on collecting their annual crop. No doubt sea buckthorn, despite being wondrously supplied with thorns, is just not suitable as a stock-proof hedge.

Hornbeam (*Carpinus betulus*)

According to Thomas Mawe and John Abercrombie's *The Universal Gardener and Botanist* of 1778, 'The hornbeam forms one of the most beautiful summer Hedges of the deciduous tribe, it being a moderate, but very close shooter, well furnished with leaves; and may be trained up from about six or eight, to twelve or fifteen feet high."' This is from a discussion about domestic hedges, but hornbeam has been and still is planted as an agricultural hedge, occasionally finding its way into one without a formal invitation.

Hornbeam deserves its name, for its timber is considerably harder than oak, and almost impossible to work (though I once turned some heavy duty mallets out of some). Combine this with its ability to grow into a very tall hedge, which keeps its leaves all the way up, and you have an impenetrable protection from troublesome neighbours. Hornbeam's bark resembles that of beech, being smooth and grey, and its leaves are similar in shape but with a finely saw-toothed edge which makes identification easy. In fact, hornbeam is more closely related to hazel and birch.

It is an ectomycorrhizal tree (symbiotic with mushroom species), but not quite so enthusiastic in this respect as beech, oak or birch. It has one species of fungus which I find quite regularly, though so far not in a hedge, and that is the hornbeam milkcap, *Lactarius circellatus*. Being host specific it is a great gift to the naturalist struggling with difficult genera like *Lactarius*. If you see something that looks a bit like *Lactarius circellatus* under a hornbeam, then that is what it is. Since hornbeam − despite its virtues − is an also ran in the hedge stakes, there is little point in further describing its associated organisms. Instead, I will move on to a tree that is often present, though rarely welcome, in a hedge, and one that has several interesting pests and diseases.

Elder (*Sambucus nigra*)

The elder is my 'desert island' tree. It is not particularly grand, or even tidy, but it has a cheerful aspect and grows two of my favourite wild foods, elderflowers and elderberries, and one of my lesser favourites – the jelly ear fungus. As a hedge shrub, its reputation is poor. An old saying, quoted in Mrs Grieve's *A Modern Herbal* (1931), claims that, 'An Eldern stake and a blackthorn 'ether will make a hedge to last forever.' (The ether being the pliable material used to bind the top of the hedge.) This is sometimes taken to mean that the elder makes a good hedge tree, but it is clearly a reference to the construction of a Midland style hedge (see p. 306), where the elder is used dead, as stakes. Elder is known for its disinclination to rot and an elder stake, it has been suggested, will persist longer than an iron fence-post.

Some writers suggest making a fence entirely out of elder, but few, if any, of these have come down to us today. *The Universal Gardener and Botanist* described it as cheap and efficient: '… the Common Elder, being a very fast grower, is often employed in forming the outward hedge along ditch-sides, or the sides or tops of banks, where it is necessary to form a hedge-fence as cheap and expeditiously as possible'.[12] The entry continues by describing how the trees thus grown were often left to reach their full size to provide berries for sale or personal use.

These days the elder is usually cut out completely as it is not welcome in a hedge since it snaps if an attempt is made to lay it and it has a bad habit of growing densely clustered stems which proceed to die, rot and leave a gap. Elder is also notorious for killing other trees around it. A well-tended hedge will be kept clear of elder, though it is often tolerated in gateways. Poor it may be for practical purposes, but the elder makes up for it by being an excellent habitat for wildlife.

The most conspicuous infestation is by the elder aphid, *Aphis sambuci*. Ranging in colour from dark green to dark grey to black, the aphids form dense colonies on the stems (usually the stem of the flower head) where they spend their time sucking sap. They don't actually need to suck, as once they have punctured the phloem vessel which carries the sap, it is forced into them – it's more like tapping

The ever-present elder in full and glorious flower.

than sucking. Most of the aphids seen on elder are clones, the mothers being alates (winged). They have a second host in various hedge plants such as docks and campions where they live on the roots. Like many other aphids, elder aphids are 'ant attended', which means that ants farm them for the honey dew which they excrete after extracting the more useful amino-acids. Ants can always be seen running up and down the branches of any elder which has aphids, defending them from predators.

The best known predators of aphids are ladybirds, though it is the ladybird larvae that feed on them. Aphids are notorious for infesting garden plants (broad beans being particularly vulnerable) and gardeners are often advised to encourage ladybirds into their garden as a protection, a piece of advice that makes little sense, as surely the best way to encourage ladybirds is to have aphids in the first place.

Few plants escape a gall or two and elder is no exception. The gall mite, *Epitrimerus trilobus* causes the leaves to roll upwards at the edge, and the gall midge, *Placochela nigripes*, takes over the flower buds to form green or red caps, each of which houses a single orange larva. A good dozen moths feed on elder, and for at least two – the

The aphid *Aphis sambuci* on an elder stem.

Phlyctaenia coronata, the elder pearl.

swallow-tailed moth, *Ourapteryx sambucaria* and the elder pearl moth *Phlyctaenia coronata* – it is their sole food plant.

I have already mentioned the jelly ear fungus, *Auricularia auricula-judaea*. This rubbery, brown and distinctively ear-shaped fungus is found on dead elder branches everywhere and at any and all times of the year. In dry weather the ears shrivel up, but reconstitute themselves completely with a little rain. Just as common, but easily overlooked, even though its presence is obvious, is elder whitewash, *Hyphodontia sambuci*. True to its name, this looks as though someone has inexpertly coated the elder branches with whitewash. There are a couple of dozen *Hyphodontia* species in Britain, some of which are host specific, which makes identification easy. Another that can be found in a hedge is *Hyphodontia pruni*.

The elder is much loved by those who find joy in the lichens and bryophytes, for its corky bark is alkaline and favoured by many of these understated organisms.

Worth a mention, as it belongs to the same family and has similar flowers to the elder, is the wayfaring tree, *Viburnum lantana*. Its sprays of white flowers are a familiar sight in hedgerows a month before elder comes into bloom in late May or early June.

Viburnum lantana, the wayfaring tree.

Domestic Apple (*Malus domestica*) and Crab Apple (*M. sylvestris*)

Drive or walk along any roadside hedge in autumn and you will seldom fail to find an apple tree. Almost invariably these will not have been planted deliberately but are the offspring of discarded apple cores. The domestic apple (easily identifiable if all else fails by its slightly hairy leaves) does not breed true, so the apples thus produced are of random genetic make-up and random value as food. The food value, and certainly the flavour, of the true crab apple is questionable, though there are some excellent recipes for it. However, it was the crab apple that was planted as a hedging tree during the enclosure period; appearing in advertised sales lists alongside hawthorn and blackthorn. Thomas Hale again:

> I have, in some few places, seen entire hedges of crab; and they are very beautiful for the regularity of their growth. They give the inclosure the look of a garden, when they are in blossom; and they have a pretty effect when in fruit. Neither are they without their farther value: for the wood is hard and serviceable; and from the fruit is made verjuice.[13]

Verjuice is the rather noxious juice of crab apples which was, and

A standard crab apple on a pastoral farm.

sometimes still is, used as a culinary replacement for vinegar, lemon or wine. Having said the above, Hale continues: 'With all its advantages we do not advise the making of entire hedges of it, for they are neither so good for shelter or fence as others.'[4]

Crab apples seem to be quite rare in roadside hedges, though they are frequently found in internal hedges, usually in the form of a standard tree. Otherwise it is found on woodland edges and occasionally – as in the New Forest in Hampshire – as a stand-alone tree.

The parlous state of most apple tree leaves by the time the fruit is ripe, suggests that there has been a free-for-all among the insects and fungi that dine on them. Several aphid species take a toll of the much put-upon crab apple. Among the most common are the apple aphid, *Aphis pomi*, a common aphid which infects many other tree species; the apple-grass aphid, *Rhopalosiphum insertum*, whose secondary hosts are grasses and members of the rose family; and the rosy apple aphid, *Dysaphis plantaginea*, effectively a gall aphid which distorts the leaves for its own purposes and whose secondary host is plantain. These aphids will be farmed by ants and have legions of predators.

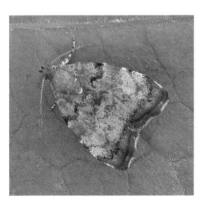

Choreutis pariana, the apple leaf skeletoniser.

Moths also do their worst. The monstrous sounding apple leaf skeletoniser, *Choreutis pariana*, is a neat looking chestnut brown moth which does what it promises to the leaves; the fruitlet mining tortrix, *Pammene rhediella*, is almost exclusively found in hedgerows as its other larval food plants are hawthorn and rowan; *Phyllonorycter blancardella* has attractive, piebald markings, reminiscent of a guinea-pig, and is found on several species of apple as well as the related quince. It would be possible to go on, but from these alone it is easy to see that the crab apple is an essential resource for many species of moth and other arthropods.

Apple species in general suffer more than their fair share of fungal infections – I counted about seventy on one published list, so it is amazing they ever make it through the day. Few are macrofungi, but the coral spot fungi, *Nectria cinnibarina*, and *N. galligena*, both infect crab apple and produce orange and red-brown fruiting bodies respectively. The latter species is particularly notorious for causing apple canker. Honey fungus too will attack crab apple, though usually only when it is already weakened. On a more cheerful note, apple trees sometimes host truffles.

Willow (*Salix* spp.)

Willows are a challenge to the naturalist as there are so many of them. The botanist Clive Stace lists twenty-seven species, but these are just that – species. In addition there are many sub-species and an eye-wateringly long list of hybrids. I gave up attempting to identify willows years ago and most of my naturalist friends have done the same, content to settle for 'under *Salix* spp.' in any record of a fungus or plant. They are sometimes known as sallow or osier, usually when describing broad-leaved willows and narrow-leaved willows respectively. Osier, however, is now generally confined to one species, *Salix viminalis*.

Thomas Hale mentions the use of willow in hedging: 'The willow is of great use also in hedges in proper soils. The stakes being made of this wood, will all grow, and at once continue firm, and thicken the hedge.'[15] J. C. Loudon, in *An Encyclopaedia of Agriculture* (1825), recommends it for wet conditions: 'The birch, poplar, alder and Huntingdon willow, are peculiarly calculated for the coldest, wettest, and most marshy parts.'[16]

Few willow-dominated hedges exist; the survey mentioned on p. 147 found only 6 out of the 1,200 hedges studied. But any hedge that can survive in wet soils is likely to support the odd willow or two, and any willow stake that is not thoroughly dead which is used in the laying of a hedge is likely to grow into a tree – wanted or not – if the soil conditions are right. It can also form an 'automatic' hedge of sorts, where it borders streams running through agricultural land, and is very common in the Fens and the Somerset Levels, usually bordering the drainage ditches.

Willows enjoy the company of several galls, one with a name to be reckoned with – *Rabdophaga marginemtorquens*. This appalling mouthful translates nicely into a description of the gall midge's mode of life: 'stick-eating edge-twister'. It forms on the edges of the narrow, stick-like leaves of osiers, rolling and twisting them inwards. Two sawflies, *Pontania proxima* and *P. bridgmanii*, produce red 'bean galls' on the undersides of narrow-leaved willows and, more striking

The sawfly gall, *Eupontania pedunculi* on grey willow, accompanied by a rust fungus.

still, are those of another pair of sawflies, *Eupontania viminalis* and *E. pedunculi*, which produce large round galls. The oddest willow gall is another *Rabdophaga* species, *R. rosaria*. This species instructs the white willow, *Salix alba*, to make a rosette of leaves in which a mass of gall midges feed. The rosettes are reminiscent of young watermint leaves, though they are usually known as artichoke galls.

Many species of macrofungi grow on willows. One of the largest is the willow bracket, *Phellinus igniarius*. This is hoof-shaped, grey on top and with light brown pores underneath. A smaller bracket fungus, the blushing bracket, *Daedaleopsis confragosa*, is ubiquitous on willow. The blushing part of its common name is a reference to the pink colour quickly attained by bruising the white pores on the underside.

Field Maple (*Acer campestre*)

Field maple has long been used in hedges and is still planted today. It lays well, despite being a little springy, and grows vigorously and contentedly in it native land. Most remain as hedges, with a few getting away as standards. It is pretty in a hedge and a delicate beauty when allowed its full expression, although William Cobbett, writing in 1825, had barely a good word to say about it:

> We have a Maple in our woods; it is a very tenacious inhabitant of coppices, hedge-rows and hedges; a very hardy thing, makes very good fuel, in fagots; but it makes no poles, no hoops, no rods, no hurdles; and it scarcely ever becomes a tree as big as one's thigh. It is mere brushwood; and of no more use as a tree, than the poppies, or wild parsnip, or wild carrot, are as cattle-food. Our Maple is a weed of the woods, and we burn it, because we know not what else to do with it.[17]

The oddly named Batty Langley (Langley was his true surname, Batty a surname adopted from a patron of his father) was a somewhat eccentric eighteenth-century garden designer. In his *A Sure and Easy Method of Improving Estates* of 1740, he is much kinder to the maple (though it is not clear precisely which maple or maples he had in mind): 'These sorts of Maple make good Hedges in a Garden, Wilderness, &c. where nothing else will live. They also thrive exceedingly under the Drip of any Sort of Tree whatever; and therefore are a very good Furniture for the Quarters and Hedges of a Wilderness.'[18]

Generally speaking, field maple tends to get through the summer without looking as though every last flying or fungal thing has tried to eat it, but a few organisms do make it their home. It has several galls, the most visible of which is the gall mite *Aceria*

The gall of the mite, *Aceria macrochela*.

myriadeum which covers the leaves with brilliant red hemispherical warts, while *Aceria macrochela* forms bright red strawberry-like galls along the veins.

The bark of the field maple is alkaline and thus a favoured substratum for many lichens and bryophytes, the older, large boles of veteran trees being particularly rich in these organisms. Two moths are particularly attracted to maple – the maple pug, *Eupithecia inturbata* and the maple prominent, *Ptilodon cucullina*. The latter looks like a woodchip and feeds on field maple and the related sycamore.

Holly (*Ilex aquifolium*)

Apart from ivy, holly is the only common hedge plant which retains its lively green during the winter. Entire hedges of holly are rare outside of the suburbs, but it is still frequently found from self-sets and original planting in many places. Thomas Hale was particularly enthusiastic about holly hedges: 'No hedge is so beautiful; none so strong. When well grown, it appears as a wall rather than a hedge, and is altogether impenetrable by cattle.'[9]

Hedgerow holly in January.

Tar spot, *Phytophthora ilicis*, on old holly leaf.

Marasmius hudsonii, the holly parachute.

Holly is a useful hedgerow tree for shady areas such as under a large, spreading standard oak. What is difficult to understand, is how you were meant to lay a holly hedge without the services of the Red Cross to hand. Perhaps the hedger's traditional sealskin glove came in handy here.

Despite sometimes being gathered as an unlikely forage plant for sheep (only the lower leaves are spikey and, no doubt, it was the upper leaves that were consumed), holly is not the most edible of trees. This is reflected in it having slightly fewer parasites than most. There is the holly leaf miner, *Phytomyza ilicis*, a fly whose larvae grow from eggs injected into the surface of the leaf; the lovely holly blue butterfly, *Celastrina argiolus* and the holly tortrix moth, *Rhopobota naevana*. As far as I know, it does not support any galls and most of its diseases come from mineral deficiencies and self-inflicted wounds. One exception is holly tar spot, a disfiguring disease caused by the fungus that bears its host's name, *Phytophthora ilicis*.

Much more attractive is the holly parachute, *Marasmius hudsonii*, a tiny mushroom that can sometimes be found at the bottom of a holly hedge on the dead leaves. A mere three or four millimetres in diameter, it is still a mushroom with cap, stem and gills (if only four or five). It looks just wonderful under a lens as it is covered in relatively long, spikey hairs.

Dogwood (*Cornus sanguinea*)

The prefix dog invariably indicates that a plant is inferior in some way. Dogwood, as a hedge tree, is certainly that. Charles Alexander Johns, in his *The Forest Trees of Britain* (1849), suggests, 'It is called Dogwood because "The fruit is not fit even for a dog;" on which account, also, it was formerly named Dogberry and Hound's Tree. It is also called Prickwood, from its wood being frequently made into toothpicks and skewers.' He also mentions what might be called the 'dogwood trick' (something I demonstrate to people during my peripatetic lectures):

The leaves and young shoots are remarkable for the number and strength

of their spiral vessels. So tenacious are these, that if a tender twig or leaf
be snapped asunder in several places, the spiral vessels may be discovered by
the naked eye, holding the pieces so firmly together that if one fragment be
lifted up, all the others will be suspended.[20]

Or to put it another way, if you very gently pull a leaf in two across
its width, one half may be suspended below the other. The 'spiral
vessels' are not easy to see and it looks like magic – hedge magic.

The fruit of dogwood is indeed bitter and thoroughly nasty
– though birds seem to find it appetising. The flowers too are
unpleasant. They form into white sprays, a little like those of elder,
and thus provide another false trail for the botanically challenged
elderflower wine maker. But it is not just the fruit and flowers that
are useless. Although found in hedges all over Britain (apart from
the tip of Cornwall, West Wales, north-west England and most of
Scotland), dogwood was seldom planted in a hedge as it is brittle and
lays very poorly.

Dogwood hosts a number of species including some galls. One of
these, the gall midge *Craneiobia corni* (also known as the rivet gall), is
a striking, bright red shiny hemispherical structure, a few millimetres across, which usually forms in clusters at the base of the leaves.
A common species of aphid specific to dogwood is *Anoecia corni*,
which alternates between dogwood and the roots of grasses, with a
winged form which is considerably better looking than the average
aphid, having a stylish black spot on its otherwise transparent wings.
Several true flies (Diptera) are known from dogwood (or at least
Cornus): *Anarete corni*, *Mydaea corni* and *Musca corni* being three obvious
species. *Antispila metallella*, a moth which depends on dogwood, is
nicely named because its wings are shiny bronze, banded with a
lighter metallic colour.

Spindle (*Euonymus europaea*)

No book on hedges can be complete without mention of the beautiful
spindle tree. It is a small tree, or a large shrub, found commonly in
hedgerows and wood edges on chalky ground south of Yorkshire,

but rare in the rest of the country and in central Wales. The tree itself is unprepossessing, but it produces attractive, pink, lobed capsules which release bright orange berries. *Euonymus* means 'of good name', indicating the high regard in which the plant was held. The strong, hard wood was used to make spindles for spinning yarn and this may be the reason it was thought of so highly – it doesn't refer to the fruit which is seriously poisonous to humans, though not, presumably, to birds. It is not generally planted in hedges, nor is it a tree that was ever sold as a hedging plant, but it finds its way there by the usual means. Spindle does not lay particularly well being hard and rather brittle. It should never be planted or permitted in a hedge near beans or beet as it is another host of the aphid which attacks these crops.

Spindle attracts several insects including the spindle ermine, *Yponomeuta cagnagella*, an attractive moth with sparse black spots on white wings, and it hosts one fairly common gall produced by the gall mite, *Stenacis convolvens*. It is fairly boring as galls go, merely curling over the edges of the leaves to form a home. The leaf miner larvae

The beautiful fruit of the spindle, *Euonymus europaea* in October.

Phylloporia ribis on spindle.

produce a single patch, rather than the usual sub-surface trackways; they also cut through the leaves.

The bracket fungus, *Phylloporia ribis*, is most often found on spindle, despite having a specific epithet indicating a preference for currants. It forms a large, multi-layered, brown bracket.

Guelder Rose (*Viburnum opulus*)

Like the spindle, the guelder rose has always struck me as a rather exotic looking tree, but both plants have been here since at least the Iron Age. The guelder rose also has bright berries, this time red and very shiny, and just about edible. Because plants break very easily when laying in a hedge, it was never planted but simply appears, growing vigorously wherever it sets seed (less commonly in Scotland). It earned the name guelder from a cultivar which came from Gelderland in Holland; it most certainly is not, however, a rose.

Elm (*Ulmus* spp.)

Although there are only a relatively small number of species of elm in Britain, it is all but impossible to determine which is which, even for professional botanists. Not that the latter will fail to give you an answer, it is just that the answer may not be the same as that of another professional botanist. Hybridisation has muddied the waters of elm taxonomy to the point where there is almost no hope. Clive Stace, the recognised authority on British plant taxonomy, is my guide here and he suggests (but no more than that) that there are four distinct native species: *Ulmus glabra*, *U. procera*, *U. minor* and *U. plotii*. *Ulmus procera* is recognised as the English elm, while *U. glabra* is the wych elm.

It seems that argument and dissent in the naming of elms is a venerable institution; Philip Miller, writing in 1735, unhelpfully calls *Ulmus glabra* the witch hazel (a completely unrelated group of plants which aren't hazel either), and goes on to complain that it is, '... by some unskilled Persons called the British Elm'.[21] Thomas Hale, distinguishes witch hazel and wych elm (which is *Ulmus glabra*) as two species of elm. There is, indeed, no hope.

Viburnum opulus, the guelder rose.

Elm existed in early hedges as a legacy tree from assarting and was planted in enclosure hedges. It is a plant that suckers prolifically, a characteristic exploited in the growing of new trees. The suckers were transplanted to an 'ulmidarium' for growing on, or straight into hedges. Herein lies the origins of elm's ultimate catastrophe – Dutch elm disease. As clonal lineages began to dominate, the plant no longer had the defence of genetic diversity.

In the eighteenth century, William Ellis related a method of planting elms to form a living palisade:

> Elms have been thus planted for supplying of Wall, Paling or common
> Hedges; accordingly this valuable Tree will answer very well, if young
> Elms are transplanted of about eight Feet high, and two inches thick in
> their Bodies, within a foot of each other …. they will, in a few Years, so
> enlarge their Bodies, and grow so near together, that a Weazel may not pass
> between.[22]

Thomas Hale writes of the abundance of elm: 'Next to the oak the elm is the most universal of the English timber trees. It is most common in hedge rows; and is thence the most familiar to the eye of all the kinds.'[23]

Elm thrives (or thrived) better in hedges, where it was often pollarded, than in woodland because it has little or no competition for light and nutrients. We can also infer from Hale that the elm was then, as some of us remember it, a standard tree, not a hedging tree. Having said that, the repeated suckers were certainly laid and incorporated into the hedge.

Hale describes the tree as '… hardy, and full of life'.[24] Not any more. Dutch elm disease – named after the country which did the research on it, not where it came from (which was North America) – has made repeated attacks on our elms, and the occasional incidence of elm decline seen in the palynological (pollen) record is almost certainly a confirmation of this. It has frequently been suggested that elm decline could be explained by the removal of elm branches for fodder, but this is most unlikely.

In the 1970s a new strain (in fact a new species) of the fungus that causes the disease, *Ophiostoma novo-ulmi*, was introduced accidentally on a consignment of timber. Britain's elms were doomed. Those that punctuated our hedgerows with elegance and serenity turned to skeletal frames. Twenty-five million of the thirty million elms in Britain died. As the bark fell away, the agent of the fungus, the elm bark beetle, *Scolytus* spp., would be revealed in the distinctive channels it created. Town and country both suffered and a massive felling operation took place in hedgerows, woodland, park and urban roadside. As a final blow, the sudden bounty of cheap elm, a wood so useful in furniture making and joinery, was all but useless, as the timber was disfigured by black marks. It wasn't even much use for firewood as it burns 'cold'.

Standard elms still exist in much reduced numbers and scattered locations, chiefly in the north, but although the standard trees of the hedgerow have gone, elm itself has not. Elm can be found in hedges all over Britain, but only as small trees or as part of a laid hedge or one that has been flailed (cut to shape and height mechanically). The disease only kills elms that reach a certain height, as the beetles are only attracted to what it considers to be mature trees. If left uncut, sucker after sucker will grow optimistically, only to die when the trunk reaches three or four metres in height. Elms are still with us, but not as we remember them.

In Gloucestershire, I once came across an area where elm-dominant hedges were common. Most were standard size and machine trimmed, but there were also some more substantial hedges, about eight feet high, protecting several large fields. Puzzled by these anomalous hedges, I drove into the farm to investigate and immediately saw why they were so high and so dense. It was a stud farm which housed horses more than capable of jumping over the average hedge. The hedge was clearly looked after and I could see no disease or infestation, in fact it was one of the healthiest hedges I have seen.

One effect of Dutch elm disease was a massive increase in the incidence of fungi that live on dead elm. The downside to this is that most of these species are relatively rare now that they have consumed their host. The prettiest by far is the wrinkled peach mushroom, *Rhodotus palmatus*, which has wrinkled, rubbery, pink-orange fruiting bodies that grow in tufts from dead elm, the caps reaching up to 10 cm in diameter. Fortunately, it will grow on small pieces of dead elm, and I recently saw it do just that, so there is hope for this species. Another species which favours elm, though not confined to it, is one of the oyster mushrooms, *Pleurotus cornucopiae*. This attractive pale cream-coloured mushroom grows in branching tufts and has gills that run from the edge of the cap to the base of the stem. For some reason it smells of coconuts.

Over fifty species of fungi and invertebrates bear the specific epithet *ulmi*, *ulmicola* or *ulmiphagus*, meaning, respectively, elm, coming from elm and elm-eater, and from this alone we can see that the elm supports many species, some of which are elm specific. Of course, a species does not need to be named after its host to be supported by it and there are many more. There is the aphid gall, *Eriosoma ulmi*, which curls up one half of a leaf blade, but also the gall *Eriosoma lanuginosum*, which changes the growth habitat of a leaf, forming, not a leaf, but a pale green 'bladder'. Most common, perhaps, is the gall mite, *Aceria campestricola*, which forms raised warts all over the surface of the leaves.

A tall elm hedge.

Aceria campestricola on elm.

Several moths are specific or semi-specific to elm. The larvae of *Stigmella ulmivora* chew their way through elm (and other leaves) as leaf miners, eventually producing a rather attractive moth with wings that look like feathers. *Carpatolechia fugitivella* and *Epinotia abbreviana* are also specific to elm. The white-letter hairstreak butterfly, *Satyrium w-album* (the 'w' refers to the wing markings), was thought to be threatened by the loss of the elm, on which it entirely depends. However, although not common, it does still survive.

Oak (*Quercus* spp.)

Oaks, especially the English oak, *Quercus robur*, support more species than any other British tree. They are an ecosystem in themselves. Oak can often be found as a hedge plant, where self-set oaks have been laid or flailed, but it is as standard hedgerow tree that it is most familiar.

According to Alexander Hunter, in a footnote to his 1786 edition of John Evelyn's *Sylva, or a Discourse on Forest-Trees*, 'We seldom see a good Oak in a hedgerow; they generally throw out large lateral branches, and form a spreading and beautiful head, but the trunk is for the most part very short.'[25] The standard hedgerow oak is still a romantic ideal in Britain, where the tree is loved for its spreading beauty and complex form, rather than its utility as timber. If you wish to make a table or fit a beam across a church, it is to forest-grown oak that you must look; unlike a hedge oak they compete with one another and reach a great height. Incidentally, my sawyer friend in the next valley told me that he would never plank an oak which grew at a village crossroads as it would invariably 'bugger the blade'. Having likely been used for a century or more as a place to post notices it would be full of nails.

The natural history of the oak deserves a book to itself, and indeed it has one in *The Natural History of the Oak Tree* (1993) by Richard Lewington and David Streeter. The book illustrates some four hundred species which live in, on and around the oak, but there are many more. It is impossible to do the oak justice in these pages, but a few of its common highlights are worth mentioning.

The oak has more galls than any other British tree, earning itself an entire chapter in the standard work on the subject, *British Plant Galls* (2011) by Margaret Redfern and Peter Shirley. They are also the most visible of the galls and come in a great variety of aesthetically pleasing shapes. There are kidney galls, artichoke galls, galls that look like eggs, sea anemones, grapes and even balls of cotton wool. The commonest are probably the oak apples, which are made by a number of wasp species such as *Biorhiza pallida*. Round, smooth and eventually brown, they are usually found with an emergence hole in their surface. Another wasp, *Andricus quercuscalicis*, builds the knopper gall, which takes over and transforms the acorns into a green then red, then brown, bluntly spiny lump, and yet another, the oak hop gall, *A. fecundator*, looks like a hop flower. The spangle gall, also produced by a wasp, *Neuroterus quercusbaccarum*, covers the underside of oak leaves with small purple discs.

Over seventy microfungi are recorded from oaks, but there are also very many larger fungi that grow on or with them. Among the most spectacular are the bracket fungi, such as the maze gill, *Daedalea quercina*, which has the typical hoof shape, but with the gills taking the shape of a complex maze. *Laetiporus sulphureus*, known as chicken of the woods, forms enormous brackets on the trunks of oak trees whose days are numbered. Egg-yolk yellow and definitely edible, they taste like tofu, only with flavour. Also edible (as the name implies) is beefsteak fungus, *Fistulina hepatica*, which commonly forms large, rubbery tongues which drip a bloody latex. Their spores are produced in thousands of independent but closely packed tubes on

Andricus fecundator, the oak hop gall.

Andricus quercuscalicis, the knopper gall.

Biorhiza pallida, the oak apple gall.

Neuroterus quercusbaccarum, the spangle gall.

Laetiporus sulphureus, chicken of the woods.

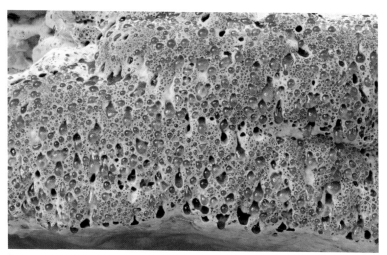

Droplets forming on *Inonotus dryadeus*.

their lower surface. Usually found at the base of oak trees, *Inonotus dryadeus* is another common bracket fungus, but one with a strange tendency to weep.

Oaks are mycorhizzal, with more associations than any other British tree and it is beneath them that most penny buns, *Boletus edulis*, are found, sometimes within hedgerows. Most of the British mycorrhizal genera are represented including *Amanita*, one of which is the death cap, *Amanita phalloides*. On one walk along a hedgerow well stocked with oaks, I found scores of edible chanterelle, *Cantharellus cibarius*, interspersed with dozens of death caps.

Chapter 16

SHRUBS AND CLIMBERS

Quite what constitutes a shrub is more a matter of taste than scientific definition, anything that is woody but not a tree usually qualifies. Multiple stems and short stature are considered to be the essentials of a shrub, but hazel – though not tall – will grow with a single stem if given the chance, so the definition is not that useful. Several of the other trees already mentioned are sometimes classed as shrubs, but I consider them to be trees, and that is that. Many hedgerow shrubs clamber all over their chosen habitat, either making an attractive display (as with honeysuckle) or a mess (like bramble) of the hedge, depending on one's point of view.

Rosa spp.

The most familiar of our wild hedgerow roses is the dog rose, *Rosa canina*; nowadays viewed as a group of species and designated 'agg.' for aggregrate. Almost as common is the field rose, *R. arvensis*, and the two are frequently confused. It is easy enough to tell them apart when flowering, as the latter's flowers are cream rather than the pure white – when not pink – of the former, and the field rose has fused

Rosa canina, the dog rose.

Rosa arvensis, the field rose.

styles in the middle of the flower which project past the stamens that surround them. Even the hips are distinguishable, as the long style structure persists on the field rose. The dog rose flowers in June and July, producing a glorious abundance of white and pink blossoms; the field rose flowers a little later. The hips of both (which are of great use to man, bird and beast) mature by August or September and hang around until November, though they can persist until well into the following year, if conditions are right.

Several other roses make their way into hedges and hedgerows, some of them as invaders. Chief among these is the highly fragrant Japanese rose, *Rosa rugosa*, which is often used for garden hedges. Anything that vigorous and hedgy will inevitably make its way into the hedgerow, usually as just a few plants although it can some-times overwhelm a hedge. It is a favourite of bumble bees, which enter the flower just as it opens into a cup.

Wild roses have a fairly large number of associated galls, including one of the prettiest of them all, the robin's pin-cushion gall, *Diplolepis rosae*. This gall wasp commandeers flower buds, turning them into fuzzy red balls with a woody centre. The related *Diplolepis nervosa* can produce two kinds of small gall – a red one known as the spiked pea or sputnik gall and a round smooth one, referred to as a pea gall.

Grapholita tenebrosana is a typically boring brown moth whose larvae infest rosehips, while the garden rose tortrix, *Acleris variegana*, is slightly more

The gall known as robin's pincushion, on a dog rose.

interesting in appearance. Its larvae begin life nibbling flower buds before turning their attention to the leaves.

As every gardener knows, roses suffer from a variety of fungal infections. One of the most common is the rust fungus, *Phragmidium mucronatum*, which takes the form of bright orange-yellow masses of urediniospores on the undersides of leaves and on stems. Life is a complicated business for rust fungi, as these spores are soon replaced by black teliospores. *P. mucronatum* also produces aeciospores. Rusts choose from a smorgasbord of up to five spore types and are sometimes classified accordingly. Precisely what they do is beyond the scope of this book, but they are all stages in the life cycle of rusts. However many types of spores this particular species produces, they make a mess of rose bushes but are a delight to mycologists.

Honeysuckle (*Lonicera periclymenum*)

Honeysuckle is perhaps the most loved of the hedgerow shrubs because of its cheerful summer beauty, its unmistakeable scent and its attraction for nectar-feeding bees, butterflies and moths. The

Honeysuckle in full flower.

shoots can become extremely dense, forming good nesting sites for birds. The berries are inedible to humans, for whom they are slightly toxic, but birds (such as thrushes, bullfinches and warblers) will eat them.

About a dozen leaf-mining larvae of flies and moths make their home in honeysuckle leaves. One of these is the fly *Chromatomyia aprilina* which forms galleries that radiate out from the mid-rib. The honeysuckle rust fungus, *Puccinia festucae*, forms circular patches on the leaves that are visible on both top and bottom. Those underneath are reminiscent of fried eggs, being orange in the middle and almost white on the edge.

Bindweed spp.

After leaving the right-handed honeysuckle, one can only move on to the left-handed bindweed. There are several British species but the commonest in hedges are the field bindweed, *Convolvulus arvensis*, and the hedge bindweed, *Calystegia sepium*. The different genus names of these two superficially very similar species are due to the extreme pickiness of botanical taxonomists who can never leave anything alone (had they been mushrooms, they would have had the same

Field bindweed nestling on a hedgerow verge.

Hedge bindweed.

generic name). The field bindweed has small pink trumpet-shaped flowers, while those of hedge bindweed are large and pure white. The former plant frequently takes leave of the hedge (and its good sense) to form dense patches in the middle of Dorset country lanes – and very pretty it looks. Both species are more common in the hedges of lowland Britain.

Black Bryony (*Dioscorea communis*)

A truly beautiful plant, its leaves are an almost translucent green, with veins of art nouveau patterning, while its late autumn berries grow like strings of green, orange and red pearls or early Christmas decorations. Unfortunately, every part of the plant is poisonous,

The art nouveau leaves of black bryony.

though not seriously so. Still, it can prove a temptation to children because the berries look so tasty. Black bryony is the only member of the yam family (Dioscoreaceae) to grow in Britain, but it is a southern plant, barely making its way north of Middlesbrough. It appears to be on the increase as a result of hedgerow neglect. Where hedges are not trimmed properly, black bryony can completely overwhelm them.

Another bryony, white bryony, *Bryonia dioica*, is a plant of the south and east of Britain and an occasional inhabitant of hedges. It too is an attractive plant with small white flowers and a fresh green tint to the leaves. It is also poisonous, possibly more seriously so than black bryony. White bryony is the only member of the squash family (Cucurbitaceae) in Britain, and the two bryonies are therefore unrelated.

Ivy (*Hedera helix*)

Few hedgerows in woodland areas escape the attentions of ivy, and it can take over an uncared for hedge. When laying a hedge, all ivy will usually be removed. Ivy will not kill a tree, it just uses it as a frame, and on standard hedgerow trees this provides shelter and nesting sites for birds. It is also harmless to walls, unless you try to remove it, at which point the whole wall risks coming down in the ensuing struggle.

The pale green flowers are late bloomers, appearing from September to December, and provide a dessert course for wasps, moths and sometimes bees. At the end of a particularly mild winter, a beekeeper friend gave me a small jar of ivy honey, explaining that it was both interesting and horrible. He was right – the taste was of sugar syrup laced with disinfectant. There is even an ivy bee, *Colletes hederae*, a European immigrant discovered in Britain as recently as 1993 at Worth Matravers in Dorset.[1] Since then it has been found in several locations in Purbeck, and subsequently in many parts of southern England.

Several moth larvae feed on ivy, though none exclusively. It has but one gall, a midge, *Dasineura kiefferi*, which takes over flower buds, swelling them and keeping them closed. Aphids found on ivy are likely to be *Aphis hederae*. The dead leaves of ivy sometimes play host to a tiny mushroom, *Marasmius epiphylloides*, which is two millimetres in diameter and pure white. Ivy broomrape, *Orobanche hederae*, is a parasitic plant that grows on the roots of ivy and has been recorded in hedges. For reasons unknown, it is frequently found in coastal areas, notably of Wales and south-west England, but also scattered more generally around the southern counties.[2]

If ivy flowers are the dessert, then the berries are the after-dinner mints, for they are the latest of the winter berries. Blackbirds are particularly fond of them and we should be grateful that such a late bounty exists to keep our overwintering birds well fed.

Hop (*Humulus lupulus*)

If proof were ever needed of the existence of God, it is provided by the hop. It is very nearly an obligate hedgerow plant, found in lowlands throughout Britain, though uncommon in Scotland. In some places it is found only occasionally, but where there are hop fields, escapees can dominate for miles around. These will be random varieties, descendants of cultivars, but *Humulus lupulus* nevertheless. The hop can be a very long plant and I have seen them escape a hedge and climb up the steel cables supporting a telegraph

Female hop flowers of an escaped cultivar.

pole. The truly wild varieties produce small flowers (the hops themselves), much smaller than those of the cultivars.

For once, it would be good to hear that a hedgerow plant had no parasites, but it is not so. As well as a rather nasty nematode worm that eats the roots and several microfungi, there is also, inevitably, the hop vine aphid, *Phorodon humuli*. In true hedgerow style, it overwinters on *Prunus* species such as blackthorn and plum then spends its summer feeding on hops and nettles.

Bramble (*Rubus fruticosus agg.*)

Bramble is an apomictic species, which means it is made up of hundreds of clonal microspecies which reproduce vegetatively or

It is difficult to know whether or not this is truly a hedge; in fact, it is a metal fence hopelessly overgrown with brambles.

from clonal seeds. Which particular *Rubus fruticosus* is which can only be determined by a specialist, though there is always the suspicion that if you canvassed ten different specialists you would get ten different answers. The specific epithet has an appropriately fruity ring to it, but is derived from the Latin *frutex* meaning 'bush'.

Bramble can be found in hedges and hedgerows almost everywhere, but like ivy tends to be removed by farmers and hedgers wherever possible because of its boundless vigour. A bramble can grow over and smother any hedge in poor condition, destroying it with its shade. Fortunately, the flail will keep the bramble under some control. It is also a plant that can create 'false hedges' by colonising a wire or timber fence until it looks just like a hedge, even when you are standing next to it. These imposters provide intractable false positives for anyone attempting to survey hedges from aerial photographs.

We have something of a love-hate relationship with the bramble – the berries are by far the most abundant and among the tastiest of all wild fruits, and nearly every child will have happy memories of picking them. On the other hand they are intractable weeds bearing thorns that can rip through clothing and skin. The leaves of bramble

Blackberries in September.

look as though they had intended to fall off during the autumn but had changed their minds and soldiered on until spring. It is certainly an untidy and disreputable looking plant and even in late summer, when the berries are full, it seems to be have been half eaten by pestilential insects. Numerous galls infest the bramble: the midge, *Dasineura plicatrix*, distorts the young leaf buds in spring, while the gall wasp, *Diastrophus rubi*, swells the young, green stems to make a home for its larvae. These swellings are remarkable structures; up to 15 cm long and eventually covered in the escape holes of scores of newly minted wasps, they look like an odd variety of wasp nest. In a way this is what they are, but not one built laboriously by the wasp itself but one made by the bramble to a design supplied by the wasp. As an aside, it is worth noting that gall species are often predated or parasitised. Chalcid wasps will pierce the galls of gall wasps with their ovipositor to lay eggs near or inside the larvae. Gall wasps respond (slowly) by evolving very hard galls, or galls covered with dense hairs, to make oviposition difficult. Other tricks to defeat their parasites are to develop quickly before the parasite can find them, or for the gall to drop to the ground where the gall wasp can develop in peace.

Brambles suffer more than most plants from leaf-mining insect larvae, one of the commonest being *Stigmella aurella*, a small furry

The ubiquitous violet bramble rust, *Phragmidium violaceum*.

Kuehneola uredinis, a very common rust fungus on bramble.

moth with a rather startling orange head. As with several other miners, its meandering track becomes wider as the larva grows. *Ectoedemia rubivora* wears its lifestyle on its sleeve in its specific epithet *rubivora*, which means 'bramble-eater'.

Insects are not the only organisms sent to trouble bramble leaves, there are also the rusts, the most ubiquitous of which is the violet bramble rust, *Phragmidium violaceum*. It is this that covers bramble leaves with purple splotches that sometimes become so large that the whole leaf turns purple. On the underside of the leaves the purple markings are matched by purple spore-masses. Another common bramble rust fungus is *Kuehneola uredinis*.

The most notorious fungus disease of the bramble is the grey mould *Botrytis cinerea*, which under normal conditions ruins blackberry crops late in the season and even earlier, if the weather is poor. The mould itself is a mass of asexual spores (anamorphic form). The fungus also has a sexual form (teleomorphic form), though it is seldom seen. It was once common for these two forms to bear different names, as they are so morphologically different that they were assumed to be different species. The rules changed recently and only one name is now used. Sadly, this means that the delightful name of the teleomorphic form, *Botryotinia fuckeliana*, is no longer with us.

Rubus caesius is a species frequently thought to be a bramble, but which isn't. It is very similar, however, though more prostrate and therefore found more on verges than clambering over hedges. The thorns are less vicious weapons than those of the bramble and the blackberry-like fruit are ill-formed, always sharp to the taste and covered with a bloom.

Redcurrant (*Ribes rubrum*), Blackcurrant (*R. nigrum*), Gooseberry (*R. uva-crispa*)

The redcurrant is common all over Britain, save the north-west of Scotland, and is a frequent inhabitant of hedges and hedgerows. The blackcurrant and gooseberry enjoy an almost identical range, but are considerably less common. Hedgerow redcurrants are a disappointment to anyone wishing to collect the berries, as despite the proliferation of frothy pink flowers in spring, by summer all that can be found are a few small berries on each spray. It may be that birds take them, but I suspect that the redcurrants are just not trying very hard. Wild gooseberry bushes are considerably more obliging, producing great numbers of small gooseberries with some reliability. I have no idea how successful wild blackcurrants are, as I have never

Photographed in Dorset in mid-April, this gooseberry bush stands out green against the bare brown of the still dormant hawthorn.

Redcurrant in flower.

found one. While redcurrants are easily spotted in the hedgerow, gooseberry bushes are much harder to find as superficially they are very similar to hawthorn. However, there is an easy trick for identifying any hedgerow gooseberry bushes at a glance. It is a common observation that hedgerow trees and shrubs come into spring leaf at different times. The gooseberry, however, is the first, enabling it to stand out dramatically against the browns and blacks of hawthorn, hazel and blackthorn.

The currants host several moths, many exclusively, including the currant clearwing, *Synanthedon tipuliformis*; the V-moth, *Macaria wauaria*; and the phoenix, *Eulithis prunata*. The currant clearwing is the most stunning of these, its purples, blacks and golds, and its stained-glass wings evidently designed by Fabergé. Also attractive, if you like this sort of thing, is the currant blister aphid, *Cryptomyzus ribis*, found chiefly on redcurrants. These raise bright red blisters on the upper surface of the leaves, while living in the hairy depressions on the underside. About five rusts are associated with currants, among them the widespread *Puccinia carcina*, which produces an orange mass that forms into tubes arranged like the suckers on an octopus tentacle.

Wild Privet (*Ligustrum vulgare*)

One would imagine privet hedges to be restricted to suburban gardens where its manageable and mostly evergreen nature is used to advantage, but it is a frequent small tree or shrub of hedges almost everywhere in lowland Britain, particularly on chalk. The paper by French and Cummins (see p. 148) found five hedges which were almost entirely made up of privet, so it must sometimes have been planted as a hedge. It is never used where stock is held, as it is poisonous to mammals in varying degrees, causing neurological and intestinal symptoms, and even death; horses are particularly vulnerable. It produces black berries similar to dogwood which birds can eat with impunity.

I have never liked privet, ever since I inexplicably fell into one as a child and came out covered in greenfly. That I have since identified these as the gall aphid, *Myzus ligustri*, helps not at all. This creature rolls the leaves forward longitudinally forming a little tube in which it spends its time. Less likely to frighten small children, as it is barely noticeable, is the nematode worm, *Meloidogyne ardenensis*, which forms small round galls on various roots, including privet, where the eggs and sometimes the adult females are harboured.

Traveller's Joy (*Clematis vitalba*)

Also known as old man's beard, traveller's joy can be a very substantial climber with long stems that can grow very thick. It usually escapes attention until the white flowers appear, and then it dominates the tops of hedgerows when the seeds festoon it with their long silky and feathered threads radiating out from the seed heads in whorls. It is a plant of the Welsh and English lowlands, its true stronghold being in the south-east of England, though scattered populations can be found as far north as Edinburgh. It is a poisonous plant that is ignored by animals.

It does have rusts and other fungi associated with it as well as insects, but few are exclusive to it. Two insects bear the name of the host: the leaf miner, *Phytomyza vitalbae*, and the mite, *Aceria vitalbae*, the latter forming a gall which upturns the leaf edges. There is also a root nematode gall, *Meloidogyne hapla*, also known as the northern root-knot nematode, which is found on many plants including traveller's joy.

Chapter 17

HERBACEOUS PLANTS AND GRASSES

It would be near impossible to provide anything like a complete flora of the British hedgerow because, as noted earlier, it would effectively be a complete flora of Britain. To avoid so pointless an exercise I shall restrict my hedgerow flora to those plants that are extremely common in hedges and those that are simply interesting. Many species found in hedges, hedgerows, hedge banks and hedge verges have been omitted from this roll call. For example, hemp agrimony, lesser celandine, the related buttercups, snowdrops and bluebells are not treated.

Cow Parsley (*Anthriscus sylvestris*)

While the dense white froth of cow parsley in bloom is a beautiful sight along the spring hedgerow, in truth the plant is little more than a weed. So common and all pervasive is it that many of the plants that could or should be growing along the roadside are smothered out of existence. Once upon a time cow parsley was just one of many hedgerow plants, but recent estimates suggest that there is now half as much cow parsley again as there was thirty years ago.[1] What has happened?

The most likely explanation is verge management. Hedges and

Anthriscus sylvestris, cow parsley, dominating an arable hedgerow.

verges are often cut and the pulverised plants (plus butterflies and bugs) are left to form a nutrient-rich mulch which encourages nitrogen-loving plants such as cow parsley, hogweed and stinging nettle. On mulched verges, tall, tough perennials flourish, while most smaller perennials and annuals fail to even get their heads above the mulch and, if they do, are shaded into oblivion. The unwelcome success of cow parsley may also be the result of changes to the timing of cutting. A Dutch research paper from 1991, published in *Journal of Applied Ecology*, suggested that cutting the plants 'at the onset of the flowering season' would help.[2] Despite the vast numbers of seeds produced by cow parsley, the plant reproduces almost entirely by vegetative reproduction (see below) and cutting these new, clonal plants early in the year would greatly reduce population size and allow greater plant diversity.

Cow parsley is a member of the carrot family, the Apiaceae (once called the Umbelliferae). This is a large family and many inhabit the hedges of Britain. Cow parsley is also what is known as a 'delayed biennial', a half-way house between a biennial and a perennial, though in good growing conditions it can become a true biennial and flower in the second year. The seeds are short-lived and do not form a persistent seed bank, and seedling survival is very low. It stores its food in rhizomes (stems that been adapted to store starch underground) for one, two or three years and then produces flowers and seeds before dying. The rhizomes from which the plant grows also throw up side rosettes to form new plants, and it is this vegetative reproduction that the plant favours.

Rutpela maculata, the spotted longhorn.

Weed or not, cow parsley is alive with spring insects which feed on the flowers and it is a favourite with bees which are the main pollinators. It has one insect gall, *Trioza apicalis*, a psyllid (also known as the carrot psyllid) that distorts the young leaves. It has this common name because it also lives on carrots (and parsnips and angelica) and is a serious pest of carrot cultivation. There are also three fungal galls that make a mess of the leaves, one of which is the rust, *Puccinia chaerophylli*. Of the nine moths that use cow parsley as a food plant, none does exclusively, though most are specific to members of the carrot family. One of the commonest of our hedgerow beetles, the spotted longhorn, *Rutpela maculata*, can be seen on cow parsley and many other species of umbellifers, though it does not seem to be a particularly fussy eater and can be found on hawthorn and several other trees.

Cow parsley is sometimes known as wild chervil, but there is a related species called rough chervil, *Chaerophyllum temulum*. Though very common, this is easily missed as it looks like underfed cow parsley, though its purple spotted stem gives the game away. It also flowers later than cow parsley, but earlier than a third member of this group, hedge parsley, *Torilis japonica*.

Torilis japonica, hedge parsley.

Hogweed (*Heracleum sphondylium*)

The Latin name of hogweed is peculiarly unmemorable, though it may help to know its etymology. *Heracleum* is named after the classical hero Heracles. It is an original Linnaean name and probably reveals nothing more than Linnaeus' fondness for classical references, though Heracles was, of course, immensely strong, and hogweed is a tough plant. *Sphondylium* is from the Greek *sphondylos* for vertebra or spine; a reference to the segmented stem.

Hogweed is, on the whole, a safe plant, unlike its relative, giant hogweed, *Heracleum mantegazzianum*, which causes photosensitisation on being touched. The wounds that occur on subsequent exposure to light are similar to burns and the effects can last for years. Fortunately, it is not routinely found in hedges, preferring, instead, river and canal banks – possibly because of the ease of seed dispersal. The more common hogweed can also cause photosensitivity in some people, so it is best to be careful when handling it.

Hogweed is an extremely common plant in hedges, with a plant every metre or so in many places, and it can grow as high as two metres. The flower heads form in summer and, to the undiscerning, resemble elderflowers. Like cow parsley, it is has begun to make a nuisance of itself by overtaking more delicate plants, growing

Hogweed in late spring.

vigorously in nearly all soil types. In fact, hogweed is among the most widespread plants in Britain, growing everywhere except on high mountain slopes. Given its abundance, it would seem a good bet to choose as a host, and indeed there are around fifty guest species with the specific epithets *heraclei* or *heracliana* (as well as plenty of others without this nomenclature).

Puccinia heraclei is a rust fungus which swells the undersides of the leaves forming pale patches on the ribs and distorting the leaves of young plants. The fungus *Ramularia heraclei* produces small brown spots on the leaves; usually each 'scale' section of the leaf is infected in turn, forming polygonal patches. *Agonopterix heracliana* is a fairly common moth that preys on most members of the carrot family including hogweed. The hogweed picture-wing fly, *Euleia heraclei*, is a fruit fly that can sometimes be seen in May mating in groups on the leaves of hogweed. Its alternative name is celery fly as it is hosted by that plant too. *Binodoxys heraclei* is a parasitoid wasp of aphids.

Sweet Cicely (*Myrrhis odorata*)

Sweet cicely, *Myrrhis odorata*.

Sweet cicely is the single member of the genus *Myrrhis* and is not a true native plant. It is rarely found south-east of Sheffield, unless it is grown in a garden as a herb. I have one in a pot but the seeds will not germinate without being primed by the cold northern winter. In the north of Britain, where it germinates readily, it often replaces cow parsley as the dominant roadside plant, and can be guilty of the same boorish behaviour in smother-ing other plants. Unlike cow parsley, sweet cicely redeems itself by being a useful plant in the kitchen. The leaves, flowers and young seed pods are all edible, and have a very sweet aniseed-like flavour.

The leaves are finely divided and the seeds pods distinctively long and upright. Sweet cicely shares the rust fungus, *Puccinia chaerophylli*, with other members of the carrot family, and hover flies and other insects are attracted to the flowers. Apart from these, sweet cicely does not seem to welcome the attentions of other organisms and I can find no species with *myrrhi* in its name. This may have something to do with its strong smell, or perhaps it has left its guest species behind in its native regions – the mountains of central and southern Europe.

Fennel, *Foeniculum vulgare*, is worth a brief mention, as it too is an imported plant with few pests. An opportunist that colonises disturbed ground, it is frequently seen as a lone plant on verges.

Alexanders (*Smyrnium olusatrum*)

Alexanders is the third species in an informal trio of imported, aromatic Apiaceae. Although not a maritime plant, it is most frequently found by the sea, usually in verges in the south of Britain. It does not tolerate frosts well, which is why it favours more temperate coastal regions. In Devon and Cornwall it dominates roadside verges for miles. The plant has broad, indented leaves and yellow flowers and has the unusual property of commencing growth in late autumn, leafing up luxuriantly just when other plants are calling it a day. The smell of the crushed leaves is vaguely reminiscent of angelica. It commonly sports a particularly beautiful orange rust, *Puccinia smrynii*.

Wild Angelica (*Angelica sylvestris*)

This is another overlooked hedgerow carrot, lost among cow parsley and hogweed. However, it is very common and even beats hogweed as the most widespread of British plants. The leaves are a dark green and made up of two or three broad, toothed leaflets. The florets are white to pink and form into distinct round umbels on the larger

Alexanders, *Smyrnium olusatrum*, in spring.   The rust fungus *Puccinia smrynii*.

umbel of the flower head. The much more impressive cultivated angelica, *Angelica archangelica*, has naturalised in some places.

   As one would expect with a widespread native plant, wild angelica has many associated organisms, as indicated by the forty or so species bearing the specific epithet *angelicae*. *Puccinia angelicae* is a rust on wild angelica; *Torymus angelicae* is a tiny wasp; *Phytomyza angelicae* is a leaf-mining fly which causes pale brown patches; and *Phaonia angelicae* is a fly similar to a housefly. The most unusual is *Plasmopara angelicae*, which is not animal, plant or fungus, but a member of the kingdom Chromista. This genus of oomycetes is known for causing downy mildew on members of the carrot family, and this one seems to have a preference for wild angelica. The name oomycete means 'egg fungus'; the egg component referring to the shape of one of the reproductive structures, the fungus part indicating that such organisms were once thought to be fungi. These organisms have never quite decided where they belong in the tree of life. At the moment they are placed in the same kingdom as brown seaweeds.

Wild Carrot (*Daucus carota*)

Wild carrot is one of the easiest species in the carrot family to identify, its leaves are very similar to those of the edible carrot (spp. *sativus*), the flower heads very large and the individual flowers greyish-white with a red floret in the centre of each. Beneath the flower heads are extremely long and conspicuous bracts which curl downwards. It is a common plant everywhere except in Scotland, where it is mostly confined to the coast.

Daucus carota, wild carrot.

Being a native species it has accumulated a substantial number of associated organisms, not unlike those we have seen already in the other carrot species. It also suffers from carrot root fly, *Chamaepsila rosae*, which finds the wild carrot just as appetising as the garden variety. Wild parsnip, *Pastinaca sativa*, is a frequent denizen of the hedgerow verge and rough ground, and sometimes lines hedges with its yellow umbels.

Hemlock Water-dropwort (*Oenanthe crocata*)

The 'water' part of this plant's common name gives a clear idea of which hedges hemlock water-dropwort prefers – those with ditches. This is a very common plant in Britain, though it has a strange distribution, occurring throughout the southern counties of England and up the entire west coast, but absent from most eastern areas of England and Scotland. Wherever it grows, however, it grows in lush abundance, filling ditches with its attractive dark green leaves in late winter. These are among the earliest leaves to brighten the year and by early summer, the brilliant white flower heads have appeared. A

Oenanthe crocata, hemlock water-dropwort.

pity then that this lovely plant is one of the most deadly in the world. It is no help that its leaves are a dead-ringer for flat-leaf parsley and I know people who have made this mistake. They suffered few ill effects beyond 'the best dreams I've ever had', but that is because they ate very few leaves and it is not the part of the plant that is seriously dangerous. The roots look like pale carrots and it is these that cause a horrible death. For most insect larvae, the plant's toxins are harmless, and for the purple carrot-seed moth, *Depressia daucella*, it is actually a primary food plant.

There are many more members of the carrot family to be found in the hedgerow, but those above are the most common by far. As a group, they are easy to tell one from another with a little practice – something that cannot be said for the notoriously difficult Apiaceae as a whole.

Garlic Mustard (*Alliaria petiolata*)

The cabbage family (Brassicaceae) is not well represented in the hedgerow as its plants are mostly produced in open ground. Garlic mustard is one of the exceptions and is found in hedges from Land's End to the edge of the western Scottish Highlands. It has several other common names, hedge garlic and Jack-by-the-hedge being the best known. The rosettes of large, kidney-shaped basal leaves are visible for much of the year, leaping upwards in the spring to produce the tall and elegant plant that it becomes. The typical four-petalled flowers are white, replaced with upright seed pods before the plant withers and dies. The common name is an obvious one for any who have tasted the edible leaves, as the flavour is both of mustard (which one would expect from a cabbage) and garlic, which one would not. These flavours are used to deter mammals from eating them, a strategy which has backfired with human beings.

Garlic mustard was introduced into North America in the nineteenth century and is now an invasive species there. Efforts have been made to find biological control agents using those organisms that control it in its native lands. One such

Alliaria petiolata, garlic mustard.

is the weevil, *Ceutorhynchus alliariae*, which attacks the stems, another is the fungus, *Leptosphaeria maculans*, which forms black dots on the stems, about a half millimetre wide.

Garlic mustard is host to at least one species of butterfly, the pretty orange tip, *Anthocharis cardamines*, which also lays its eggs on the cuckoo flower, *Cardamine pratensis*, another cabbage species.

Other Brassicaceae such as rape (*Brassica napus*), charlock (*Sinapis arvensis*) and the various cresses such as hairy bittercress (*Cardamine hirsuta*) and wintercress (*Barbarea vulgaris*) make odd appearances along the hedgerow verge. Horseradish (*Armoracia rusticana*), however, has shown a slightly more determined effort to colonise hedges, forming the odd patch here and there, and even establishing itself as a dominant plant of road verges in parts of East Anglia. Wild radish (*Raphanus raphanistrum*) is also found in hedges, its deeply incised leaves with their distinctly radishy flavour making them unmistakeable.

A male orange tip, *Anthocharis cardamines*, here settled on greater stitchwort.

Bedstraws (*Galium spp.*)

Galium species seem to have made the hedge and hedge verge their home, as few rural walks will fail to find at least one of them. The best known of the fourteen or so British species is cleavers, *Galium aparine*, a plant thought of with affection and amusement by many because of its Velcro-like hooks which enable it to stick to almost anything. This odd ability has provided it with another name (the cause of some small joy), sticky willy. It is also commonly known as goosegrass. The small round fruits are similarly hooked, allowing them to attach to passing animals and thus be distributed. Typical of the genus, the leaves are arranged in whorls at intervals along the stem, which in this species reaches up to three metres in length. The white, four-petalled flowers form in little sprays from the same point on the stem as the leaves.

Similar in appearance but smaller (and blessedly free of hooks) is the very common hedge bedstraw, *Galium mollugo*. Its flowers are white, which helps distinguish it from the third common species of this genus to inhabit hedges, lady's bedstraw, *G. verum*, which has abundant, bright yellow flowers.

Galium species harbour about twenty galls, some of which are host specific. Some distort the leaves, for example, the mite *Cecidophyes*

Young *Galium aparine*, cleavers.

Galium verum, lady's bedstraw.

calvus; some, such as the psyllid 'fly' *Trioza galiiare*, are 'artichoke' galls, which change the shape of the leaf; some swell the stems, spectacularly so in the case of the midge *Geocrypta galii*; and many, like the midge *Dasineura hygrophila*, swell and distort the leaf buds. Rusts also infect the bedstraws. The most frequent is *Puccinia punctata* which can be found on both hedge bedstraw and lady's bedstraw, disfiguring the leaves with small brown dots.

The bedstraws are larval food plants for half a dozen moths. The many-lined moth, *Costaconvexa polygrammata*, and the striped twin-spot carpet, *Nebula salicata*, are specific to the genus. The first of these is strange in appearance, with horizontal markings running from side to side like wood grain. The substantial bedstraw hawk-moth, *Hyles gallii*, enjoys the hospitality of several plants; four of them are *Galium* species, including hedge bedstraw and lady's bedstraw.

Stellaria media, chickweed.

Greater Stitchwort (*Stellaria holostea*)

Greater stitchwort drapes its long, brittle stems over many hedges. Its pretty white flowers look as though they have ten leaves, though they only have five, each deeply incised. The main joy of this plant is its seed dispersal mechanism, which takes place with a popping sound, often when it is disturbed. It is home to the cloaked carpet moth, *Euphyia biangulata*.

The other, extremely common, *Stellaria* species is chickweed, *S. media*, which in addition to taking over vegetable plots across the land, is often found in hedge verges. Galls form on all *Stellaria*, among them *Microbotryum stellariae*, a fungus which thickens the anthers and turns them purple with spores which also discolour the formerly bright white petals.

Daisy Family (Asteraceae)

This is a large family with around 23,000 accepted species in 1,600 genera, so you will be pleased to hear that just a handful will be described here. Let us start with the 'daisy' that is found most often – the dandelion. In fact, there is no 'the dandelion' about it, as what most people are happy to call a dandelion will be one of 235 microspecies, all apomictic in that they reproduce clonally without bothering with all that sex nonsense. The generally accepted name for the dandelion is *Taraxacum officinale*, with agg. tagged on the end to indicate that it is an aggregate species, or, in other words, you are not sure which dandelion it is. Even the best botanists struggle with dandelion identification, leaving the unrewarding effort to a diminishing number of specialists known as taraxacologists. Two such are A. A. Dudman and A. J. Richards who wrote *Dandelions of Great Britain and Ireland* (1997) which contains detailed descriptions of most of the 235 microspecies, each accompanied by silhouette drawings, and all of which look exactly the same. I have a copy on my bookshelf and it is a much-treasured possession.

So, for all but the very few, a dandelion is a dandelion and that is that. It is a little regarded plant despite its beauty – perhaps if it smelled like a rose we would love it more. But a field of dandelions in late April is one of the delights of the British countryside. Hedgerow verges too turn a brilliant yellow, which quickly changes to a fluffy white as the famous dandelion clocks appear.

As with most of our common native plants, there are many organisms that depend on the dandelion for their livelihoods. There are a dozen or so leaf miners, most of them flies, with one weevil, *Orthochaetes setiger*.

Many fungi exist which routinely discolour dandelion leaves. Among those that are host specific are the two rusts, *Puccinia hieracii* (black dots) and *P. variabilis* (orange dots), and the common *Protomyces pachdermis*, which forms small purple swellings. Moths enjoy the succulent leaves of dandelions, with the stout dart, *Spaelotis ravida*, and the barred marble, *Celypha striana*, found solely on dandelions.

There are many dandelion look-alikes in the hedgerows, though it is really just the flower that has a dandelion-like appearance. Plants such as the hawkbits, hawksbeards, hawkweeds and catears are the ones that cause the most head scratching among neophyte botanists, as well as quite a few experienced ones.

Nearly twenty species of thistle grow in Britain and eight species of sow thistle (sow thistles belong to a different genus). Two of the three found on my two hedge surveys are typical species of hedge verges – creeping thistle, *Cirsium arvense*, and spear thistle, *C. vulgare*. I also found the common prickly sow thistle, *Sonchus asper*. All are troubled by the galls of weevils, nematodes, rusts and flies, the most interesting being the fruit fly *Urophora stylata*, which transforms the receptacle and achemes of *Cirsium* flower heads to form homes for its grubs.

Lesser Burdock (*Arctium minus*)

Appealing and annoying in equal measure, lesser burdock finds a place along both roadside and internal hedges. It is also a plant that can infest pastoral grassland, where the infamous sticky seed heads can make a considerable mess of sheep's wool. It is, in short, a weed, which establishes itself in disturbed ground. Its soft, downy leaves are enormous and its thistle-like flowers a lovely purple. The roots are still used to make drinks, both alcoholic and otherwise, usually in combination with the roots of dandelion. With both plants, it is chiefly the bitterness which provides the flavour.

Arctium minus, lesser burdock.

Burdocks are well provided with moths such as the pretty and common garden tiger moth, *Arctia caja*; the thistle ermine moth, *Myelois circumvoluta*; and the spotted white plume moth, *Pterophorus galactodactyla*, though some of these are restricted to the greater burdock. As well as half a dozen fungi with a burdock association, there are many others that are not host limited and which usually inhabit stems.

Mugwort (*Artemisia vulgaris*)

This relative of wormwood is extremely common in roadside hedges, but for some reason is known by few. It lacks showy flowers, but is a substantial plant at four feet tall, with finely crafted, grey-green leaves. It also likes to live dangerously by frequently growing at the very edge of the road. Those that grow further back may be used in making traditional ales, though the flavour is not entirely suitable to modern palates. While it is a graceful plant to see, it is generally classed along with hogweed and cow parsley as an indicator of high fertility and low biodiversity.

Artemisia vulgaris, mugwort, in high summer.

Pea Family (Fabaceae)

I try quite hard to learn the flowering plants but I must confess to having long ago thrown in the towel when it comes to the pea family. Apart from black medick, *Medicago lupulina*, horseshoe vetch, *Hippocrepis comosa*, and bird's foot trefoil, *Lotus corniculatus* – all of which are highly distinctive – I am mostly at a loss. Tufted vetch, *Vicia cracca*, however, is just within my grasp as it is among the showiest of the vetches and common in hedges. The pretty purple flowers form dense tufts, while the strikingly pinnate leaves boast eight to twelve pairs of leaflets, the whole tangled in a sprawling mass. Bush vetch, *V. sepium*, which has lilac flowers, is also a frequent inhabitant of hedges and, indeed, both these vetches were found in the survey on pp. 138, 140.

Tufted vetch has a few galls, one of them, the gall midge *Contarinia craccae*, takes over the flowers with several jumping grubs. Despite the very small leaves it also has at least one leaf miner, the fly *Liriomyza congesta*.

Stinging Nettle (*Urtica dioica*)

For reasons that are painfully obvious, the stinging nettle is the first plant that people learn. It is common wherever the nitrogen level is high and, like cow parsley, is a blanketing weed in hedges, although it is determinedly perennial. The specific epithet could be applied to many plants as it means that it is a dioecious species, having both male and female plants. It literally means 'of two houses' (from the Greek) and was a term used by Linnaeus who liked domestic metaphors.

What makes the stinging nettle so interesting is the enormous numbers of organisms that it supports. My friend Bryan once proudly showed me a very dead stinging nettle stem he had found that day. On it he had found six species of fungi – one basidiomycete (a major division of the fungi which includes most mushrooms as well as much else) and five ascomycetes (another major division of the fungi, which includes cup fungi, morels and yeast). The most conspicuous, if that is the word, was a white 'disc' fungus called *Lachnella villosa*; in fact it was not a disc fungus (in the ascomycetes) at all but a basidiomycete – but whatever its evolutionary lineage, it was a true beauty – a white cup clothed in white filaments.

There was a 'genuine' white disc fungus (in that it is a member of the ascomycetes) with a conical cup and a short stem called *Calyptella capula*, an orange disc fungus with no stem called *Calloria neglecta*, a pale yellow disc fungus which did have a stem called *Crocicreas cyathoideum*, and, finally, *Leptosphaeria acuta* which looked like a collection of minute, black nipples (the only way to describe them). This list, more than anything else in this book, shows the complexity of hedgerow life, indeed of the natural world itself.

Most parasites are, perforce, smaller than their hosts (the cuckoo is the most notorious exception to this rule). However, a plant known as greater dodder, *Cuscuta europaea*, challenges its stinging nettle host by being nearly the same size. It has recently been placed in the Convolvulaceae family, and from its twining, climbing habit, it

Urtica dioica, stinging nettle.

is easy to see why. The characteristics found in convolvulus species that are lacking in dodder are leaves and chlorophyll because it needs neither. Although it starts life in the soil, it soon entwines the nettle, and penetrates its vascular system to draw out water and nutrients. Despite its sinister lifestyle and entirely pink colouration, it is a beautiful plant. It parasitises other plants too, and can be found in England south of the Wash.

Inevitably, the stinging nettle has its own rust gall, *Puccinia urticata*, which substantially swells 5 cm lengths of stem and has the typical orange, octopus-sucker appearance of many *Puccinia*. A fly gall, *Dasineura urticae*, raises small, fused lumps on leaves, petioles or flower stalks.

The most noticeable guest

Lachnella villosa. each disc is about a millimetre across.

species on nettles (apart from the imposing dodder) is the cater-pillar of the small tortoiseshell butterfly, *Aglais urticae*. Nettles heave with hundreds of these hairy, black and yellow striped larvae, wrapped in their silken hammocks, which develop from the bright green eggs laid on the leaves. Four other butterflies use nettles too, though they also feed on other plants. It is the sole food plant of the spectacle moth, *Abrostola tripartite*; the snout moth, *Hypena proboscidalis*; the Paignton snout moth, *Hypena obesalis*; and the small magpie moth, *Eurrhypara hortulata*, and a non-exclusive food-plant for thirty more.

Although most people are aware that nettles can be eaten (prefer-ably cooked), few realise that the seeds are edible too. They are not picked, as such, but the entire flower spike laid out on a sheet of plastic or paper and allowed to dry. The seeds will then shake off. Lightly toasted, they are quite delicious. But it is not just us that eat nettle seeds; they are a frequent source of food for seed-eating birds.

Deadnettles (Lamiaceae)

The Lamiaceae family of plants was once called the Labiaceae, a reference to their lipped flowers. Apart from the flowers, a helpful clue is that all the Lamiaceae have a square section stem. This enables any in this family to be rotated through ninety degrees by rolling the stem between finger and thumb. As well as the deadnettles them-selves, the family contains hedgerow stalwarts such as woundworts, bugles and mints. Most, but not all, are woodland species.

White deadnettle, *Lamium album*, is extremely common in hedges, its nettle-like leaves providing an irresistible opportunity to wow friends by popping a leaf into your mouth. Red deadnettle, *Lamium purpureum*, is sometimes seen in disturbed hedges but is really a plant of cultivation. The beautiful yellow archangel, *Lamiastrum galeobdolon*, is less frequent and always a delight to see. It is sometimes used as an indicator of hedge age or woodland assart origin, though this is not an entirely reliable method. Ground ivy, *Glechoma hederacea*, much despised by gardeners, is a low creeping plant with deep purple flowers which rise up on stems which at least attempt to be vertical.

The ivy part of its name is presumably for its carpeting habit and is repeated in the specific epithet *hederacea*.

The lipped flowers of the deadnettle family are designed to attract nectar-eating pollinators, and the white deadnettle is sometimes called the bee nettle. It is a very useful nectar source, so much so that the flowers – or at least the base of the flowers – taste distinctly sweet.

In addition to these welcome visitors, this group suffers from several species that do not have the plants wellbeing close to their hearts. The larvae of several moth species infest these plants and there are a number of gall associations. Ground ivy has only one gall, the fly *Dasineura glechomae*, which turns the two terminal leaves into a pouch. The white deadnettle is less fortunate in having five, one of which, *Dasineura lamiicola*, forms a pea gall on the tips of the shoots.

Every plant must have its associated rust or smut – *Puccinia glechomatis* on ground ivy and the smut *Melanotaenium lamii* on white and red deadnettles. White deadnettle also suffers occasionally from the ascomycete fungus *Septoria lamii*.

Hedge woundwort, *Stachys sylvatica*, is frequently found in hedges and woodland (as its names suggest). It has upright stems, bearing attractive spikes of purple flowers, is conspicuous on hedge banks. Selfheal, *Prunella vulgaris*, is a plant of grassland and only encountered on verges; bugle, *Ajuga reptans* is a woodland edge plant and thus found on hedge banks. Wood sage, *Teucrium scorodonia*, finds its way into nearly every hedge on acid ground but is a disappointing plant. Its sage name suggests that it is a useful wild herb, but crush one between your fingers and you will smell only mice.

Some hedgerow plants are a pleasure to come across because of their beauty or rarity. Others, however, are genuinely useful, such as the genus *Mentha* and the genus *Calamintha*. The commonest by far is wild marjoram, *Origanum vulgare*. This calamint is strictly a plant of alkaline soils and is often found on chalky hedge banks, forming large swathes of fragrant leaves and pink flowers. Less common, but found in similar locations, is wild basil, *Clinopodium vulgare*. Both these plants smell and taste exactly as one would expect. Spearmint, *Mentha spicata*, appears occasionally in a hedge, but the commonest true

Clinopodium vulgare, wild basil.

Stachys sylvatica, hedge woundwort.

Eysarcoris venustissimus, the woundwort shieldbug.

mint is watermint, *Mentha aqua*. Strictly speaking, this can hardly be described as a hedge plant as it always grows in damp or wet ground. However, there are enough damp hedges and hedge ditches for it to be found with some frequency.

The strong smell of mints and calamints is thought to deter animal species and with the mints it seems to work – the mint bent-wing, *Pseudopostega crepusculella*, being one of the few moths which feeds on *Mentha* species. The mint smell does not deter fungi, however, and the very common *Puccinia menthae* is found on most *Mentha* species. The hedge woundwort also uses smell as a repellent, with an unappealing odour especially when crushed. This is not enough to put off the woundwort shieldbug, *Eysarcoris venustissimus*, whose nymphs feed on the plant. Last (but least only in terms of size) is the tiny, pale yellow disc fungus, *Calycellina chlorinella*, which sometimes occurs on the blackened areas of wood sage stems.

Red Campion (*Silene dioica*)

Very few hedges and hedge banks fail to provide a display of this

Silene dioica, red campion.

straightforwardly pretty plant that is common all over Britain. Slightly less common but even more straightforward is the bladder campion, *Silene vulgaris*. *Silene* species are fairly well provided with microfungi, including four rusts and one smut, and several galls.

I hesitate to mention herb robert, *Geranium robertianum*, with red campion as it belongs to a completely different family, that of the cranesbills (Geraniaceae). However, it is equally common in hedges and on hedge banks, enjoys the same extensive range and looks rather similar from a considerable distance, though herb robert is much smaller with typically lobed leaves. Despite its encouraging name, it does not taste particularly pleasant.

Germander Speedwell (*Veronica chamaedrys*)

Many speedwells find their way on to hedge banks or verges, though really they are plants of grass or water. Germander speedwell is the best known of them. The plant made the survey listed on p. 143, but there was something odd about this particular plant, as the photograph shows. Where the terminal buds should have been, there was

The gall of the midge, *Jaapiella veronicae*.

a strange, pink, furry ball. Such balls are made by a midge fusing the two terminal buds together, the capsule thus formed being clothed in hairs (presumably stimulated hairs of the plant itself). Inside there will be several orange larvae of the midge, *Jaapiella veronicae*, a common gall and one that is well worth looking out for.

Foxglove (*Digitalis purpurea*)

Born in the countryside but brought up in a city, I had little understanding of wild flowers, but recall my grandmother (a lady of impeccable rural credentials, having been the daughter of a Wiltshire village thatcher) talking of cowslips and foxgloves. I wondered what they looked like and felt the touch of shame that I did not know. A confession, of sorts, but at least I wondered. Now I can spot a foxglove from half a mile and I am always pleased to see one. It is, perhaps, the most flamboyant of our summer flowers which would, no doubt, have been introduced as a garden plant had it not been a native. Beautiful it may be, but it is also deadly. It contains two heart stopping chemicals, digitoxin and digoxin. In the precisely correct dose these, or their modern analogues, can strengthen heart function and are (or were) one of the most important drugs at the disposal of medicine.

Foxglove, a plant of woodland, forms glorious upright stands in hedgerows and on hedge banks. The finger-glove flowers are designed with precision to encourage access by, mostly, bumblebees. The bee has to climb completely inside the flower to reach the nectar at the base, covering itself with pollen in the process. Several fungi are recorded from foxgloves, at least four of which have *digitalis* (or something similar) in their name. These include a downy mildew, *Peronospora digitalis*, and an ascomycete, *Phomopsis digitalis*, which forms black dots on the stem. The foxglove hosts around half a dozen moths, one of which is specific, the appropriately named foxglove pug, *Eupithecia pulchellata*. Disappointingly, few galls form on foxgloves.

Mercurialis perennis, dog's mercury, with its associated rust *Melampsora populnea*.

Dog's Mercury (*Mercurialis perennis*)

A thoroughgoing woodland plant, dog's mercury is found in shady hedges which were originally woodland, or are near to woodland, where it carpets hedge banks and sometimes strays on to verges. A small green plant with small green flowers, it has none of the grand displays of foxglove or wild marjoram, but it is poisonous, though not deadly. It rarely appears nibbled or damaged in any way, so it is no surprise to learn that it has few parasites. Apart from a rust, *Melampsora populnea*, which frequently paints both leaf and stem bright orange.

Willowherbs

Great willowherb, *Epilobium hirsutum*, grows by running water and also in damp soil. Though it is a riverside plant, it will grow just about anywhere that is at least a little damp, including in hedges. Its flowers are larger than those that form on the long spikes of the common rosebay willowherb, *Chamerion angustifolium*, a plant of disturbed soils and a regular of hedgerows. Both willowherbs form large, dense stands, alongside or displacing other tall plants. A Danish friend told me that in Denmark the rosebay willowherb is colloquially called the summer holiday plant, as all the flowers are in bloom at the start of the holidays, then gradually die from the bottom upwards, the topmost falling with the mood of children due to return to the gloom of the classroom.

Both are host to some very substantial moths, among them are the elephant hawk-moth, *Deilephila elpenor*, and the striped hawk-moth, *Hyles livornica*. Leaf, stem and flower bud are infected with a variety of gall organisms: *Mompha sturnipennella*, a small black and white moth and the fly *Dasineura epilobii* being two out of five recorded from rosebay willowherb. Great willowherb has its own galls, including a rust, *Puccinia pulverulenta*.

Chamerion angustifolium, rosebay willowherb.

Meadowsweet (*Filipendula ulmaria*)

Like great willowherb, meadowsweet prefers damp areas but will put up with most conditions if pushed. In summer the hedges fill with its white downy flowers and its heady and somewhat cloying perfume. Reluctant to let the summer go, meadowsweet can bloom as late as early November. Its aroma can be too much for humans, but it attracts bees, for whom it is an important nectar source.

If a stand of meadowsweet is examined and the leaves turned over, there is a good chance the rust, *Triphragmium ulmariae*, will be revealed in all its orange glory. While you are there, it is also worth studying the stems, alive and dead, to see if any of the twenty or so disc fungi hosted by this plant are present. Few are larger than half a millimetre across, so you will need a lens. Meadowsweet is home to a further dozen or so fungal species.

Filipendula ulmaria, meadowsweet.

Wood Avens (*Geum urbanum*)

Also known as herb bennet, this is a woodland plant and very frequent on hedge banks and verges. It has five yellow petals and conspicuously lop-sided, triple-lobed leaves, and its root, when crushed, smells of cloves. Wood avens is not particularly welcoming to pests, with only a few associated fungi and two galls – a fly and a mite. The mite, *Cecidophyes nudus*, produces pale green blisters on the leaves.

Common Fumitory (*Fumaria officinalis*)

This is the commonest by far of our fumitories. The masses of grey leaves can look like smoke from a distance, hence the common and generic name. It is a rather floppy plant and scrambles for a place on hedge banks. It hosts gall weevils which cause the stems to swell.

Nightshades

People rightly worry about deadly nightshade, *Atropa belladonna*, as it lives up to its name. The specific epithet means 'beautiful lady', a reference to the plant's ability to dilate the pupils when applied in eye-drop form. The genus name derives from *Atropos*, one of the three Fates of Greek mythology, uncompromising ladies who governed all. Atropos, which means 'unturnable' or 'immoveable', was the one who cut the thread of life. Unfortunately, deadly nightshade is a rather rare plant and I have seen it only once, bordering the car park at Old Trafford, but it does appear in hedgerows (usually near habitation), so is worth looking out for.

Much more common everywhere, in hedgerows in particular, is woody nightshade, *Solanum dulcamara*, otherwise known as bittersweet. The bright purple and yellow flowers and intense red berries make it a very good looking, if slightly straggly, plant. It is poisonous, but not very, and I know of some people who eat the ripe berries. There is also enchanter's nightshade, *Circaea lutetiana*, also seen in hedges, but much happier as a garden weed.

There are well over a dozen fungi on the nightshades, many of which are host, or at least, family specific, with several of them bearing *solani* as their specific epithet. But the most infamous organism to infect them is *Phytophthora infestans*. The potato – which belongs to the same family – is also attacked by this oomycete, hence its dread common name, potato blight.

Solanum dulcamara, bittersweet.

Plantains (*Plantago spp.*)

Plantains are really species of rough pasture, and their progress and distribution through the ages – recorded in the pollen record – has been used to follow the historical progress and distribution of pasture. The main hedgerow location for plantain is rough verge edges, where it has found a whole new life. Ribwort plantain, *Plantago lanceolata*, and greater plantain, *P. major*, are the most frequently found; the former identifiable by its long, thin leaves, the latter by its broad, round ones. *P. lanceolata* is more commonly seen in alkaline soils. Plantains host half a dozen galls (none very exciting) and a dozen fungi.

Docks

Scarcely a hedgerow or even a wall in the country is without a few docks (and sometimes many). Nearly two dozen moths depend at least partially on docks, as well as thirty or so fungi and fourteen galls made by a variety of organisms. Docks belong to the large Polygonaceae family, and two that are familiar in hedges – redshank, *Persicaria maculosa*, and bistort, *P. bistorta* – are well worth looking at. Polygonaceae means 'many joints', which redshank certainly has, as well as a dark patch on its leaves (macula is the Latin for 'stain'). Its small pink spike

Bistorta officinalis, bistort.

of flowers is also seen in its more elegant sister species bistort, a plant with a wide distribution, but which is most frequently seen on damp hedge verges in the north. Bistort has a venerable history as an edible and medicinal plant, but sadly it is mostly just that – history – due to an astringent taste that is unacceptable to the modern palate. The superseded Latin name of bistort, *Bistorta officinalis*, clearly shows its former importance in an apothecary's store cupboard. The name bistort derives from its corkscrew shaped root which is 'twice twisted'.

Modern humans find bistort difficult to swallow and for moths it seems to be a dinner of last resort. However, half a dozen galls are found with *Persicaria* species in general, each deforming the plants in their own special way.

Lords and Ladies (*Arum maculatum*)

The first monocotyledonous plant in this list, lords and ladies is a familiar plant of woodland and often nestles in the darker recesses of hedges. A common alternative name is cuckoo pint. It takes an unusual approach to life: leaves are produced in the depths of winter (they are among the first green of the year), these then die to be replaced by the flower spike and sheath (spadix and spathe, respectively), which in turn is replaced by the fruit – the familiar 'berries-on-a-stick'.

Lords and ladies is a plant with less than its fair share of associated fungi or galls, and appears to be the food plant of almost

Arum maculatum, lords and ladies.

nothing. The protection of a cocktail of noxious chemicals has done its job, with every part of the plant being poisonous and extremely unpleasant to eat. The one guest species that I can discover is the rust fungus, *Puccinia sessilis*. It has the bright orange colouration typical of the genus. It is also true that the spadix is sometimes nibbled by rodents and the berries eaten by birds, pheasants in particular. The unusual flower attracts insects by its slight but unpleasant smell of dung. The insects descend into the chamber from which the spadix arises and are partially trapped there for an anxious few minutes while they are inadvertently and thoroughly dusted with pollen.

One fungus, *Ramularia ari*, infects the leaves and causes brown spots. However, *Arum maculatum* is partially symbiotic with species of fungi whose services are limited to facilitating germination. So essential are these fungi, that it is impossible for seed to germinate without it. Having served this purpose it is payback time and the fungus receives a free ride for the life of the plant. This particular mycorrhizal process was first described by French researcher I. Gallaud in 1905, leading it to be known as the 'Arum type'. Orchids are famous for displaying the same behaviour.

Wild Garlic (*Allium ursinum*)

Also known as ramsons, wild garlic is a common and welcome inhabitant of woodlands throughout Britain, being notably absent only from the Scottish Highlands and parts of East Anglia. Being a woodland plant, it is found in shady hedgerows too, though more often in woodland hedgerow areas. The first leaves appear as early as February and linger until June or July when they become an olfactory hazard. Wild garlic is host to several fungi including one of the life stages of the previously mentioned *Puccinia sessilis*.

Allium ursinum, wild garlic or ramsons, on a Dorset hedge bank.

Claviceps purpurea, ergot.

Grasses

Many grasses or related plants can be found on verges and hedge banks, but five are ubiquitous: false brome, false oat grass, Yorkshire fog, rough meadow grass, creeping soft grass. The microfungi of grasses are extensive and hard to identify, but one fungus stands out above all others as historically important and is clearly visible, if you know what you are looking for. This is ergot, *Claviceps purpurea*, the small, black sclerotia (a dormant or resting structure) of which look like the wild rice one sometimes sees in shops. It is, however, highly poisonous, containing a vasoconstricting toxin which causes gangrene and a neurotoxin which is the precursor chemical to LSD. Ergot can be found in grasses during wet autumns.

Chapter 18

LICHENS, MOSSES, LIVERWORTS, FERNS AND FUNGI

The trees and plants of the hedgerow are obvious to all, less so are the smaller organisms that grow on and with them. Thirty metres of a good hedge may contain seven trees, but on those trees may be thirty lichens and twenty mosses, and beneath them a hundred fungi. These organisms are usually passed by unnoticed, but they are beautiful and important in themselves. Few trees will fail to sport a moss, but they are not easy for the layman to distinguish. The trunk of the hedgerow ash tree in the photograph, for example, appears to be covered by a single moss, but closer investigation reveals that there are many more – no less than seven, in fact, plus one liverwort which looks just like a moss. The mosses present are: *Isothecium alopecurioides, Thamnobryum alopecurum, Homalothecium sericeum, Anomodon viticulosus, Neckera complanata, Hypnum cupressiforme* and *Isothecium myosuroides*. The liverwort is *Radula complanata*. Higher up the tree there are more species of moss to be found – those which can tolerate such elevated and dry conditions. Mosses are rather fussy about where they grow with different species inhabiting different parts of a hedge or a single tree. Some will chose a damper, north-facing side, some prefer the crooks and folds of a trunk where nutrient-rich water runs down from above.

A moss-rich ash, which shows signs of having been laid into the hedge.

Other common mosses of the hedgerow are the supine plait moss, *Hypnum resupinatum*, and the frizzled pincushion, *Ulota phyllantha*. Typical hedgerow liverworts are *Frullania dilatata* and *Metzgeria furcata*. Mosses and liverworts are often identical to one another as far as the uninitiated are concerned, but they are only related in as much as they are both plants. They are found in different divisions on the tree of life and only look similar because their way of life and habitats are similar.

Also visible on the trunk is a fern called western polypody, *Polypodium interjectum*. Ferns too are frequent inhabitants of hedges and hedgerows, more often in shaded locations. The photograph overleaf shows three ferns in one place: these are the male fern, *Dryopteris filix-mas*; the hart's tongue fern, *Asplenium scolopendrium*; and the soft shield fern, *Polystichum setiferum*.

Moss, liverwort and fern species are all fairly numerous, lichens even more so with around 1,900 British species. They tend not to be specific to a host, but to certain conditions – acid, alkaline, high levels of nutrients or low levels of nutrients. They respond quickly to

Three fern species.

a change in these environmental considerations by simply dropping down dead. Their modern nemesis is pollution, with entire populations being wiped out by an increase in sulphur dioxide levels. This particular threat has recently diminished, replaced by nitrogen compounds, due to the high levels of nitrous gases in the atmosphere and – especially bad for hedges and hedgerows – pollution from over-enthusiastic slurry sprinklers. Although they die easily and quickly, lichens do not recolonise well even when conditions return to what they once enjoyed. Instead, their previous niche is colonised by common generalist species, rather than the specialist species that were there before.

Just how prolific lichens can be when left in peace is seen in the photograph of a single length of young ash trunk. There are no fewer than five species in a barely two foot section of trunk. They are *Bacidia laurocerasi, Lecanora chlarotera, Opegrapha sorediifera, Parmotrema perlatum* and *Phlyctis argena*. It is worth revisiting the mosses and liverworts at this point, for there are also three of each in the photograph: the mosses, *Hypnum cupressiforme, Orthotrichum affine* and *Ulota crispa*, and the liverworts, *Frullania dilatata, Metzgeria furcata* and *Radula complanata*.

Many of the fungi that inhabit hedges and hedgerows, particularly

This two foot length of live ash trunk sports no fewer than five species of lichen. Also present are three mosses and three liverworts.

the microfungi, have already been discussed in conjunction with their host plants, but many are not so fussy about the company they keep and will occur in hedges and hedge verges because that is the general habitat that suits them. Many of these are saprotrophs, which live on dead organic matter such as leaf litter and compost material in the soil.

The clouded funnel, *Clitocybe nebularis*, is one saprotroph that seems to appear more often than all the others and usually in large troops. It is a large, grey mushroom with a distinct cloudy bloom to the cap. I am frequently sent photographs of this striking mushroom from people who wonder if they can eat it. They can't. A more encouraging assessment of edibility can be made for the common shaggy inkcap, *Coprinus comatus*. This grassy verge species forms large troops, often along roadsides. It seems to prefer disturbed ground, but there may also be some benefit accruing to it from nutrient elements that occur in car fumes (maybe not so encouraging an assessment after all).

The fairy ring champignon, *Marasmius oreades*; the parasol mushroom, *Macrolepiota procera*; and a substantial proportion of the large 'true' mushroom genus *Agaricus* are typical of grassy verges, though many more are found there. The shaggy parasol, *Chlorophyllum rhacodes*, is more a mushroom of woodlands, so is found beneath hedges rather than alongside. Slender *Mycena* species appears on twigs and in moss, as well as growing in vast tufts on standard trees or simply out of the ground. The smaller species of puffball such as the common puffball, *Lycoperdon perlatum*, can be found on hedge banks, and the stump puffball, *L. pyriforme*, on recently deceased trees.

Chapter 19

MAMMALS

Nearly the whole range of British terrestrial mammals makes some use of hedges, either as a home or a temporary refuge. Many hedges are designed to keep deer out of fields, so it would take a very substantial and poorly managed hedge to accommodate so large an animal within it, though deer may gather beside a hedge for a little cover. The extremely tasty roebuck I once stalked (on my first and last foray into deer hunting) crept quietly along a hedgerow, and to my inexperienced eye was invisible in the evening gloom. Not being able to see something rather precludes one from taking a shot, so this was left to my professional companion. He put a bullet through the animal's heart with great accuracy and it fell without a sound. In fact, one species of deer, the muntjac (*Muntiacus reevesi*), can and does find a home in our hedges. This newcomer to the British countryside seldom stands more than two foot at the shoulder, so a hedge proves no barrier. To the chagrin of some, their repeated incursions can make a mess of a previously useful hedge.

Much more common, however, are the diggers – badgers, foxes and rabbits – who dig their setts, earths and burrows in hedge banks. These creatures are less welcome to whoever manages the hedge because their extensive excavations will compromise it very quickly and cause much damage. In the case of the badger (*Meles meles*), legislation has made combatting the problem difficult, and impossible to do as it used to be done, which was first to evict the badgers and then repair the bank and hedge. The fox (*Vulpes vulpes*) is less of a problem as its earth forms temporary breeding accommodation and is usually just an expanded rabbit burrow. Rabbits (*Oryctolagus cuniculus*) are the worst hedge offenders, however, undermining them on an industrial scale with holes every three metres or so, all intricately connected underground. At least these may be removed without fear of prosecution and the bank repaired (though if the hedge bank suits them, they will be back). Rabbits are particularly disastrous to the Cornish hedge because when these are undermined they simply collapse. A Cornish hedge is effectively a narrow, wall-lined bank with hedging trees planted on the top (see p. 311). The earth between the cladding stones falls into the burrows and the entire edifice comes tumbling down.

Damage to hedge and wall is but a small part of the depredations suffered by farmers from these three animals. Rabbits eat crops and foxes take lambs and poultry. The badger is accused of spreading tuberculosis, though the truth of the matter is hard to know. A good farmer friend of mine was beside himself on discovering a dead and diseased badger inside his cattle shed and, sure enough, his herd tested positive a few weeks later. Badgers are also capable of turning over acres and acres of prime, herb-rich chalk downland in their search for pignuts, in the process destroying plants, fungi and invertebrates by disturbing the ground and raising the nutrient levels in the necessarily poor soil.

These stories of rural woe are mentioned to show another reason why those whose livelihood depends on the land do not universally love hedges – hedges harbour creatures that can be destructive as well as fascinating and beautiful, and the many pests of hedgerow plants are equally adapted to crops.

While badger and fox no longer have any natural predators in Britain, the rabbit has many – not least the badger and fox. But there are several more rabbit hunters, among them the stoat (*Mustela ermine*) and the weasel (*Mustela nivalis*). On the Dorset farm where I once lived, I used to watch a weasel run up and down the hedge, although I never saw it catch a rabbit, as it would probably do so within the burrow. The stoat is the larger of these two cousins and otherwise distinguished by a black tip to the tail ('a weasel is easel to tell from a stoat, which is totally different,' as the saying goes). Stoats will eat almost anything they can catch, with rabbits a favourite. Both species are strongly associated with hedgerows, making their

Weasel in a hedge bank.

dens (which are sometimes fur-lined) in the tunnels dug by their prey. The most secretive of creatures, they use the centre pathway of hedges, if there is one, or the edge of hedges to make their way around their home patch. They are also known to use stone walls for cover.

Although my treatment of hedgerow mammals is brief, it would be impossible for me to leave out the eponymous mammal of the hedgerow, the hedgehog (*Erinaceus europaeus*). True to its name, and as a species of woodland edges, it is found in and around hedges. It has suffered much over the years: from hedgerow loss, the increase in arable farming, getting run over by cars and, more recently, by being eaten by the out-of-control badger population. Hedgehogs put up temporary daytime shelters made from leaves wrapped around with twigs and bramble and a much more substantial 'hibernaculum' in which they overwinter. Their diet is foraged from grassland and consists of earthworms and other invertebrates.

Another signature mammal of the hedgerow is the hazel dormouse (*Muscardinus avellanarius*), which can be found, with some effort, in hedgerows all year round. It is a southern species with its largest range and density being in the coastal counties of England. Dormice feed on the flowers and fruits of shrubby plants found within hedges, seldom leaving the safety of their preferred habitat. This must be sufficiently dense and overgrown to provide good cover and sufficient food, so they will not be found in a typical, low, thin and flailed hedge. More than most mammals, the dormouse relies on hedges as a corridor. Despite its common and Latin names, the hazel dormouse does not insist on living with and on hazel, it is more of a generalist.

The grey squirrel (*Sciurus carolinensis*) is now very common in hedgerows throughout most of Britain having notoriously outper-formed the native and considerably more attractive red squirrel (*Sciurus vulgaris*). It is a creature for which the British have mixed feelings – better a grey squirrel than no squirrel? They have, however, made a nuisance of themselves beyond usurping their native rival, not least in eating vast quantities of hazelnuts. They also consume the eggs of nesting birds, compete with other mammals and birds for food, and strip bark from trees (mostly on plantations). An orni-thologist friend is unequivocal in his opinion of the grey squirrel and will, he tells me, always try to run one over if he sees that fluffy grey tail in the road ahead. They are quite tasty, though.

Small mammals are by far the most abundant in hedgerows and their relationship with the habitat has been studied repeatedly and in some detail using capture and count. The surprising finding is the enormous difference between the levels of population in seemingly similar species. One study found that in over 3,000 captures made from hedgerows, the wood mouse (*Apodemus sylvaticus*), yellow-necked mouse (*Apodemus flavicollis*), bank vole (*Myodes glareolus*) and common shrew (*Sorex araneus*) accounted for 97 per cent of the animals found.[1] The paltry 3 per cent was made up of the harvest mouse (*Micromys minutus*), field vole (*Microtus agrestis*), pygmy shrew (*Sorex minutus*) and water shrew (*Neomys fodiens*). This despite the fact that the hedgerow is all but essential for the harvest mouse as a refuge. Another study found that the wood mouse accounted for 77 per cent of captures, the bank vole 10 per cent, the field vole 7 per cent and the common

Hedgehogs.

shrew about 5 per cent. Overall, the wood mouse, field vole and common shrew were found in all the hedgerow (and other) habitats examined during the study. The wood mouse comes out as king of the hedgerow by a long way in both studies. It is a very appealing creature with pretty round ears, loveable enough until it attempts to overwinter inside your house. With most of these small mammals, it is only the well-established hedge that provides a good habitat, though the wood mouse seems able to tolerate a hedge in almost any condition.

Mammals come with pests and few people realise how many they can harbour. The standard and compendious work on British mammals helpfully includes tables listing these pests and they make grim reading.[2] Small rodents suffer from no less than sixteen species of flea, two flukes, seven tapeworms and nine nematode worms. The bank vole is the most flea-ridden small rodent in the British Isles. The eternally itchy hedgehog also has a lot to contend with, receiving an entire, page-long table of endopathogens all to itself. It also suffers from the host-specific hedgehog flea, *Archaeopsylla erinacei*,

267

The rabbit, a notorious destroyer of hedges.

plus numerous ticks and mites. These troublesome pests are just a matter of everyday life to wild animals. My own observations of badgers suggest that, on arising at dusk, they spend the first ten minutes scratching themselves with a loud ripping sound. For the recorder of hedgerow species, they are yet more things to add to the list – another way in which the hedgerow is so alive.

Chapter 20

BIRDS

If hedgerows are good for anything, most people would say they are good for birds. While even the ubiquitous wood mouse will go unnoticed, birds are always there to draw the eye. Hedgerows support around 80 per cent of our woodland birds, but it is not hard to believe that all our woodland birds will visit hedgerows at one time or another. The populations will rise and fall and much head-scratching by amateur and professional ornithologists takes place. I have little interest in birds, considering them to be nasty, feathery things that fly away before you can even identify them. But even I have noticed the decline in the yellowhammer (*Emberiza citronella*) – for which I am willing to admit a small affection – in the local hedges. Thirty years ago the hedges swarmed with them, now they are only seen occasionally. There seems to be little that has changed beyond an increase in arable, though a 1994 study on birds and hedges suggests that the yellowhammer likes tilled ground. Perhaps it is a subtle change in cutting regimes that has done the damage, or an increase in the population of birds of prey?

The theory that the rise in birds of prey is a cause of songbird decline is not particularly convincing. If raptors have had any effect,

Male bullfinch.

then it is merely a further imposition on top of several indignities songbirds have suffered. Basically, there is little left for them to eat: arable weeds have declined through increased herbicide usage and invertebrates have declined through increased use of insecticides. It is not the hedgerow that changed or the behaviour of birds of prey, it is the loss of the surrounding habitat.

The hedge itself still provides breeding locations and food for many birds, but also winter food for migratory thrushes such as redwing, fieldfare and song thrush. Holly berries and hawthorn berries are the favourites, as they are abundant and persist when little else remains.

The size and composition of a hedge has a profound effect on the birds that might inhabit it. Generally speaking, a large, tall, lush hedge with many woody species will have more birds, though some bird species (for example, dunnock, willow warbler and lesser whitethroat) prefer smaller hedges with only one or two tree species. These issues were examined in the 1994 paper mentioned above, which studied the behaviour of eighteen bird species in forty-six farms in lowland England. The surveys took place during the breeding season. The results were quite remarkable, proving the fundamental importance of hedge height, width and number of woody species. For the robin, song thrush, willow warbler, long-tailed tit, great tit and chaffinch, it was a strong and clear case of the higher the better, although the long-tailed tit seems to lose patience beyond six metres. The yellowhammer and the linnet preferred short hedges. The frequency of wren, robin, blackbird, lesser whitethroat, yellowhammer and blue tit increased markedly with hedge width, though, this time, several species were not interested in hedges over five metres wide. The number of woody species in a hedge was also important – usually, the greater, the better. The robin, song thrush, whitethroat, lesser whitethroat, blue tit and yellowhammer showing a remarkably clear and linear increase up to about eight species of woody plants. Other species of bird disliked such variety.[1]

Overall, the study concluded that tall hedges were better for birds, with fifteen of the eighteen bird species finding the average hedge too short. However, a better reading of the results suggests that no one size fits all in providing a perfect habitat for hedgerow birds. This will, of course, affect hedgerow cutting regimes – if you wish to encourage birds, there is no preferred height and hedges should be trimmed, or allowed to grow, to a range of heights, not just one. The RSPB recommends a minimum height of between 1.2 and 1.4 metres to support bird populations, particularly when nesting, where cover is essential. M. D. Hooper provides data on both the levels of bird numbers and bird species for various hedges.[2] Remnant hedges come out worst, followed by recently laid hedges. A well-grown and properly trimmed hedge was beneficial for bird life, but the clear winner was a very overgrown hedge that had begun to invade the fields with escaped blackthorn. This provided thirty-four breeding birds of nineteen different species in a length of hedgerow of 1,000 metres, compared to nine breeding birds and seven species in the same length of well-trimmed hedge. For birds, bigger really is better.

Passerine birds – those belonging to the order Passeriformes (which includes most songbirds) – are not the only birds found in hedgerows. Anyone who has ever walked along a hedge and been scared to death by the sudden and extremely noisy flight of a sheltering partridge or pheasant, will know that game birds use hedges for cover. Birds of prey are frequently seen in hedges, taking a rest after putting in the required number of flight hours. Just up the road from my home, not far from Eggardon Hill, buzzards can always be seen perched in the roadside hedges, taking a breather and looking like an out-take from Alfred Hitchcock's movie *The Birds*.

Chapter 21

SPECIES FOUND ON DRY STONE WALLS

A stone wall is a very different matter to a hedge, hedgerow or hedge bank. Although it can accrue trees and shrubs and their associated under-storey plants, it is fundamentally a habitat of rock and supports several invertebrates, a few reptiles, many flowering plants, mosses, liverworts and lichens. There is none of the flamboyance paraded by the hedgerow; this is chiefly a habitat to be explored by the loupe-wielding connoisseur. Stone walls vary considerably in how much plant life they will support with many – perhaps most – walls being almost naked save for some vegetation at their foot. Climate seems to be the deciding factor here, though the rock used will also have an effect. The mossiest walls I have ever seen are around Oban in western Scotland, an area that boasts a temperate rain forest.

English stonecrop, *Sedum anglicum*, is found all around the coast due its fondness for clifftops, shingle and rocky shores. It is found most extensively, however, on the rocky western extremities of Britain, both on the coast and inland, most notably on stone walls. The plant pictured here was taken on Bodmin Moor. The related and aptly named navelwort, *Umbilicus rupestris*, is chiefly a plant of the

A very mossy dry stone dyke near Oban.

Sedum anglicum, english stonecrop on Bodmin Moor.

Umbilicus rupestris, navelwort in flower.

A single rock from a Dorset dry stone wall, species-rich with lichen.

rocky west of England, though those pictured here were found in the Lake District.

Pellitory-of-the-wall, *Parietaria judaica*, is more common in the south. It may come as something of a revelation to learn that it is a very close relative of the stinging nettle, though close examination will reveal clear similarities between the two plants. Ferns too are grateful for a rocky home, the best known being the spleenworts.

While plants cling to cracks and crevices in walls, lichens are entirely at home on bare rock. Few people realise or care just how many species exist, nor how many can be found on a single rock. On a walk along a mostly fallen wall with my friend Bryan, I found a small boulder which appeared to have three or four lichens on it and challenged him to name them. He rattled off four names, but did not stop there.

Here is his complete list:

Ramalina siliquosa
Lecanora gangleoides
Aspicilia calcarea
Caloplaca dalmatica
Verrucaria baldensis
Poronia linearis
Caloplaca flavescens

Diploicia canescens
Acrocordia conoidea
Lecanora crenulata
Belonia nidarosiensis
Lecanora albescens
Verrucaria nigrescens
Ochrolechia parella

I do think this is astonishing and it reminds us how great the variety of life in Britain truly is. The list is also interesting because it contains two ecological groups – those who like an alkaline substratum and those who prefer something a little more acid. The rock concerned was sedimentary and consisted of two successive layers: one of Jurassic limestone and one of Chert.

PART IV

HOW BOUNDARIES ARE MADE AND MAINTAINED

Chapter 22

HURDLES

Quite what a hedge looked like in, say, the Bronze Age or the depths of the Dark Ages, is difficult to say. Despite the best efforts of palaeontologists and academics, it is not even possible to know if they were used extensively at all. Herding of stock by labourers or individual farmers was most likely the commonest method of control and protection. Tethering, too, has a long pedigree and could be viewed as a moveable, circular, virtual hedge. Not only was the animal prevented from wandering off to get lost or eat the corn, its grazing was controlled down to the inch. A farm labourer friend of mine in Wales told me that sometimes animals needed no confinement at all, provided they were away from any crops. Sheep, he told me, would remain in and around a certain sheltered location indefinitely once the farmer had put out food for them for a few days, because they had come to associate the area with safety and food; it had become home. Things may have been more difficult in prehistoric times as there were wolves and perhaps bears to contend with – perils that modern Welsh farmers need worry about no more.

It may well be that permanent hedges were few and far between in prehistory and that herding was complemented or replaced by

A simple hazel hurdle.

hurdles and tethering, which could easily be moved when an area of land became over-grazed. Hurdles can also be used to protect crops. However, hurdles fare little better than hedges in the archaeological record, although examples of the related wattle and daub construction have been found in late Iron Age roundhouses, making it likely that hurdles would have been used in a more thoroughgoing agricultural context.[1] They are exactly the sort of thing that primitive farmers were likely to have used, being easy to make with simple tools and highly effective.

A hurdle is simply a moveable fence that is light to carry and easy to erect. Hurdles have been used throughout history and are still in use today, though their purpose – to form a temporary enclosure for stock – has largely been usurped by the considerably less elegant electric fence. Nowadays they are employed as much for their rustic charm as their utility, but there is still a strong tradition of hurdle making in Britain and no county show is complete without at least a hurdle-maker or two showing off their skills and their wares. The most usual form seen at such shows is the woven hurdle, but there is another form which looks rather like a farm gate. This latter type was advertised in the *Rochdale Chronicle* of 1861 at two shillings and ninepence a hurdle:

> These FLAKES or HURDLES are some of the best in this Country, are very
> strong, eight feet long, four feet seven inches high, and iron clipped [bound]
> and are all made of CLEFT [split or riven] ENGLISH OAK. They are
> particularly adapted for Fencing out FIELDS, ROADS, &c., and are easily
> put down and taken up, and will endure many years.[2]

A conspicuous line of such hurdles, enclosing a pasture of grazing
cattle, can be seen in the foreground of John Constable's painting
Wivenhoe Park (1816). At first glance the barrier looks like an ordinary
fence made of hefty riven timbers, but in fact it is clearly made up of
sections which would have been constructed away from the site and
fixed in place by driving the sharpened spikes of the end posts into
the ground and then tying them together with ropes. Some hurdles
had metal fittings at each end so that they could be fixed together
and the spikes may be iron-clad. A contemporaneous drawing of
both the woven and the gate-like types of hurdle can be seen in R. W.
Dickson's *Practical Agriculture; or, A Complete System of Modern Husbandry* (1805).

Much more familiar are those hurdles constructed from
coppiced or pollarded timber. Typically these are made from hazel
on a seven-year rotation, though almost any wood can be used, and
advertisements for hurdles of chestnut, willow and other timbers
can be found. Willow hurdles are particularly attractive.

Coppices or copses (the terms are effectively synonymous) are
found almost everywhere in Britain and are the remnants of an agricultural resource that has outlived its practical use. Few copses are
coppiced nowadays, and dense forests of massive, untended hazel
stools, as much as six feet in diameter and consisting of hundreds
of individual stems, can often be found. On the land once owned by
my former landlord, Snowy Eyre, there are two contiguous copses;
one called Maiden Newton Copse and the other Parson's Copse. The
former was, probably, a resource in common for the parish; the
latter, an income for the church. It is now a magical place of bluebells
and enormous hazel coppices which have not been cut in living
memory. However, a few active copses serve the needs of hurdle
makers and also those of some hedge-layers, who use them in the
stakes and etherings (see p. 296) of certain hedge styles.

Detail of *Wivenhoe Park*, by John Constable.

Hazel does not improve with keeping, so hurdles are, or were, made in the copse itself from timber cut that day. Pliability is an essential characteristic of anything that needs to be woven and hazel is at its most pliable when freshly cut. Winter and early spring is the only time when hurdle making is practical as hazel is too sappy at other times. Hurdles can be made in the summer and autumn, but they often warp or split and are less resistant to rot. A hurdle maker will clear-fell an area and sort the hazel into a variety of grades, only some of which are used in hurdle making.

The vertical components of a hurdle are round sections of hazel up to two inches in diameter and known, for reasons that are obscure, as sails. Two of these (those at the ends) are longer and sharpened to a point. Ten sails are used to make a hurdle and they are arranged into ten holes drilled into a substantial, curved piece of timber called a mould – pointy sticks pointing upwards.

Most of the horizontals are riven (split) lengths of hazel of smaller section (about one inch). Thinner lengths are used which are not split. These must be thin enough to be woven without splitting and are used to form two or three twisted runs (a paired spur) at the top and at the bottom of the hurdle. It is with these, of course, that the weaving starts and finishes. Between these two layers, the bulk of the weave consists of split hazel woven in and out between the uprights and twisted and

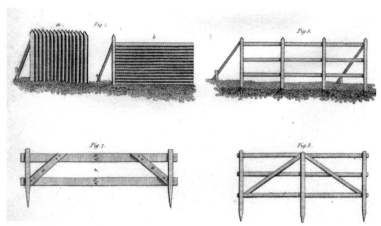

Dickson's drawings of hurdles.

wrapped around the end poles. The half twist that occurs at each end pole is not an artistic flourish but made to prevent the hazel from breaking during its 180 degree turn. As so often in these crafts, the devil is in the details – such as what should happen to the ends and on which side the bark should be displayed. Inevitably, local traditions use different methods and those fine people who still make hurdles no doubt meet once a year in a pub to argue over what works best.

One intriguing use of hurdles is the annual ceremony of the Penny Hedge, also known as the Horngarth, in the upper harbour at Whitby, on the bank of the River Esk. The historical reasons suggested for this custom are all rather implausible, but what is of interest to the student of hedges is that both custom and design go back to the twelfth century and thus an ephemeral item of ancient agricultural utility has been preserved. The Penny Hedge is a hurdle-cum-dead-hedge, erected to very precise instructions: nine hazel stakes are driven into the mud with the use of a mallet of some antiquity; nine 'yethers' (slender branches) are woven through the uprights at the top and some brushwood woven at the bottom. The whole structure is encouraged to remain upright by braces at each end.[3] As hedges go – even dead hedges – it is a most unimposing construction, but it is designed to, and invariably succeeds in, withstanding three tides, which is a little over a day and a half.

Chapter 23

'DEAD' HEDGES AND LIVE ONES

Despite their relative simplicity, it is unlikely that hurdles were the first fences ever built. Stone walls were among the earliest boundaries as they were often a natural result of clearing the land. However, the first true fence was probably a dead hedge, a barrier made from dead wood (and not a live hedge that has died). Assarting was an essential first step in agriculture, and if you have cleared an area of land you will be in possession of a vast quantity of timber of different sizes. Much would have been burnt and much used as building material, but the brash, the small branches trimmed from larger trees or just immature trees, could be piled up along the edge of a clearing to form a rough and ready, but nevertheless effective, stock-proof fence. Perhaps there was even a level of sophistication, with the forest edge trees used as supporting uprights, against which all the brash was piled.

It is impossible to believe that such a simple and obvious structure was not used in prehistoric farming, but is there any physical evidence that they were? Not far from the Fengate excavations (see p. 29) at Must Farm near Whittlesey, a distinct dead hedge was revealed, 70 metres long with a row of coppiced stakes, which has been dated to the early Bronze Age (2200–1950 BCE). Preserved in the anoxic wet clay, it is one of many remarkable finds at the site. The dead hedges at this site were used to enclose several small paddocks.[1]

As well as forming semi-permanent fences, dead hedges have been used to protect new hedges from the depredations of cattle and sheep. Here is William Ellis, writing in Volume I of his *The Modern Husbandman* of 1744:

> For the better securing the Safety of new-made Hedges against Cattle, there is generally a Covenant inserted, in almost all Chilturn Leases, for defending them with a Dead-hedge, or Rails, &c. The Dead-hedge is made by driving down Stakes of four Feet and a Half long, about four or six Inches into the Earth, at two Feet asunder, and then by weaving in long Thorn, Bush, Hasle, Sallow, Ash, Maple, or other Hedge-wood, it will last two Years, and then may be made into Faggots, for Burning.[2]

Dead hedges are still occasionally made today, but with posts hammered into the ground in two rows, forming a two- or three-foot gap. The brash is laid between the posts and a substantial and

A dead hedge in Hertfordshire built to protect a hawthorn coppice from goats.

surprisingly neat fence is produced very quickly indeed. It can be made neater still by first weaving any supple lengths of timber through the post before filling the centre with brash. In time, the brash will settle and rot, and eventually the height of the hedge will sink. This is easily remedied by simply topping it up with more brash and any rotten posts replaced. It is surprising that they are not more popular today. In fact, dead hedges have enjoyed a minor renaissance because, as well as being simple to make and maintain, they are both effective as fences, extremely attractive to wildlife and effectively carbon-negative (they act as carbon sinks, albeit a temporary one).

If assarting was carried out on a field-by-field basis (rather than clearing a vast area and dividing it up later), then the narrow strips of woodland that were left between the fields could form the basis of a hedge. Much has been made of this by many authorities who cite the species-rich, woodland aspect of many ancient hedges. These, it is argued, are simply narrow strips of primal forest. Quite how this would work depends on the woodland that is cleared. If it is not primal forest but instead relatively young regrowth following a long period of neglect, then the slender trees remaining on the border strips may immediately provide the raw material for a laid hedge (see p. 288).

Primal woodland is quite different, consisting of mature trees, fallen trees, a few that are young and a great deal of open space occupied by grass, moss, ferns and herbaceous plants. A two- or three-metre strip, left after the clear-felling and shallow ploughing of the woodland floor either side, would consist of a few mature and immature trees and substantial lengths of bare or mossy soil. This is likely to have acted just like a forest clearing, with seedlings able to make a bid for freedom in the open light. Indeed, in some forests mature trees are surrounded by half-starved neighbours of varying maturity, biding their time waiting for their elders to drop down dead and give them some light. Thus it may be that a relatively barren looking strip will burst into life and produce enough growth to provide trees suitable for a hedge, perhaps aided by a little judicious planting.

Chapter 24

THE LAID HEDGE (1): GENERAL FEATURES

The use, or not, of laid hedges before Saxon times is still contentious, but it is difficult to believe that the banks that surround so many ancient field systems (such as that at Valley of Stones in Dorset) were not hedged. That live hedges have been laid since ancient times seems certain and there are a few hints in the archaeological and historical record of their existence. We have seen the suggestion of a Bronze Age hedge at Fengate, found as a remnant of two pieces of bent blackthorn (see p. 35). Also encouraging is the earliest documentary record of a laid hedge. It comes from the pen of Julius Caesar who writes in *The Gallic War* (c.58 BCE) of a defensive strategy of the Belgae:

> To hamper the cavalry of their neighbours, whenever these made a raid on them, they cut into young saplings and bent them over, and thus by the thick horizontal growth of boughs, and by intertwining with them brambles and thorns, they contrived that these wall-like hedges should serve them as fortifications which not only could not be penetrated, but not even seen through.[1]

Two obvious problems exist for any attempt to offer this as support-ive evidence. First, it is in Belgium not Britain. However, Iron Age technology was common to all of northern Europe so there is no reason why the British should not have known about this technique. Second, it was a device of warfare, not agriculture. But it does dem-onstrate that the laying of hedges was a known practice at the time and there is no reason to suppose that so useful a technique would not have been employed in a more peaceful context.

Finding one or two hedges in one or two locations does not prove that they were used extensively, only that they were used at that time. But it is not too great a leap of faith to assume that the use of hedges was fairly widespread. Furthermore, if a laid hedge about the farm was thought to be useful 4,500 years ago, and such hedges are still in use today, it is reasonable to assume that they also existed in the intervening centuries. It seems entirely plausible to me that laid hedges have been the main form of hedge over a long period, as it is both an obvious technique to use and the only workable and effective method of managing a hedge. It is true that most modern hedges dispense with laying, relying instead on the mechanical flail to control them, but few such hedges are stock-proof without the addition of a wire fence.

Hedge laying, we must therefore conclude, is an ancient practice; one that is used today in many forms and at differing levels of sophis-tication. The principle, if not the detail and the practice, is simple. I have spent a total of three days laying hedges, under the direction of people who actually knew what they were doing, and I enjoyed the single-minded tranquillity of it. However, having laid hedges for those back-breaking three days, I feel no need to do so ever again, as it is far too much like hard work. What follows is an outline of the basic method of planting and laying a hedge:

A row (or two rows) of saplings, called whips, is planted and is usually protected from animal damage by temporary fencing, possibly using a dead hedge (see above). In many places, particu-larly pastoral areas and where drainage is a pressing issue, a ditch will be dug and the hedge planted on the resultant bank. Planting is generally done in two rows, the whips staggered and allowed to grow for about ten years. The stems are then trimmed a little, and are chopped or sawn on a shallow diagonal, just above soil level, leaving a thin and fairly bendy strip of live wood attaching the small tree to the base of the stem. The trees are then laid almost horizontally and held in place by pinning them down with crooks of wood or woven around stakes. Such a hedge laid in the winter will produce a mass of new side shoots by the spring. These become denser and denser as the years go by and will need to be trimmed to a sensible height to form a neat, stock-proof hedge. New growth from any trees that had been cut to just above ground level (because they were not needed for laying) will also shoot up, increasing the density of the hedge.

A laid hedge will remain stock-proof for decades, though only if it is occasionally trimmed and repaired. Eventually, it will become gappy and leggy, and some of the stems will become trunks. At this point the hedge is laid again, but from well-established and much denser stock. The hedge therefore goes through a cycle, though it is one of indeterminate length – you fix a hedge only when it is broken, not to a timetable.

The earliest description of hedge planting and tending is that of

A half-laid Devon hedge complete with ditch.

Sir Anthony Fitzherbert (see p. 70). Writing in 1534, he makes his enthusiasm for hedges clear enough, as long as you take a moment to decipher his pre-Shakespearean English: 'If a housbande shall kepe cattell well to his profytte, he muste have severall closes and pastures to put his cattell in, the which wolde be wel quickesetted, diched, and hedged, that he maye sever the byggeste cattell frome the weykeste at his pleasure, and specyallye in wynter tyme, whan they shall be fodered.'[2]

Fitzherbert's *Boke of Husbandry* is a practical tome, so he goes into laborious detail on the methods of setting and laying a hedge. On the choice of tree for the hedge he suggests, 'whyte thorn and crabtree', and maybe 'holye and hasell' for the 'woode countreye', and 'ashe, oke, and elme' for the 'playne countreye'. It is possible that his references are to the woodland areas and the open-field areas respectively, but perhaps his differentiation is merely topographical. Fitzherbert held a particular dislike for blackthorn, imploring his readers: 'But get no blacke thorne for nothynge, for that wyl grow outward into the pasture, and doth moch hurte in the grasse, and tearing the woll of the shepe.'[3]

Whichever tree he recommends, they were almost certainly planted as 18 inch (or more) whips, which were uprooted from scrub and woodland, and not nursery-grown plants. His advice on when to plant a hedge is exactly that which would be given today – from early November to early April, though he puts it less prosaically: 'fro the tyme the leaves be fallen, unto oure lady daye in lente'.

He is a little unclear on the matter of ditches, and one can only assume that his hedges were set on grassy banks which had been previously raised during 'diching'. There is mention, at one point, of a wide (five foot) ditch which would 'fence it selfe' and that the 'lower hedge will serve'. It is impossible to know what he is talking about here, and it may be that Fitzherbert wasn't altogether sure either. It is worth mentioning that he and many other writers on agricultural practice of the sixteenth to the early nineteenth centuries were not necessarily working farmers in the sense that they got their hands dirty. They may have owned land and overseen farms, but it is doubtful if many of them ever ploughed a field or laid a hedge.

Some of what they tell us no doubt comes from observing workers in the field and perhaps talking to them about what they did, but some is likely to be well-intentioned advice based on armchair invention. Certainly, a few of their more outlandish designs for hedging were either reportage of something that has long been discontinued, or was never practicable in the first instance.

Fitzherbert is considerably more coherent and helpful about hedge laying or, as he entitles this section of his book, 'To plasshe or pleche a Hedge'. The two words (in their modern spelling of plash and pleach) are synonymous and mean the bending of a partially cut-through stem which is then laid to form a hedge; the bent stem itself being called a pleacher or plash. Here's how Fitzherbert puts it: 'If the hedge be of x or xii years growing sythe it was first set, thane take a sharpe hatchet, or a handbyll, and cutte the settes in a playne place, nyghe unto the erthe, the more halve a sonder, and bende it down towards the erthe, and wrappe and wynde theym together.'[4]

This is a perfect description of the first stage of laying a hedge in several of the styles that are still seen today at county shows and hedge-laying competitions, as well as in the field. He does miss out all the messy tidying up of the extraneous growth that would have accumulated in those ten to twelve years since the hedge was planted, but, to be fair, there should not be too much of it in so young a hedge. Partially chopping through the young trees just above the ground, bending them, laying them down and fixing them in place, pretty well sums up hedge laying. There is considerably more detail, the most notable of which is that he tells the hedge-layer to leave single stems standing every two or three feet and to cut them to a height of four feet. These act as living posts, around which the pleachers are woven, something that is still found today. Here, in essence, we have a very early record of a hedge-laying style. It is simple and practical and there is little doubt that it existed long before Fitzherbert recorded it. In fact, this style, where living trees act as posts, still persists in Wales and is also used in France and Germany.

R. W. Dickson's *Practical Agriculture; or, A Complete System of Modern Husbandry* was published in 1805. His views on hedges and fences are

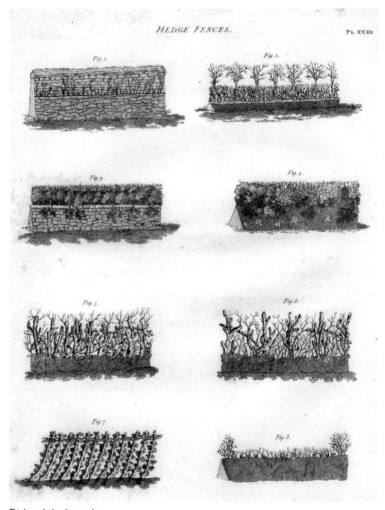

Dickson's hedge styles.

fascinating, and the book boasts some fine illustrations, one of which is shown here. Dickson writes a great deal about planting hedges and caring for them by trimming, though he is more eloquent on the methods that should be avoided at all costs than he is on those that the farmer should pursue – which amount to little more than what the average gardener does in trimming his roses (Figures 5 and 6). His most surprising revelation is that he distinguishes plashing from laying. Plashing, for him, is where the stems are 'nicked a little', bent over slightly, and fixed by ethering (Figure 7), and laying is where the stems are laid horizontally. This merely reflects the Midland style and the Devon-Somerset respectively (see below), but it is interesting to see the terms differentiated, and he goes on to say that laying is reserved for young hedges. Figure 3 appears to be a version of a Cornish hedge, while Figure 8 shows a simple, if undernourished, hedgerow on a bank, and Figure 1 appears to be a bizarre and impractical arrangement in which a turf-topped wall has a hedge growing from it half-way up.

The neat hedges proposed by Dickson suggest a past when rustics spent much of their time fussing over them as though they were about to be entered into a national competition. In fact, attending to hedges would have been a very long way down the to-do list of the farmer or farm labourer. It may have been a relatively inexpensive process during a period when labour was cheap, but not so low in cost as to be thought of as trivial. More than that, it was – and still is – the amount of time it takes to lay or tend a hedge that was the problem. In *The Whole Art of Husbandry* (1708) John Mortimer estimates how long it should take: 'A man may ditch and quick-set three poles or more in a day, where the ditch is three foot wide, and two foot deep. A man may make a hedge five foot high, bind it well, and lay it thick, and do two pole in a day; if lower he may do double.'[5] He then goes on to suggest what the cost might be: 'To make a hedge and lay the quick is three-pence a pole. To make a hedge and cleanse a ditch, the common way is five-pence a pole; but if he plash it well, and cleanse the ditch two spit deep, and sets it with quick where any is wanting, 'tis worth from six-pence to eight-pence a pole.'[6] A pole is only five and a half yards so a square, ten-acre field (which has a circumference of half a mile) would, at two poles a day, take forty days and cost anything from £1 to £3. Bear in mind, though, that fields share hedges, so the cost on a large farm would be nearly halved.

My low estimate of farmers' enthusiasm for hedge laying and tending is based on knowing farmers who are just too busy with other things – making sure a new calf is being cared for by its mother or worrying about a TB test on their herd – to be overly

CLOSE OF THE HUNTING SEASON : MENDING THE GAPS.—DRAWN BY JOHN LEECH.—(SEE PAGE 344.)

Mending the Gaps, by John Leech.

concerned with hedges. There is also the evidence provided by artists during the enclosure period. For every romantic cameo of farm labourers tending a hedge, such as the one illustrated here, there are many more drawings, paintings and prints in which hedges are incidental. One outstanding example is Turner's superbly observed *Frosty Morning* (1813), which accurately portrays the experience of the farm labourer and the state of the average hedge – untidy, with some scrawny looking standards. The workers, incidentally, appear to be engaged in ditching.

If you want to know what a hedge looked like in the eighteenth or nineteenth century, there is no better place to look than in a representation of a fox hunt. I have viewed scores of these and can say with authority that few hedges are neatly trimmed and none that I have seen depict the hedges as being recently laid or plashed. The ideal for many areas was to keep the (usually hawthorn) hedge to a remarkably low height of four or five feet, a minimum of four foot wide at the base and more or less triangular in section. The planting regime was typically two rows, twelve inches apart and staggered

Pollarded trees can be clearly seen in this representation of the hunt.

with eighteen inches between them. They were pruned severely after a year, and laid after ten.

Rural art also reveals some of the details of old hedges and even hedge-laying practices. The fox hunting scene shows a hedgerow with some fairly neat hedges, set with pollarded trees. The latter are interesting because most hedgerow trees were indeed pollarded as the timber formed by the new growth could not be damaged by stock and grew reasonably straight. A pollarded tree is effectively a 'wooden post factory', with the added benefit of delivering its wares to the point of use – in hedges. They were also a resource for plain fencing and fuel.

Anyone attending a hedge-laying competition will encounter a large number of enthusiasts, copious quantities of beer and cider and a bewildering number of hedge styles. The main styles are Midland, South of England, Lancashire and Westmorland, Derbyshire, Yorkshire, Welsh, and Devon and Somerset. Having said that, every county seems to have its own, and indeed around thirty styles may be identified by anyone who cares enough to look closely. No matter how many styles there are, there are really only three basic types: 'barrier',

A 'crook' holding down the pleachers.

'stake and pleach' and 'crop and pleach'. The first is found in Devon, Somerset and Dorset and is the simplest; in fact, being the simplest, it can be found almost anywhere in one form or another. The pleachers are bent over and held in place by crooks – small branches, driven into the ground, with a short piece of branch sticking out at an angle to form a hook. In the second type, the pleachers are woven around stakes, and in the third they are woven around a living stem (as in Fitzherbert's hedge).

Stylistic details include such things as the use (or not) of 'ethering', where the hedge is finished off with thin hazel twisted into a rope at the top of the stakes; whether or not the pleachers all lie in the same direction; and the existence of sawn timber in a laid hedge to form a hybrid hedge-fence. There are so many variations that there really is no end to the styles one could differentiate. Some hedge-layers have begun to take their craft a little too seriously with talk of standardisation, as if there should be an EU directive governing a pursuit that is no one's business other than the hedge-layer and his employer.

Quite why different styles developed is lost in history, but three factors dominate: the material available to the hedger, the purpose for which the hedge is being made and tradition. Generally speaking, most hedgers will have little problem in obtaining any species of hedge tree they wish for, but if a large quantity of cheap sawn timber is available to make the stakes, there is no reason why they should not make use of it. Much more relevant is what the hedge is to be used for. A hedge acting as little more than a marker between two arable fields need not be high, thick or strong – it just has to be there. One that is used to keep bullocks, however, will need to be substantial and stock-proof. One that is required to keep two bulls apart must be tank-proof.

Chapter 25

THE LAID HEDGE (2): DEVON AND SOMERSET STYLE

I have, inexpertly, laid two styles of hedge, so I shall describe these first and in detail. They are the Devon and Somerset style and the Midland style, and they encompass the main techniques used in hedge laying. The hedge I helped lay in Devon, under the gentle and patient tuition of George, consisted of a double row of trees (a 'double comb', in the trade), most of which were around two or three inches in diameter, set on a relatively low bank and with a ditch to one side. I arrived first and claimed the row of trees on the side opposite to the ditch – why make things hard for yourself?

That there were two rows of trees was not immediately obvious, the hedge was just a mess of tangled young trees, slightly older trees and ivy. The first thing that needed to be tackled was to remedy this by removing ivy and bramble. Also for the chop were over-size trees that could not be laid and were not worth keeping as standards, any trees that had decided to plant themselves next to the hedge, and overhanging branches which were likely to get in the way. Dense clusters of stems were thinned. Ideally, all that should be left is a row (two rows for the complete hedge) of trees spaced a foot or two apart which can easily be laid. In fact, we were left with a row of

A double hedge, the right-hand side laid by the author, with help.

contenders for the honour of being part of the hedge, the decision on which to keep and which to dispense with being left for later. This decision nearly always turned out to be an agonising one and was the most difficult part of the hedge-laying experience.

The process now was simple. A likely looking stem was cut with a billhook, near to the ground, with one – or, in my case, a series of – diagonal cuts which left a sometimes perilously thin piece of wood and bark connecting the roots to the rest of the tree. In fact, George took pity on me in the end and allowed me to use a saw. As the stem is cut, it is gently bent over in the direction of the lay to make cutting easier. Once the cut has gone sufficiently far to allow the stem to flex, an axe is forced into the cut in order to split the base of the stem downwards. This leaves a longer piece of thin stem which bends easily without breaking – or it does most of the time. One thing to watch out for is 'pleating' where the bark peels away from the wood. This will kill the tree in short order, though it is difficult to know how to avoid it. The next stem is selected and laid on top of the last one and perhaps woven in with it. The bits left sticking up from the cut stem base are cut off with a saw or billhook. Any stems that don't make the grade are cut out completely.

The laid stems are now pleachers, except that in Devon they are

A laid pleacher, showing the cut. The spur will be cut short and levelled with a saw.

called steepers and the process of laying is called steeping; and in Dorset they are called pleachers too, but sometimes laying a pleacher is called plushing. Anyway, they tend to spring up a bit and are held in place, where needed, by crooks – forked branches, cut into the shape of a hook and hammered into the ground.

Parts of the same hedge, photographed a year apart, showing the rapid growth of side shoots from hazel.

I was assured by George that the hedge was stock-proof – on the ditch side at least, though it was more treacherous to cross than impassable. But such a hedge bursts into life almost immediately (it was early March) and discourages both escapees and intruders within a year.

Quite frankly, any fool in possession of a billhook, saw, mallet and axe can lay a perfectly functional hedge, though it is unlikely to win any rosettes. Winning awards is of little interest if utility is the only aim, but where the amateur falls down is speed. It took me the best part of a day to complete barely ten metres and that was only one half of the hedge – and I had help. I estimate that I was working at a quarter of the speed of a professional. It was also very hard work. An experienced hedger, using only hand tools, can complete twenty metres in a day, or to put it more authentically, one chain.

George did give me a few bits of hedge-laying lore, such as always lay the pleachers uphill if the hedge is on a slope. If it is on flat or flattish ground alongside a road, then it should be laid in the direction of the traffic, presumably to prevent people and horses being horribly impaled should a pleacher wrest itself free. If other considerations allow, then a hedge should be laid towards the rising sun – or was it the setting sun?

The Devon hedge deserves a little more attention beyond a description of how it is, or can be, laid. A true Devon hedge (not the Devon style of laying, which is a separate matter) has a bank. In the past, a Devon hedge was considered to be a bank; now it is the combination of bank and the vegetation atop it that qualifies as a hedge. It is not, however, any old bank thrown up during the digging of a ditch, but a faced bank. The commonest facing is turf, but stone too is used in some places in Devon (see the Chapter 27 on the Cornish hedge).

Devon hedges are remarkable structures and the building of one something of an art.

The turfs are not of the type one finds in the garden centre to repair patches in the lawn. About 300 mm long, 100 mm wide and a very substantial 200 mm thick, they are more like grass bricks, and it is as bricks that they are used. A shallow foundation, typically 1,850 mm wide, is cut in the soil and two rows of turfs are laid along the inside, green side out. The gap in the middle is filled with soil which should have a high clay component to make it structurally sound. This is usually taken from alongside the new hedge bank, its removal eventually forming a ditch. The process is repeated until a height of 1,200 mm is reached, each row of turf being set back a little from the previous row and aligned to create a brickwork effect. The width at the top should be 900 mm. To prevent the entire edifice collapsing, the outside surface thus formed is made slightly concave. Herein lies the artistry and craft. The whole structure is topped with soil and, after a respectful interval to allow for settling, trees are planted along the top.

Building a Devon hedge is extremely labour intensive, not least the cutting of the enormously thick turf. A rather clever alternative has been devised in which the turf is replaced with hessian sacks filled with earth and grass seeds. Sometimes the seeds are omitted and the whole construction is sprayed with seeds and mud – something which sounds like great fun.

Chapter 26

THE LAID HEDGE (3): THE MIDLAND STYLE

My next bit of hedge took two days to lay. I went to Chipping Norton to tackle a young hedge in a rather unprepossessing location that had never been laid before. It was a single row (though the whips had been planted in a zigzag pattern with eight inches between neighbours) and had no bank or ditch. This proto-hedge consisted of a random selection of ten-year-old trees that clearly had aspirations to become a wood. The main culprit was the blackthorn which, true to its reputation, had thrown up hundreds of suckers some distance from the line of the hedge.

The hedge I was tasked with laying (this time under the tutelage of John) was a Midland hedge, a completely different style to the one in Devon. This type of hedge is a strange thing indeed, which, once completed, looks like a neat fence on one side and an untidy bush on the other.

The cutting of the pleachers is just the same – except that no saw is permitted and the correct pronunciation of billhook is billuk – but instead of being laid on top of one another in a linear heap, the pleachers are woven around and tucked behind a series of stakes set in the ground every 18 inches, as you work your way along the

Laying a Midland hedge.

A Midland hedge, the foreground part of which was wrought by the hand of the author.

hedge. The weaving around and tucking behind is what gives the Midland hedge its striking fence one side, bush the other, character. But there is also a final flourish of neatness and artistry in the way a Midland hedge is finished – the hedge is 'ethered'. This looks impossible to do until you are shown how. Long, thin lengths of hazel are twisted around the top of the stakes that hold the pleachers to form a rope-like finish. In fact, there is no twisting to be done, you simply hold a small bundle of two or three hazel lengths with one hand and wind another bundle over it and behind the stakes. Extra lengths are added as you go to create a continuous 'rope'. The etherings and pleachers are then leant on to press them down, or encouraged downwards with a mallet, until the top is straight and of the correct height of about a metre. The stakes are cut to an even height, odd bits of twig are cut off or tucked away and the hedge is complete.

Unlike the Devon hedge, it was obvious that once completed this hedge was immediately stock-proof, and from both sides. However, the fence side would traditionally be for arable, while the side with thousands of twigs sticking out was for pastoral. These two aspects of a Midland hedge are known as 'plough side' and 'bush side'. Both sides would leaf-up fairly quickly at which point the distinction becomes moot, but for a newly laid hedge the fence aspect provides more room for the plough, while being less protected from the cattle rubbing and grazing.

The hedge I worked on in Somerset and the one in Oxfordshire were, respectively, 'barrier' and 'stake and pleach', fundamental arrangements on which endless variations are wrought, though there are more possibilities for invention in the latter. The only notable variation on the Devon and Somerset style is in the method of holding the pleachers in place. Around my way, in Dorset, they seem to use anything that comes to hand such as lengths of hazel looped over the pleachers or, at a pinch, that ultimate agricultural standby, baler twine.

Variations on the theme of the Midland style abound: the Southern style is 'bushy' both sides, because the pleachers are woven so that half of them project on one side, half on the other. Presumably this was designed to serve a largely pastoral landscape. In the south-east of England, the ethering is woven as a basket weave, rather than a rope weave; in Lancashire, the stakes are driven in on either side of the pleachers and placed alternately; the Yorkshire style replaces both stakes and ethering with sawn timber, and the brush is dispensed with altogether, giving a very bare and fence-like appearance to a newly laid hedge.

The two major classes described, exemplify the distinction between the boundaries of wooded country and those of the much later inclosure. The barrier hedge is better suited to the leafy, pastoral countryside of Devon, Somerset and Dorset.

I learned one more thing in my time with George and John – how much difference there is between tree species when it is time to lay them. The Devon hedge was almost entirely of ash, and laid easily. Ash is a very flexible wood, even when dried and sawn, but much more so when the wood is still live. The Midland hedge seems to have been planted as a stern lesson to would-be hedgers on the pitfalls and perils of planting the wrong tree. The blackthorn and hawthorn could be laid with ease, as could the sole apple tree. Less pliable to my will was dogwood – a common tree of the hedgerow, despite its problems. The second worst was guelder rose, which was almost impossible to lay as it often snapped off before it could be properly laid. The worst by far (and this will come as no surprise to anyone who has attempted to reach the flowers or berries by pulling a branch towards them) was the elder which would shatter at the slightest push.

My two experiences of hedge laying took place in the early spring. This, of course, is because trees will tolerate being laid much more readily while they are dormant. Towards the end of October to the beginning of March is the period during which laying is normally done, though Owen from up the road extends the season for a couple of weeks more by tackling the hedges on top of the hills last. These are dormant longer as they leaf-up later in the slightly cooler climate.

Chapter 27

THE CORNISH HEDGE AND THE CLAWDD

Devon hedges are sometimes faced with stone, but it is really Cornwall that is famous for its stone-faced hedges. A Cornishman once told me that such hedges of Devonish provenance were degenerate affairs and poor things indeed. However, in greener north Cornwall there are turf-faced hedges and no doubt these are viewed with a derisive eye by hedgers in Devon. As a teenager on a touring holiday near Fowey, I was puzzled by the dangerously narrow country roads which seemed to have been cut out of bedrock. Why would anyone bother to dig out mile upon mile of rock to make a road when there was clearly not the slightest need to do so? But, of course, I had been driven (in a fog of ignorance) between stone hedges and not along a gully. In fact, the stone of the Cornish hedges is often hidden by the vegetation that it supports. Perhaps the plants had threatened to narrow the roads out of existence and had been cut back by the council. To see them in their naked glory one must either be lucky or travel to West Penwith, at the tip of Cornwall, where few hedges support much vegetation.

As with the turf bank of the Devon hedge, it is the stone-faced bank of the Cornish equivalent that is considered to be the hedge,

A lightly vegetated Cornish hedge in West Penwith.

not what grows on top of it. Should anyone refer to them as walls in Cornwall, the error of their ways will be politely but firmly pointed out. Use of the word hedgerow will also mark you down as a know-nothing outsider. To be on the safe side, you should call everything a hedge, even if it is obviously just a stone wall. If you are wrong then at least it will look as though you were making an effort.

Cornish hedges are ancient structures, with some 'walls', dated to the Iron Age, showing signs of having been filled with earth and thus qualifying as Cornish hedges. If properly constructed, they can attain a great age without the necessity of being rebuilt. Cornish hedges seem to belong in the landscape; they seem to be landscape. Unfortunately, some are now being built without the benefit of what has been learned over the centuries and have been known to collapse within six months.

Cornish hedges are constructed in much the same way as the turf bank hedges of Devon, but there is considerable variation in the laying of the stonework. Although I must have passed many more that were concealed beneath vegetation, I found three styles in as many hours on a drive round Cornwall, and they were all quite beautiful. As with stone walls, it is the availability of materials, tradition and the personal quirks of the craftsman that dictate the design details of a Cornish hedge. One was constructed out of large, rectangular stones, laid like a vertical cobblestone road, another from thin, sedimentary rocks, horizontally laid and capped with a herringbone flourish (Jack and Jill style, as it is known). The third, which I fancy to be quite rare, was made of very thin stones oriented vertically. Cornish hedges are made, among other things, from granite, shale, quartz from mining operations and slate.

The dimensions of a Cornish hedge are similar to those of their Devon counterparts. The width at the base should be around 1,500 mm, the width at the top about 750 mm and the height 1,500 mm. Such a wall will support small plants and hawthorn, though not generally a standard tree. If standard trees are to be planted, then the width of base and top is increased by one metre. There is both artistry and science in the building of these walls. The sides are not straight slopes, but curve upwards, first gently, then more steeply,

Four of the many styles of Cornish hedge, the last being a new build.

until they are vertical, or even leaning slightly outwards, near the top. Anyone with an eye for such things can see that it is the perfect curve required for stability. A straight-sided facing would bulge out from the weight of soil pressing down from above. So important is this curve that hedgers use carefully crafted forms to ensure consistency and the curve even has a name – the batter.

Hedges are laid on subsoil, which in Cornwall is usually reached by digging a trench of six or eight inches. Fairly massive stones, called grounders, are laid and made level with 'fillers', thus providing a flat surface on which the next row of stones can be neatly laid. As each row is added, the hedge is filled with soil that is packed down very firmly. There must be no organic matter in the soil as this will rot and partially hollow out the hedge. The soils used have suitably rural sounding names: rab, growan and shillet (rab, I am told, being the best). All stones should be laid with a short edge facing outwards. This uses a great deal more stone than having a long edge facing outwards but makes for a much stronger hedge. Despite this, there are no through stones (single stones running from front to back) as are often found in dry stone walls. Some Cornish hedges, especially near gateways, incorporate stones of enormous size which require the services of a digger or tripod frame to move into position. It is a tribute to the skill of the hedgers that these monster rocks are invariably incorporated so neatly.

Doomed to make way for a much-needed widening of the A30 on Bodmin Moor, this Cornish hedge reveals its shape and structure.

The top row is usually, though by no means always, vertical, regardless of the orientation of the stones in the rest of the hedge. Vertical stones are more stable and bind well with the grass and plants that will soon grow there. The hedge is finished by mounding up soil on the top and, above this, pegging down two rows of 'tobs', one on each side of the top of the hedge. A tob is a six inch thick turf that has been saved from the original clearance of the site. This ensures that the plants growing on the hedge will be local. It is pegged with bits of twig and branch. The gaps between the tobs are filled with soil and that, for the moment, is the hedge complete.

Planting with thorns is best done in the early autumn when the hedge can look forward to several months of rain and has a chance to settle. Cornish hedgers are commendably fussy about what they plant on their hedges, insisting on only local stocks of hawthorn and blackthorn, and western gorse (*Ulex gallii*), rather than the much more common European gorse (*U. europaeus*). While thorns and other plants are often planted intentionally on top of Cornish hedges, some hedges are left entirely to their own devices to grow what they will. Soon the entire hedge becomes covered in plants – the reason that they are so prized as wildlife habitats. Once any trees have grown to a reasonable size, they (and any side vegetation) are, ideally, trimmed back at a sensible time of year by hand or with a gentle powered hedge trimmer. Or at least they should be. The Cornish hedge, and more generally the biota that it once supported, has suffered much from the introduction of the mechanical flail. This instrument of convenient destruction is discussed on pp. 335–6.

The Welsh clawdd (which means hedge, dyke or embankment) is similar in construction and size to the Cornish hedge, though many are much shorter at only a metre. These too have a hedge on top, though less frequently than the Cornish hedges. In a leaflet detailing the specifications of a clawdd, the Dry Stone Walling Association of Great Britain insists that they are absolutely not earth filled stone walls (which they clearly are), but stone-clad earth banks (which they clearly are as well). The stones used are igneous or granite boulders which have been nicely rounded by glaciers, the sea or in streams. Almost invariably, the stones are 'pitched', that is, laid vertically and with the narrow edge on show, rather than the long edge, which is set into the bank for stability. The main difference between a clawdd and a Cornish hedge is that the Welsh hedge lacks a curved batter. The sides lean inwards, but are perfectly straight, except on particularly tall walls where an inward curve is all but essential.

Chapter 28

DRY STONE WALLS

Dry stone walls – walls built of stone without the use of mortar – are among the most persistent of archaeological relics and a few truly ancient examples are still in use. Some have survived since Neolithic times, and I suspect that many stone walls that grace Cornwall, Dartmoor and the hills of Wales, northern England and Scotland, saw their birth in prehistory. Stone walls do, of course, fall victim to cattle rubbing, subsidence on soft soil, frost damage and 'freeze and thaw' which can gradually pull them apart. But they are repeatedly rebuilt in the same place from, mostly, the same stones. While there are many ancient stone walls in Britain, typically head-dykes and walls surrounding farmsteads (the latter known as in-bye), most of those we see are of much more recent vintage – the period of parliamentary enclosure. This is clear from the straight lines of walls which march across lower reaches of the Peak District, Northumbria, Cumbria, the lowlands of Scotland and many other places.

Treeless coastal areas, such as those that may have existed in prehistoric Cornwall, required nothing more than the removal of stones from the rocky, grassy hills to provide an area for cultivation. If you remove stones, then you have to put them somewhere. The

Dry stone wall in the Peak District.

two obvious solutions are to heap them up into a pile (a clearance cairn), or to place them, more carefully, around the edge to form a wall. It has been suggested – by a Cumbrian dry stone walling friend – that the original fields were circular, with a diameter twice that of the distance it is possible to throw an average rock. Such walls are known as consumption walls or accretion walls because part of their job is to consume unwanted stones from the field. For those who refer to walls as dykes, as they do in Scotland, consumption dyke is an alternative name.

It is worth pausing briefly at this point to examine the terminology of dry stone walling, if for nothing more than to explain why a dyke – which most people consider to be a drainage ditch – should refer to a wall. A dyke was once understood by the Scots to refer to the ditch which was thrown up whenever a wall and ditch was to be constructed, but by the sixteenth century dyke had become synonymous with the wall thus created. To make matters slightly more complicated, the Scots have never settled on a single spelling, so it may be rendered 'dek', 'deak', 'deik', 'dick', 'dike' and a dozen or so more. Of course, a dyke is any old wall as far as the Scots are concerned, so a dry stone wall is referred to as a 'drystane dyke'.

Nick Aitken, one of a body of people for whom dry stone walls are the stuff of life, has compiled a remarkable (and, sadly, unpublished) glossary of dry stone walling terms. A rough count found over 800 definitions, from 'A-frame' (a wooden frame, propped up vertically, which acts as a guide to the shape of the wall being built) through 'garsty' (stone wall, usually collapsed and covered in grass) and 'jingle' (Galloway name for 'shingle') to 'yawnie' (a stone too big to lift). You will be pleased to know that the remaining 796 definitions will only be described if and when required.

Thousands of miles of dry stone walls still exist, largely because while it is easy enough to grub out a hedge, it is a major operation to remove a wall. They are still the agricultural boundary of choice in the uplands of Britain, but are by no means restricted to such areas. If stone is easily come by without the effort of moving it great distances, then stone walls will appear. The low hills of Purbeck in Dorset and the gentle rolling plains of West Lothian and Fife, all sport stone walls because stone is all around for the taking. One wonders if hedges would have become so pervasive in Britain if stone had been available everywhere. Stone walls are permanent and, if built properly, low maintenance – you never have to trim a low wall (well, occasionally, if it becomes overgrown with ivy or bramble) and you never have to lay it. Finally, of course, you can erect a stone wall in cold and windswept places that would defeat a hedge.

Like hedges, dry stone walls come in many forms and are similarly determined by the availability of material, the use to which the wall will be put, local traditions and the artistry of individual craftsmen. Unlike hedges, where usage and tradition predominate, it is the material that sets the style of the wall more than any other consideration. A wall made from large, irregular lumps of 'tuff', a consolidated volcanic ash, as found in parts of Scotland, will be completely different from one constructed from neat layers of Dorset limestone.

Very nearly every type of rock can be used to form a wall, though sedimentary rocks are arguably best because they have bedding planes along which they may be split to form flat stones of a convenient thickness. Some sedimentary rocks are so effective in this respect that they need not be laid at all but stood upright to form what can only be called a stone fence. Examples include the Brathay flag walls of Cumbria, found around Ambleside, Coniston, Hawkshead and Langdale, and the remarkable slate fences of Wales, most notably in Snowdonia, where large slates are arranged in a row and tied together at the top with thick wire. Sadly, these stark but attractive wall-fences are fairly rare, and slate walls, where the slates are laid horizontally, are rather more common.

Sandstone too has bedding planes and can be formed fairly easily into rectangular bricks, albeit of random dimensions. These produce neat, attractive walls which would grace any suburban garden, and were, in fact, reserved for estate boundaries where display mattered. Possibly the most common material for dry stone walls is limestone in its many forms. This splits into reasonably flat stones and is relatively light, certainly in comparison to granite.

The Dry Stone Walling Association in Cumbria has a magnificent display of a dozen or so regional styles of wall, all of them built

A slate fence at the Dry Stone Walling Association headquarters in Cumbria.

by the appropriate craftsmen who made the trip to Cumbria, as did the stone they used. Some did not have to travel far as four of the styles came from Cumbria itself. But even this, literally, monumental attempt to characterise the stone walls of Britain fell far short of representing the wealth of invention, artistry and skill of dry stone craftsmen. Missing, for example, was the quirky, sloping pattern of Purbeck, or the fancy walls I once saw in south-eastern Scotland which had two courses made entirely of through stones which projected several inches from the main surface of the wall.

Even several of the extremely varied styles found in Cumbria were missing, for example the 'stone and turf' walls, known as 'kests', which are found near the Cumbrian coast. These consist of alternating layers of large, round cobbles and turf, topped with more turf and often planted up with a hedge, as in Cornwall. Not far away, near Matlock in Derbyshire, is an even more impressive display of dry stone walls. The Millennium Wall Project boasts eighteen examples of wall style, but even so grand a project could not cover all the styles that exist in Britain.

Stone walls are generally classed into 'coursed', where the stones are laid in distinct rows or courses, and 'not coursed', where the

A sandstone wall at the Dry Stone Walling Association headquarters in Cumbria.

The beautiful sloping style used in Dorset. Photograph taken near Worth Matravers.

A Northumbrian wall with two rows of tie stones.

arrangement is more random. A further division is between 'single' and 'double'. Double walls, which are more common, consist of two partially interlocking sides, with any gaps in the middle filled with small stones and the whole thing tied together with through stones (see illustration above). Single walls are made from stones (usually different sized pieces of granite), most of which span the full width of a wall and are not generally laid in courses. They are often untidy looking structures (though still beautiful) as it is difficult to lay them with a neat, flat surface, and most will not be coursed. What follows are a few of the more common possibilities.

The most basic, primitive wall is sometimes called the 'random rubble' and is a single wall which can look like a narrow, linear spoil heap. These are made from large, irregular igneous rocks that cannot be dressed with a hammer and which have to be piled up in as stable a configuration as rock and skill will allow. There are 'vertical' arrangements where (mostly) long thin stones are arranged vertically, often in rows which seem to flow and merge as progressively larger and smaller lengths are used. 'Pinned' walls combine large stones, interspersed with small stones which are used to wedge their larger cousins in place. Some small stones are long and thin, helping

A 'single' or 'random rubble' wall with single stones spanning the entire width of the wall. And a work of art. Dartmoor.

to tie the wall together and form layers on which the larger rocks are placed. There are herringbone pattern walls, walls with distinct courses, walls that look as though they had set out to have distinct courses but lost interest half-way. In most coursed walls the stones become progressively thinner as they reach the top; some single walls are the other way round with the bigger rocks on top. These can be found, for example, in the broad, cattle-farming vales of Lanarkshire and may be designed that way to prevent cattle knocking off the capping stones. If the main supply of stone is flat sedimentary material of the same thickness, then an even thickness all the way up is what you get.

Styles are often thought to be regional, and are sometimes referred to by a regional name, but, as with the Cumbrian styles, there can be many more than one in any county. The sloping style of Purbeck pictured on p. 320 shared a field with a wall made in a horizontal style. The importance of the stone is nicely shown in the Millennium Wall Project where each of the eighteen walls is made using a different mineral, including quartz dolerite, Blue Pennant sandstone, basalt laval flow and Burlington slate.

Many walls are capped (also known as coped) and the commonest capping (or coping) is with upright thin stones. Upright, at least, when first put in place, as the loss of a single capping stone

An 'upside down' wall in Lanarkshire.

(or a slight movement in the wall) will result in them all sloping. When walls run down a steep slope it is necessary to ensure that they lean a little uphill when set; if they lean downhill collapse is all but inevitable. But capping can also be horizontal or even crenellated by using alternate tall and short stones. Walls built to impress can be capped with large, long, well-dressed stones. Even plain upright stones have variations – neatly rounded, random angular, or squarish. In some cases horizontal capping stones overhang the wall, either on both sides or on one, the latter sometimes being an indication of ownership. Large and heavy capping stones overhanging substantially on one side are apparently there to make a wall wolf-proof. Apart from keeping out wolves, the main purpose of capping a wall is to prevent it gradually deteriorating from the top down. Walls in which the stones become gradually smaller are particularly prone to slow erosion by stock and the elements. Capping stones can also appear vulnerable, but are surprisingly tenacious and seldom fall. Vertically arranged cappings look particularly at risk, but they are always wedged together and if they begin to lean they merely become even more tightly wedged and can last for decades.

I once spent a day with a couple of very kind and helpful dry stone

A rather untidy but effective capping on a dry stone wall in the Lake District.

wall enthusiasts who had taken on the task of rebuilding the wall that runs alongside the South West Coastal path above Chesil Beach in Dorset. No doubt they were

A neatly rounded capping.

going as fast as quality control would allow, but progress seemed to be glacial. Looking back at the 200 metres they had already completed, I wondered if they had begun working on it just after the Second World War. But building a wall is a very slow process, with every stone examined and chosen and positioned with care. Some need to be lightly dressed with a deft blow from a hammer. Speedy it was not, but the finished wall was a work of art.

It was a restoration project, so the old wall was carefully

Part of a newly restored wall above Chesil Beach in Dorset.

disassembled and the stones placed alongside where the wall had been with a gap left for working. The original stones were cleaned with a light brushing, but that was all, as they wished to preserve the lichens that had grown on them. Inevitably, some had been damaged beyond their use as facing stones (usually as a result of frost fracturing), so a fresh consignment of matching stone from a nearby quarry had been delivered and carefully sorted.

The area around a length of wall had been cleared, the footings dug out (where necessary) to give four inches of depth, and the path and height of the wall were set out with mathematical precision. A series of frames, which provided the shape and height of the intended wall, were set in the ground and string was drawn taut between them to mark the intervening gaps. The frames were called batters, a word we have come across before in the setting out of a Cornish hedge (see p. 312). The wall's dimensions were one metre at the base, half a metre wide at the top and one metre high.

The building process was staggered gradually over an advancing twenty metres or so, giving a shallow sloping top edge to the unfinished wall. The footing or foundation stones do not need to be attractive as at least four inches of them will be below ground, but they do need to be big. In some walls the foundation stones and the shallow trough in which they sit are wider than the wall; this is termed 'scarcement'. In this example, however, they were the same width as the wall. The stones making up the surface – the bulk of the wall – are positioned either side, long edge inwards for stability and with any gaps in the middle filled with smaller stones which become known as the 'hearting'. Better stones (and slightly more effort) are put into the side of the wall which could be seen by walkers than on the side seen only by sheep; a practice with a long pedigree, as every workman who wishes to please his master will place his best work where it is most likely to be seen. Through stones, which prevent the two sides of the wall drifting apart, are placed at knee height. The large stones needed for this purpose can be in short supply, so through stones which go most, but not all, of the way through the wall may be used instead. The wall was coped with vertical stones, packed tightly together. They were of dramatically different sizes and heights and the whole thing looked like a bookshelf on which the Dewey Decimal System has been taken too seriously.

My new friends showed me a couple of the flourishes that can make these walls so interesting. Walls often have a tree growing along their base which will eventually distort it to the point of complete collapse. Removing even a fairly small tree down to the roots is extremely difficult without a digger, and if simply cut off at ground level will spring back to life to continue its siege. Better to live with it and place a long 'bridging stone' to allow the tree to grow without demolishing the wall. Walls are not just stock-proof, they are badger-proof too – at least they are unless a sett is established beneath a wall. The previous, fallen wall had allowed badgers to pass unhindered and their trackway was clear in the grass. To allow them to continue their nightly forays, a badger run was built through the wall in line with the established track.

Such details are a characteristic of dry stone walls everywhere. In Cornwall I came across a charming method of keeping the stone part of a Cornish hedge stock-proof at the point where it crossed a ditch. Three, long, thin stones, set in the bank either side, neatly bridged the gap between hedge and ditch. These are sheep-creeps: low,

The painstaking reconstruction of the South West Coastal path wall.

A badger run.

square openings through the wall which allow the passage of sheep but not of cattle. Cattle-creeps (basically adjustable sheep-creeps) also exist as do water smoots which are similar to the opening that allows badgers through (I guess we should call these badger smoots) but are designed for very small streams. Other small openings include 'rabbit smoots' and 'bee boles' – the latter accommodating an old-fashioned beehive and usually placed in walls around orchards. Stiles are also constructed in a variety of different ways. Very long through stones are sometimes fitted into a wall to give two or three steps projecting from either side. This relies on the weight of the wall above the through stones to hold them in place, so the top one is vulnerable to collapse. Particularly endearing is the squeeze stile, which allows the passage of human legs but not of cattle or sheep (except very thin sheep, perhaps).

The Dorset Ridgeway wall, or at least, the particular stretch of it that my friends were working on, was almost perfectly level. Not all dry stone walls are built on level ground and techniques have been devised to allow the construction of these sometimes precipitous structures. If the slope is fairly gentle, then there is no need for special measures; the wall will look the same, but will just undulate a little. For steep slopes, however, it is impossible to lay courses parallel to the ground as the entire wall will simply slide down the hill. For

327

A mortared wall in Fife.

walls running down a steep slope, the courses need to remain horizontal – if the wall does not have courses, then the individual stones must be arranged as much as possible with their horizontal surfaces horizontal and their vertical surfaces vertical. Foundations are more important when a wall runs down a hill than when they are on the flat, and are arranged in a series of steps. Walls can run around a hill as well, in which case the wall itself is built in the same way as it would be on the flat, but the foundation stones will ideally have a scarcement projecting from the downhill side, but not usually the uphill side.

There is something very personal about a dry stone wall. A hedge can be a thing of beauty, but while man determines its form, it grows entirely on its own. In a dry stone wall every stone is placed there by someone who selected it, possibly trimmed it, and then positioned it with thought and care – the wall bears the mark of its creator.

Although dry stone walls are by far the most common type used for agricultural boundaries, walls can also be mortared. They are rather frowned upon by the purist dry stone waller as both a needless affectation and a tacit admission of a lack of faith in one's ability to build a 'proper' wall. A more substantial objection is mortared walls are necessarily inflexible structures. Any subsidence in the footing will result in the wall cracking at one or several points, and perhaps even collapsing. The latter is certainly true, but I have seen some magnificent mortared walls in Fife which look set to last centuries. They go on for miles, but there were no cracks in them. The key here, no doubt, is that they were well made and possessed of solid foundations.

Chapter 29

FENCES

Although the word fence will likely bring to mind a creosoted garden fence or a wooden fence around a paddock, it is a word often used for boundaries in general, notably in the past. The word is a shortened version of defence, showing its original meaning as a protection from attack. But agricultural fences as they are understood now have always been built in one form or another. For the last 100 years or so, a fence around a field has increasingly come to mean a barbed wire, plain wire or broad mesh fence and it is this that is most likely to be used in place of hedges and stone walls. Even where hedges and stone walls still exist, they are almost invariably accompanied by a wire fence, except in strictly arable country. The history of this useful, but nevertheless much hated, invention will not be examined here, but I could not resist the photograph of what is very likely to be an ancient tensioner, found on a post in Scotland. Before the widespread use of barbed wire, a fence would have been made of wood or, more latterly, of iron.

R. W. Dickson, who had so much to say about hedges (see pp. 291–3), also had advice on the construction of fences. His illustrations of them in *Practical Agriculture* make them look very neat,

A vintage barbed-wire tensioner.

which is probably more than can be said for the fences that were actually built, if contemporary landscape paintings and drawings are a reliable guide. Figure 1a, which appears to show riven timber, is a typical fence of the period, though the uprights are placed much closer together than was the actual practice. Figure 1b shows a more usual construction, but using the more expensive sawn timber. The other figures show a variety of rustic arrangements. Figure 3b shows a fence 'warped with thorns' (warped in this context being a term borrowed from weaving). In fact, fences with a 'weft' of longer sticks such as willow and hazel are common. Figure 4a which depicts upright willow stakes woven together with willow sticks is interesting, as just such a fence is depicted in a German woodcut of 1547 entitled *Peasants Behind the Hedge* by Hans Sebald Beham. This is an amusing if not particularly attractive scene: two figures are working on the fence, two are doing something best enjoyed in private and a fifth is evidently suffering from an excess of refreshment. If the eye can be drawn away from the enthusiastic couple, a pollarded tree can be seen on the left that probably supplied the uprights for the fence. It also provides firm evidence that pollarding is a venerable practice.

During the main enclosure period, fences were essential to

Dickson's drawings of fences.

protect new hedges while they became established, and were often demanded by Enclosure Commissioners. This resulted in a great deal of woodland being lost in order to supply timber to build thousands of miles of fencing, as well as the creation of a large, if short-lived, saw-milling industry. It may be that the timber so supplied was sufficiently cheap in Yorkshire to inspire the Yorkshire hedge, also visible in Dickson's plate as Figure 3b. The hunting pictures that tell us so much about hedges are also revealing on the matter of fences, and the plate on p. 333 clearly shows a double fence protecting a hedge.

Wooden fences are still used with surprising frequency in agricultural settings – not in a systematic way, but popping up here and there, seemingly at random. Iron fences too are sometimes seen.

A wooden fence on Bodmin Moor colonised by gorse.

They are attractive in their own way as the photograph of this one in Lanarkshire shows. While they are something of a legacy feature of the country-side, unlikely to be replaced once they have rusted away, they are still manufactured in order to provide a deluxe option for the grander estates.

A rare iron fence in pastoral Lanarkshire.

This nineteenth-century drawing, entitled *A Crumpler*, nicely shows a hedge protected by two fences.

Chapter 30

A FINAL PLEA

The problem of outright hedgerow loss has been, if not solved, then at least ameliorated by legislation, subsidy and education. Nevertheless, hedges continue to decrease in quality if not quantity. The vigorous annual flailing of many internal hedges at a consistent metre or less has produced artistically formed but biologically sterile hedges of little interest. The hedges most people see are those of the roadside, and it is these – not internal agricultural hedges – that provoke repeated (and frequently justified) letters to local papers and to local councils. Roadside hedges are usually the responsibility of the farmer, while everything up to the hedge – the verge – is maintained by the local highway authority.

I once wrote that when I ruled the world, the trimming of our hedges, hedge banks and verges would be placed under my personal control. But I was being a little hasty. No cutting regime pleases everyone and I would find myself with more enemies than friends. Cutting and mowing is a constant problem in another area of conservation – grassland management. A field mycologist will prefer a field (or verge) to be cut short; those who love butterflies will wish it to be left long. In the work that has been done with bird populations,

The fate of many an internal hedge – left to wither.

it has been discovered that some birds like tall hedges and some like them short. Fortunately, there is sufficient serendipitous variation for all these considerations to be addressed, but a single, strict application of a rule for cutting at a particular height – whether it be grass or hedge – would likely cause damage to certain populations. Variation, then, is the key.

There can be little doubt that the traditional laid hedge is best for wildlife. Cut and laid, it gradually grows and thickens; its erstwhile occupants of bird, beast, plant and fungi returning, supplied by neighbouring hedges which are cut to a different timetable. It is trimmed of its excess growth, perhaps shaped a little and otherwise left to its own devices to grow as it will. After twenty, forty or even more years it is laid again. It is impossible to hand lay the thousands of miles of hedges in Britain so a more feasible solution must be found. There have been a few experiments with semi-mechanical hedge laying – each stem is nicked with a chain saw, then the whole row laid flat with the assistance of a tractor. The results have not been encouraging.

Unfortunately, the most practical is the mechanical flail. This, basically, is a mower-on-a-stick; a fearsome beast which slays all before it. Having said that, it is not so bad in itself, more in the way it is sometimes used. A hedge, repeatedly cut to the same height, fails to thrive, as there is no opportunity for branching. The hedgerow hawthorn, blackthorn and hazel grow to a certain height, but then are forced to stop, lateral branching is prevented and the trees become leggy. The solution to this little conundrum is to raise the flail every time by ten centimetres to allow branching; an exercise that will produce a dense, stock-proof and long-lived hedge. Eventually, it will reach its natural height and a gentle trim will keep it in check.

There is also the less popular circular-saw-on-a-stick. This looks like a prop from a particularly nasty horror movie, but in some circumstances makes a neater hedge than the flail. Some consist of four blades that are able to make a clean sweep of the average hedge. Most roadside hedges are cut alternate years, but a three-year cycle has been suggested as a better alternative. Three years' growth produces thick stems not easily cut by the flail. The appalling sight of rows of hedge shrubs with a case of terminal split ends is familiar to all who live in the countryside and an eyesore that this device could eliminate. The circular saw has the advantage of not shredding the timber it cuts and so prevents the damaging mulch that otherwise accumulates at the foot of a hedge. It also supplies a bio-fuel – what we used to call firewood.

Hedge banks may require an even more sensitive touch. The following tale of what happened to the Cornish hedges (which are effectively all hedge bank, albeit clad in stone) is an extreme example of what may happen to hedge banks in other localities. In 1972 a lady in Cornwall, Sarah Carter, was pushing a pram along a country lane at West Penwith, revelling 'in the masses of wild flowers in the hedges', the buzzing of bees, the susurrations of the grasshoppers and the swarms of dancing butterflies. Like the opening scene of a disaster movie, within moments it was all gone. The twisted flowers, shredded butterflies and mangled bees lay at her feet. The man from the council had come along with his tractor and flail to 'mow' the hedge. In a normal hedgerow, some of the animals might have escaped, but on a Cornish hedge, there is nowhere to hide; the flail can reach right to the stone removing all the plants down to their roots. Even if the flailing is done on alternate years – one part of an area one year, another the next – recolonisation does not occur because it cannot happen that quickly. Seed banks are destroyed and the flora and its associate fauna are lost and the hedge infested with nitrogen-loving weeds and invasive plants.

Sarah Carter has carefully recorded the losses over the years she ascribes to the indiscriminate use of the flail. It makes for grim reading. In one mile of typical roadside hedge over a fifty-year period, ninety species of herbaceous plants were lost, five shrubs, twenty grasses, sixty mosses, forty birds, twenty butterflies, two hundred and fifty larger moths and perhaps a thousand other insect species.

Sarah has attempted to remedy the situation by the time-honoured practice of making a thorough nuisance of herself to those responsible for the trimming of Cornish hedges. Flailing regimes have improved, with less cutting during the spring and summer, but it may take generations for species to recover. The traditional method was to cut, where necessary, with shears, and a modern powered version akin to the domestic hedge-trimmer can be used, either attached to a tractor or hand-held. However, it is very slow and roads would be blocked for much longer if they were used instead.

Where hedge banks along roadsides exist, councils and farmers are sometimes very good at timing the frequency, period and height of their cuts. Most councils now have policies like the 'blue-post' scheme, which marks the herb-rich hedge banks and verges which are exempt from a haircut until autumn. Such schemes can be a little hit and miss, and many lovely banks find themselves treated to a short back and sides just when they come into full bloom. The wild basil pictured on p. 246, for example, had disappeared within two days of the photograph being taken! In most cases there are absolutely no concerns about traffic visibility or safety involved, it is just a case of an over-tidy mindset that requires keeping everything trim. Devon took a lead in not cutting verges and banks unless necessary for safety reasons, but soon received complaints that it looked a mess. As noted, you can't please everyone.

With the cutting of roadside hedge, hedge bank and verge timing is absolutely crucial. Spring is not a good time for hedges

Well managed hedges viewed from Pilsdon Pen in West Dorset.

and hedgerows because that is when the flowers grow and the birds nest, while in summer fruits and nuts are setting and later blossoms appearing. By autumn the fruit and berries that will feed the birds have ripened and these are still being eaten in early winter. This leaves the tiny window of late winter in which the hedges may be cut without causing too much collateral damage. Except, that is, for butterflies and some of the true flies which fare better if hedge cutting is in September. But, of course, it may be that winter weather makes it entirely unsuitable for tractors to traverse a field alongside a hedge, or perhaps the time clashes with whatever is happening in the field. These are some of the reasons why hedges are often cut at sub-optimum times. There are laws in place to limit the times of cutting and, rather oddly, these are stricter for farmers who receive subsidies, who (at the time of writing) are permitted to trim from 1 September until the end of February.

These slightly tedious details of hedge maintenance have not been, nor ever will be, settled to the satisfaction of everyone. Many councils are now taking a greater interest in the hedges and roadsides under their direct or indirect care and will often mark trees for salvation if they show promise as standards. Collecting what is cut rather than leaving it behind to encourage weed species is, or would be, a great step forward.

We should, perhaps, all follow Sarah's example in treasuring what we have in our wonderful hedges and hedgerows and make an almighty fuss about that which we perceive to be lost through bad hedge management along the roadside or indeed anywhere else. Then, maybe, we can have our hedges back.

NOTES

Chapter 1 In the Beginning

1. Frans Vera, *Grazing Ecology and Forest History*, CABI Publishing, 2000.
2. Tony Brown, 'Clearances and clearings: deforestation in Mesolithic/ Neolithic Britain', *Oxford Journal of Archaeology*, vol. 16, issue 2, July 1997, pp. 133–146.
3. J. B. Innes and J. J. Blackford, 'The ecology of late mesolithic woodland disturbances: model testing with fungal spore assemblage data', *Journal of Archaeological Science*, vol. 30, issue 2, February 2003, pp. 185–194.
4. Keith Wilkinson and Vanessa Straker, 'Neolithic and Early Bronze Age environmental background', in C. J. Webster (ed.), *The Archaeology of South West England*, Somerset County Council, 2007.
5. John G. Evans, *The Environment of Early Man in the British Isles*, University of California Press, 1975.

Chapter 2 The Neolithic Clearances

1. Francis Pryor, 'From Neolithic to Bronze Age, 8000–800 BCE'. www.bbc. co.uk/history/ancient/british_prehistory/overview_british_prehistory_01. shtml.
2. Rodney Castleden, *The Stonehenge People*, Routledge and Kegan Paul Ltd, 1987.
3. P. J. Fowler, *The Farming of Lowland Britain*, Cambridge University Press, 1983.

4. R. W. Dennell, 'Prehistoric crop cultivation: a reconsideration', *The Antiquaries Journal*, vol. 56, issue 1, March 1976, pp. 11–23.

5. Lucy Verrill and Richard Tipping, 'Use and abandonment of a Neolithic field system at Belderrig, Co. Mayo, Ireland: evidence for economic marginality', *The Holocene*, vol. 20, issue 7, November 2010, pp. 1011–1021.

6. Julian Thomas, 'Current debates on the Mesolithic-Neolithic transition in Britain and Ireland', in Joshua Pollard (ed.), *Prehistoric Britain*, Blackwell Publishing Ltd, 2008.

7. Sofus Christiansen, 'Infield-Outfield systems: characteristics and development in different climatic environments', *Geografisk Tidsskrift*, Bind 77, 1978, pp. 1–5.

8. Richard and Nina Muir, *Fields*, Macmillan, 1989.

9. W. Groenman-van Waateringe, 'Hedges in the west European early-Neolithic', *Bericht van de Rijksdienst Oudheidkundig Bodemonderzoek*, 1972, pp. 295–299.

Chapter 3   The Bronze and Iron Ages

1. Andrew Fleming, *The Dartmoor Reaves: Investigating Prehistoric Land Divisions*, Batsford, 1988.

2. Barry Weiss, 'The decline of late Bronze Age civilisation as a possible response to climatic change', *Climatic Change*, vol. 4, issue 2, June 1982, pp. 173–198.

3. Christopher Taylor, *Fields in the English Landscape*, J. M. Dent & Sons, 1975.

4. *An Inventory of the Historical Monuments in Dorset, Volume III: Central*, HMSO, 1970.

5. Francis Pryor, 'Seasonal farming in the wealthy Fens', *British Archaeology*, issue 38, October 1988, pp. 12–13.

6. Tom Williamson, 'Parish boundaries and early fields: continuity and discontinuity', *Journal of Historical Geography*, vol. 12, issue 3, July 1986, pp. 241–248.

7. Stephen Rippon, 'Early planned landscapes in south-east Essex', *Essex Archaeology and History*, vol. 22, 1991, pp. 46–60.

8. Chris Wardle, 'The late Bronze Age and Iron Age in Staffordshire: the torc of the Midlands?', West Midlands Regional Research Frameworks, Seminar 2.

9. 'Flying Through Cornwall's Past: The Prehistoric Landscape'. www.historic-cornwall.org.uk/flyingpast/preland.html.

10. R. F. White and P. R. Wilson (eds), 'Archaeology and Historic Landscapes of the Yorkshire Dales', Yorkshire Archaeological Society Occasional Paper No. 2, 2004.

11. 'A pound-like feature, relic field boundaries and post medieval building platforms', a survey of the Blackdown Hills, Devon, The Community Landscapes Project, University of Exeter.

12. Francis Pryor, *The Making of the British Landscape*, Allen Lane, 2010.

13. Andrew Mudd, 'The excavation of a late Bronze Age/early Iron Age site at Eight Acre Field, Radley', *Oxoniensia*, vol. 60, 1995, pp. 21–65.

14. James Greig, 'A possible hedgerow flora of Iron Age date from Alcester, Warwickshire', *Circaea, The Journal of the Association for Environmental Archaeology*, vol. 11, issue 1, 1994, pp. 7–16.

Chapter 4 The Impact of the Romans

1. George Lambrick and Mark Robinson, 'Iron Age and Roman Riverside Settlements at Farmoor, Oxfordshire', Council for British Archaeology Report No. 32, 1979.

2. C. A. Ralegh Radford, 'The Roman villa at Ditchley, Oxon', *Oxoniensia*, vol. 1, 1936, pp. 24–69.

Chapter 5 The Anglo-Saxons

1. Christopher Taylor, *Fields in the English Landscape*, J. M. Dent & Sons, 1975.

2. Dorothy Whitelock, *Anglo-Saxon Wills*, Cambridge University Press, 1930.

3. From http://www.langscape.org.uk/index.html.

4. Ibid.

5. F. L. Attenborough (ed.), *The Laws of the Earliest English Kings*, Cambridge University Press, 1922.

6. Ibid.

7. Stephen Rippon, 'Infield and outfield: the early stages of marshland colonisation and the evolution of medieval field systems', in Tom Lane and John Coles (eds), *Through Wet and Dry: Essays in Honour of David Hall*, Heritage Trust of Lincolnshire, 2002.

8. Ibid.

9. Quoted in P. H. Sawyer, *The Age of the Vikings*, Edward Arnold, 1962.

10. Oliver Rackham, *Trees and Woodland in the British Landscape*, J. M. Dent, 1976.

Chapter 6 The Open-Field System

1. C. S. Orwin, *The History of Laxton*, Oxford University Press, 1935.

2. William Langland, *The Vision and the Creed of Piers Ploughman*, c.1370–90.

3. Quoted in Margaret Davies, 'Rhosili open field and related South Wales field patterns', *The Agricultural History Review*, vol. 4, 1956, pp.80–96.

4. I. F. Grant, 'The highland openfield system', *The Geographical Teacher*, vol. 13, issue 6, Autumn 1926, pp. 480–488.

Chapter 7 Inclosure and Enclosures
1. Graeme J. White, *The Medieval English Landscape 1000–1540*, Bloomsbury Academic, 2012.
2. Quoted in ibid.
3. Quoted in Rowland E. Prothero, *English Farming Past and Present*, Cambridge University Press, 1912.
4. Sir Thomas More, *Utopia*, transl. Ralph Robinson, 1556.
5. Quoted in Tristram Hunt, *The Civil War at First Hand*, Weidenfeld and Nicolson, 2002.

Chapter 8 The Enclosure of the Fens
1. Quoted in H. C. Darby, *The Draining of the Fens*, Cambridge University Press, 1956.
2. Quoted in W. H. Wheeler, *A History of the Fens of South Lincolnshire*, Simpkin, Marshall & Co., 1896.
3. Ibid.

Chapter 9 Parliamentary Enclosure
1. G. E. Mingay, *Parliamentary Enclosure in England*, Longman, 1997.
2. Ibid.
3. Oliver Rackham, *Trees and Woodland in the British Landscape*, J. M. Dent, 1976.
4. Thomas Hale, *A Compleat Body of Husbandry*, London, 1758.
5. Ibid.
6. *Windsor and Eton Express*, 1801.
7. Thomas Hale, *A Compleat Body of Husbandry*, London, 1758.
8. Ibid.
9. *Exeter and Plymouth Gazetteer*, 1849.
10. Ibid.
11. Robert C. Allen, *Enclosure and the Yeoman: The Agricultural Development of the South Midlands, 1450–1850*, Clarendon Press, 1992.
12. *Chester Chronicle*, 1809.
13. Thomas Hale, *A Compleat Body of Husbandry*, London, 1758.
14. Ibid.
15. Ibid.
16. Ibid.

17. Elihu Burritt, *A Walk from London to John O'Groat's*, Sampson Low, Son & Marston, 1864.

18. Ibid.

Chapter 10 Hedgerow Loss

1. P. Bolton, C. Baker and M. Keep, *Agriculture: Historical Statistics*, House of Commons Library Standard Note SN/SG/3339, 3 February 2015, Fig. 1.

2. *Northampton Mercury*, 1937.

3. P. Bolton, C. Baker and M. Keep, *Agriculture: Historical Statistics*, House of Commons Library Standard Note SN/SG/3339, 3 February 2015, Fig. 1.

4. *Portsmouth Evening News*, 22 March 1952.

5. Ibid.

6. *Portsmouth Evening News*, 12 September 1953.

7. Quoted in A. J. Youngson, *Britain's Economic Growth 1920–1966*, Routledge, 1967.

8. The Agriculture Act 1947, section 95.

9. Quoted in E. Pollard, M. D. Hooper and N. W. Moore, *Hedges*, Collins, 1974.

10. N. W. Moore, M. D. Hooper and B. N. K. Davis, 'Hedges 1. Introduction and reconnaissance studies', *Journal of Applied Ecology*, vol. 4, issue 1, May 1967, pp. 201–220.

11. T. Cornulier, R.A. Robinson, D. Elston, X. Lambin, W. J. Sutherland and T. G. Benton, 'Bayesian reconstitution of environmental change from disparate historical records: hedgerow loss and farmland bird declines', *Methods in Ecology and Evolution*, vol. 2, issue 1, January 2011, pp. 86–94.

12. 'Land Cover Change 1940s–1980s: Hedgerow', Scottish Natural Heritage Trend Note, No. 009, December 2003.

13. 'Hedgerows', Denbighshire Habitat Action Plan, May 2004.

Chapter 11 Protecting the Hedgerow

1. House of Commons Debate, 20 March 1997, vol. 292, column 1083.

2. House of Commons Debate, 20 March 1997, vol. 292, column 1088.

3. Rutland County Council, Development Control and Licensing Committee Report, No. 91/2012.

4. Ibid.

5. Tim Stewart, 'Alan Curbishley's neighbour taken to court for cutting down 100-year-old hedgerow', *London Evening Standard*, 11 September 2009.

6. D. Kleijn et al., 'Mixed biodiversity benefits of agri-environment schemes in five European countries', *Ecology Letters*, vol. 9, issue 3, March 2006, pp. 243–254.

7. Ibid.
8. Paul Silcock, Ben Allen and Kaley Hart, 'Land Stewardship in England Post-2013: CAP Greening and Agri-Environment', IEEC and Cumulus, Report No. CC-P-570, 21 November 2012.

Chapter 12 Habitat

1. Michael Woods, *Rural Geography: Processes, Responses and Experiences in Rural Restructuring*, Sage Publications, 2005.
2. Robert Wolton, 'UK Biodiversity Action Plan: Priority Species Linked to Hedgerows', Report to Hedgelink, November 2009.

Chapter 13 Species

1. Robert Wolton. 'Life in a hedge', *British Wildlife*, vol. 26, issue 5, June 2015, pp. 306–317.

Chapter 14 What can be found in a hedge?

1. Stephen Howard Jones, 'The Landscape Ecology of Hedgerows with Particular Reference to Island Biogeography', PhD thesis, University of York, 1992.
2. D. D. French and R. P. Cummins, 'Classification, composition, richness and diversity of British hedgerows', *Applied Vegetation Science*, vol. 4, issue 2, December 2001, pp. 213–228.
3. NBN Gateway (data.nbn.org.uk).

Chapter 15 Trees of the hedgerow

1. Anonymous (A Society of Gentlemen), *The Complete Farmer: Or, a General Dictionary of Husbandry*, Third edition, 1777.
2. William Ellis, *The Timber-tree Improved*, Part II, 1742.
3. The Rev. St. John Priest, *General View of the Agriculture of Buckinghamshire*, 1810.
4. William Ellis, *Ellis's Husbandry, Abridged and Methodized*, Volume II, 1772.
5. Stephen Switzer, *Ichnographia Rustica: Or, The Nobleman, Gentleman, and Gardener's Recreation*, Volume I, 1718.
6. *The Gentleman's Magazine*, vol. 95, 1804.
7. George Buchan Hepburn, *General View of the Agriculture and Rural Economy of East Lothian*, 1794.
8. Ibid.
9. R. W. Dickson, *Practical Agriculture; or, A Complete System of Modern Husbandry*, 1805.
10. Thomas Hale, *A Compleat Body of Husbandry*, Second edition, Volume I, 1758.

11. Thomas Mawe and John Abercrombie, *The Universal Gardener and Botanist*, 1778.
12. Ibid.
13. Thomas Hale, *A Compleat Body of Husbandry*, Second edition, Volume I, 1758.
14. Ibid.
15. Ibid.
16. John Claudius Loudon, *An Encyclopædia of Agriculture*, 1825.
17. William Cobbett, *The Woodlands*, 1825.
18. Batty Langley, *A Sure and Easy Method of Improving Estates*, Second edition, 1740.
19. Thomas Hale, *A Compleat Body of Husbandry*, Second edition, Volume I, 1758.
20. The Rev. C. A. Johns, *The Forest Trees of Britain*, Volume II, 1849.
21. Philip Miller, *The Gardener's Dictionary*, Volume II, 1735.
22. William Ellis, *The Modern Husbandman or, The Practice of Farming*, Volume IV, 1744.
23. Thomas Hale, *A Compleat Body of Husbandry*, Second edition, Volume I, 1758.
24. Ibid.
25. Alexander Hunter (ed.), footnote in John Evelyn, *Sylva, or a Discourse on Forest-Trees*, 1786 edition.

Chapter 16 Shrubs and climbers
1. Stuart Roberts and Nicolas Vereecken, 'Ivy bee (Colletes hederae)', Hymettus and BWARS information sheet, September 2009. (www. naturespot.org.uk/sites/default/files/downloads/IvyBee.pdf)
2. Online Atlas of the British & Irish Flora (www.brc.ac.uk/plantatlas/index. php?q=plant/orobanche-hederae).

Chapter 17 Herbaceous plants and grasses
1. Michael McCarthy, 'Cow parsley: the countryside killer', *The Independent*, 19 May 2014.
2. J. E. M. van Mierlo and J. M. van Groenendael, 'A population dynamic approach to the control of Anthriscus sylvestris (L.) Hoffm.', *Journal of Applied Ecology*, vol. 28, issue 1, April 1991, pp. 128–139.

Chapter 19 Mammals
1. G. C. Kotzageorgis and C. F. Mason, 'Small mammal populations in relation to hedgerow structure in an arable landscape', *Journal of Zoology*, vol. 242, issue 3, March 2009, pp. 425–434.
2. Stephen Harris and Derek Yalden (eds), *Mammals of the British Isles*, Mammal Society, 2008.

Chapter 20 Birds

1. R. E. Green, P. E. Osborne and E. J. Sears, 'The distribution of passerine birds in hedgerows during the breeding season in relation to characteristics of the hedgerow and adjacent farmland', *Journal of Applied Ecology*, vol. 31, issue 4, November 1994, pp. 677–692.

Chapter 22 Hurdles

1. Barry Cunliffe, *Iron Age Communities in Britain*, Fourth edition, Routledge, 2005.
2. *Rochdale Chronicle*, 1861.
3. Whitby Museum. www.whitbymuseum.org.uk/whist/penn.htm

Chapter 23 'Dead' hedges and live ones

1. Jonathan Tabor et al., 'Archaeological Investigations at Must Farm, Whittlesey, Cambridgeshire: The Phase 2 Extraction Area', Cambridge Archaeological Unit Report no. 251, June 2010.
2. William Ellis, *The Modern Husbandman*, Volume I, 1744.

Chapter 24 The Laid Hedge (1): General Features

1. Julius Caesar, *The Gallic War Book II*, trans. H. J. Edwards, William Heinemann, 1917.
2. Sir Anthony Fitzherbert, *Boke of Husbandry*, Walter W. Skeat (ed.), English Dialect Society, 1882.
3. Ibid.
4. Ibid.
5. John Mortimer, *The Whole Art of* Husbandry, 1708.
6. Ibid.

FURTHER READING
AND RESOURCES

History

Ault, Warren O., *Open-Field Farming in Medieval England: A Study of Village By-laws*, London: Allen & Unwin, 1972

Devon Hedge Group and Devon County Council, *Devon Hedges*, 2014

Evans, John G., *The Environment of Early Man in the British Isles*, Berkeley and Los Angeles; University of California Press, 1975

Fleming, Andrew, *The Dartmoor Reaves: Investigating Prehistoric Land Divisions*, London: Batsford, 1988

Fowler, Peter, *Farming in the First Millennium AD: British Agriculture between Julius Caesar and William the Conqueror*, Cambridge: Cambridge University Press, 2002

Fowler, P. J., *The Farming of Prehistoric Britain*, Cambridge: Cambridge University Press (1981), 1983

Hammond, J. L. and Barbara Hammond, *The Village Labourer 1760–1832: A Study in the Government of England before the Reform Bill* (1911), new edition, Stroud: Sutton Publishing Ltd, 1987

Hoskins, W. G., *The Making of the English Landscape*, London: Hodder & Stoughton, 1955Jessel, Christopher, *A Legal History of the English Landscape*, London: Wildy, Simmonds & Hill, 2011

Mingay, G. E., *Parliamentary Enclosure in England* (1997), London and New York: Routledge, 2014

Muir, Richard and Nina Muir, *Fields*, London: Macmillan, 1989

Pollard, E., M. D. Hooper and N. W. Moore, *Hedges*, London: Collins, 1974

Pryor, Francis, *The Making of the British Landscape: How we Transformed the Land, from Prehistory to Today*, London: Allen Lane, 2010

Slater, Gilbert, *The English Peasantry and the Enclosure of Common Fields*, London: Constable, 1907

Taylor, Christopher, *Fields in the English Landscape* (1975), revised edition, Stroud: Sutton Publishing Ltd, 2000

Natural History

Blamey, Marjorie, Richard Fitter and Alastair Fitter, *Wild Flowers of Britain and Ireland*, second edition, London: Bloomsbury, 2013

Chinery, Michael, *British Insects: A Photographic Guide to Every Common Species*, London: Collins, 2009

Eastoe, Jane, *Hedgerow and Wildlife: A Guide to Animals and Plants of the Hedgerow*, London: National Trust, 2008

Ellis, Martin B. and J. Pamela Ellis, *Microfungi on Land Plants: An Identification Handbook*, second edition, Slough: Richmond, 1997

Manley, Chris, *British Moths: A Photographic Guide to the Moths of Britain and Ireland*, second edition, London: Bloomsbury, 2015

Nelson, Raphael, *Birds of the Hedgerow, Field and Woodland* (1948), London: Unicorn Press Ltd, 2014

Redfern, Margaret and Peter Shirley, *British Plant Galls*, second edition, Shrewsbury: FSC, 2011

Sperry, Paul and Barry Hughes, *Collins Complete Guide to British Mushrooms and Toadstools*, London: Collins, 2009

Stace, Clive, *New Flora of the British Isles*, third edition, Cambridge: Cambridge University Press, 2010

Practical

Brooks, A. and Sean Adcock and edited by Elizabeth Agate, *Dry Stone Walling: A Practical Handbook*, Doncaster: British Trust for Conservation Volunteers, 1999

Maclean, Murray, *Hedges and Hedgelaying: A Guide to Planting, Management and Conservation*, Ramsbury, Marlborough: Crowood Press Ltd, 2006

Radford, Andy, *A Guide to Dry Stone Walling*, Ramsbury, Marlborough: Crowood Press Ltd, 2001

Foraging

Wright, John, *Hedgerow*, River Cottage Handbook No. 7, London: Bloomsbury, 2010

Online Resources

www.dswa.org.uk Dry Stone Walling Association, Cumbria

www.ediblebush.com Author's website

www.fwag.org.uk/ Farming &Wildlife Advisory Group

www.gwct.org.uk/ Game & Wildlife Conservation Trust

www.hedgelaying.org.uk/ National Hedgelaying Society

www.hedgelink.org.uk A comprehensive site devoted to hedge management, law and conservation.

www.nbn.org.uk/ National Biodiversity Network Gateway Provides invaluable records on the distributions of species of animal, plant and fungus.

ACKNOWLEDGEMENTS

As always, it is impossible to write a book such as this without help. In this case, a great deal of help. It has been given with undue selflessness by fellow enthusiasts of hedgerow, wall and dyke, and I thank them all.

First among them is Bryan Edwards who took me on so many walks and suffered with patience my constant question: 'So what's this plant/grass/ lichen/moss, Bryan?'. Adrian Boots has been most helpful with the history and, not least, encouragement.

Thank you to Alan Portas for sharing his compendious knowledge of hedges with such enthusiasm, Monica Wilde for driving me for hundreds of miles around Scotland looking at drystane dykes, George Pidgeon and John Hall for showing me how to lay a hedge, Charlie Kitchin for taking me on an informative but bitterly cold walk across the Fens, Dr Rob Wolton for showing me his Devon hedge and to Sally Fielding for introducing me to the ways of walls. My thanks go to Joy Allison for imparting her knowledge of Laxton, Michael Bamforth for helping me track down some ancient hedges and Sarah Carter for sharing her passion for the Cornish hedge. Others who deserve my gratitude are James Fitzharris, Pip Taylor, Susan Eberley of wyrtig.com, Nigel Adams, Graham Stanley, Mark Forrest, the staff at the Dorset History Centre and Allison Shaw of the Dry Stone Walling Association. If I have missed anyone then they have my heartfelt apologies, but receive my thanks nevertheless.

My profound thanks go to my editor, John Davey, who has remained courteous and helpful despite his patience being tested to the limit. I am grateful to Penny Daniel for guiding the editorial process with such care and also to Paul Forty. To Joe Staines I owe a particular debt of gratitude. As my copy editor he showed great skill in what he did, but also a quite remarkable dedication to the rooting out of error. Thank you Joe, for saving me so much embarrassment. Thanks go also to Jonathan Harley for taking such care with the layout and to Hannah Ross for her expert publicity campaign.

As always, many thanks go to Gordon Wise of Curtis Brown for his encouragement and assistance throughout this project.

Picture Credits

The author and publishers would like to express their thanks for permission to use the following images: Allan Portas 285; Andy Wood 265, 267; Bodleian Library 59, 60; Bryan Edwards 164, 169 (left), 174, 184 (bottom left), 184 (bottom right), 197 (bottom right), 200 (right), 209 (bottom), 227, 236, 246, 250, 270; Dorset History Centre 41 (ref: D/FSI), 82 (ref I.5); Google © Infoterra Ltd & Bluesky 32; John Waller (www.underwoodsman.co.uk) 280; Tom Tams 170, 176, 190 (right), 192 (bottom). All other photographs are by the author.

While every effort has been made to contact copyright-holders of illustrations, the author and publishers would be grateful for information about any illustrations where they have been unable to trace them, and would be glad to make amendments in further editions.

INDEX